Contents

Introduction	v
May	1
June	22
July	41
August	59
September	78
October	100
November/December	118
January	132
February	154
March	177
April	204

*This book is dedicated to my immediate family for putting up with
my year long absence from them
Dean, Beth, Norbert, Alyssa, Sandy, Darren, Austin and Kara*

Introduction

Boulders that took two men to lift, wheelbarrows full of rocks and two hundred mile an hour winds were only some of the stories we heard about our lighthouse home, Eshaness, on the north mainland of the Shetland Islands in Scotland. My husband Dean and I purchased the lighthouse in May 1999 after a long and difficult search, which is told in *The Last Lighthouse* published by Luath Press. Ever since the purchase I had been staying at the lighthouse for a few months at a time in the fall and spring.

Mark Rykards, a producer for BBC Radio Scotland, had followed me for three days during one of my early trips looking at lighthouses. Mark and I had stayed in touch and kept talking about doing a feature, which would document my staying for a year at the lighthouse. That was the beginning of *A Year at the Lighthouse*.

For this pensioner-age American born in the Midwest, who had lived the majority of her time on a farm in the middle of a cornfield, it was scary to think of living alone at the mercy of the Atlantic Ocean for a year, especially considering the stories I had been told. Dean could only be with me for short visits. If I did it I would have to do it alone.

Another major concern was being away from my family and friends. Dean was supportive but others didn't want me to be gone for so long and became angry and resentful. Discussion continued until Dean and I decided I should give it a try. I signed contracts for the audio diary with BBC Radio Scotland and this book. I was going to live at the lighthouse from May 1st 2001 until April 30th 2002.

One of the first big hurdles was getting a visa to stay in the UK for the year. It seemed a simple process since the United Kingdom allows writers to stay in the country up to a year without a work permit but it took countless faxes, many phone calls and enormous frustration before I finally got my permit. The visa arrived only four days before I was to leave for the lighthouse.

Saying goodbye to friends and family was difficult but the sadness was softened a little knowing my youngest daughter's family would be coming to the lighthouse in the summer accompanied by Dean. But it would be a long time until I would see my oldest daughter's family and my friends again. Our three grandchildren are at the ages where they change daily and I wouldn't be able to watch them grow for a year. Surprisingly I was also upset every time I thought of leaving my beloved dog, Kiri.

I was more than a little scared about what lay ahead. As the time for leaving got closer I tried to focus on how happy I had been at the lighthouse on previous visits and that I would be returning to my family in a year. I had so many details to attend to before I left because of the length of the stay that my mind was constantly occupied. However, getting on the plane for the UK was one of the more difficult things I have done in my life.

This book is a journal of my activities, written early every morning.

Tom Williamson, the caretaker of the lighthouse, is a main character. Living at Bordigarth, a croft about three miles from the lighthouse, he became my guide and teacher about Shetland and helped me get the most out of my stay.

Eshaness is a brilliant place to learn about the ocean, its creatures, and Shetland in general. I spent hours watching seals and birds and fishing the lochs around the lighthouse. I arrived in early spring and was immediately busy, assisting Tom with lambing and observing all of the returning birds nesting which was extremely helpful in getting over my anxiety at leaving my family and the US.

The weather is major feature of this journal. The lighthouse sits on a rocky cliff 200 feet above the ocean and is exposed to the elements from all directions. All activities are determined by the weather and to be caught unaware by a severe storm can be life-threatening. Like all Shetlanders, I became preoccupied with watching the weather forecast and talking about it. Winter taught me in a graphic way through some horrendous storms how important knowledge about advancing weather can be.

Most of my life I have had a pet of some kind so one of my most difficult challenges was finding a pet to live with me at the lighthouse. During the year my pets included two hedgehogs, three orphaned lambs, a wild orange rabbit and four rare breed chickens. Some were my companions for a short time and others for many months.

The most traumatic things that took place during the year did not happen at the lighthouse but back in the United States. These events radically affected my life at the lighthouse and my happiness. The most dramatic was the terrorist attack on the USA on September 11th, but a tragic accident at home turned out to be the most devastating.

From the beginning, one of my fears was that I would begin to take the splendour of the lighthouse and the surrounding area for granted. Shetland is physically beautiful and almost every day it presents another dramatic aspect. As winter set in and I became more and more house-bound, I found myself living as I did at the farmhouse in Michigan. I got up, ate breakfast, went to work on the computer until evening and then either watched TV or read a book. I got frustrated as I felt when I was at the lighthouse I should be outdoors enjoying the ocean. It got so bad some days I did not even look out of the window to watch the surf.

I probably will not stay a long time in the winter again unless I have lots of writing to do. I have always described the lighthouse as my writing retreat. That is what it became during most of the winter. The weather keeping me inside made me a prolific writer.

The last months of the journal became a description of what I go through getting a book ready for publication. Many authors find that part of a book's development the most difficult as it is tedious and time consuming. This part of the writing process is usually hidden from the readers so it adds an unusual dimension to the book.

When the year came to an end I was anxious to see my family again and ready to go back to the hustle and bustle of my life on the farm in Michigan, but now that I am back on the farm I desperately miss the ocean, the sea birds and my snug little house with its light on top. Living in a lighthouse is a unique experience. It was not easy because of the isolation and the difficult weather but it was an experience I treasure. I am anxious to get back to see how much my lambs have grown, walk to the Bruddans to see the seals, ride in the wee red boat to Dore Holm and to finally catch a big, elusive brown trout. The weather no longer frightens me as I have learned how to deal with dangerous storms and understand that following one, I can watch some of the most dramatic and stunning surf imaginable. I have bought an airline ticket to return to Shetland in a few months. Until Dean retires I may not be able to stay for a full year but I will return often and for fairly lengthy stays.

A Year at the Lighthouse taught me I am okay on my own, even when tragedy strikes. I like having birds, seals, chickens and lambs for my daily companions instead of people, and the ocean is both frightening and remarkably beautiful. Even though I did not tend the light I now understand why it was difficult for the redundant lighthouse keepers to find a new way of life.

Sharma Krauskopf

Acknowledgements

This book is dedicated to my daughters Beth and Sandy and my sons-in-law Norbert and Darren, along with my three grandchildren, Austin, Kara and Alyssa. Austin asked me recently how long could they have me before I returned to the lighthouse, which illustrates how much they deserve mention.

Tom Williamson was helpful in every way and without him it would not have been such an exciting and fulfilling year. I cannot forget to thank Tim Harrison and the *Lighthouse Digest* for letting me use some of the material from my monthly *Light Reflections* column.

A special thank you also goes to the 20 or so people who were bombarded daily with the e-mails which became the draft of this book.

Kiri, my beloved dog, who I often feel I hurt the most with my absence deserves a special mention. The saddest part is I will never be able to tell her how sorry I am and how much I missed her because she died while I was away.

May

April 29th

It is a peaceful springtime Sunday with hazy sunshine and a gentle wind, an unusual Shetland day for this time of year. Most of the morning I spent planting flower seeds in containers. Some are herbs for my windowsills and some are flowers I will transplant outside when they are large enough. The daffodils that I forced last winter and bloomed on my windowsill are in the ground, hopefully to survive and bloom next year.

Sometimes I think all things have a battle to survive on Shetland. Tom had a lamb born this morning that was attacked by a 'hoodie crow'. The bird ate the lamb's eye and damaged his tongue. We are not sure if the tongue is badly injured but it was bleeding. The wee one is alive or was an hour ago but survival is not likely so Tom took it home. If it lives it will be my first 'caddy' or orphan lamb.

It seems ironic that hoodie crows are a protected species here when they are such mean birds. Margaret Macdonald is always telling me – nature is sometimes cruel.

Yesterday I got supplies while in Lerwick to take care of the caddies but had to call our good friends the Macdonalds at Grantown-on-Spey for technical advice on how much to feed the newborn lambs. Margaret was really helpful so I think I am ready to take on my flock. Later today I will put bedding in the garage, as that will be my nursery for the caddies.

I have a beef roast in the Rayburn, as Tom will be up for dinner. I will make dinner for him in the evenings for the next two weeks as a way to help him with the lambing. He takes two weeks off from his fish hatchery job to oversee lambing in his flock. He works unbelievably hard with very little return but that appears to be the fate of crofting these days. I will be glad when my five days of self-imposed quarantine for foot and mouth disease is up so I can actually help him with the lambs. I could probably do it now but I would feel dreadful if I somehow contacted the virus on my travels here and spread it to Shetland.

April 30th

I'm taking a coffee break while link-checking software goes through the new issue of my Internet magazine, *Scottish Radiance*. It is a beautiful day with bright blue sky and a few puffy white clouds so I decided to take my coffee outside on a rock. The sea was tranquil and I saw some birds floating at the bottom of the cliffs. My first reaction was that the puffins were back early but running to get my binoculars I was disappointed to find that it was only some seagulls.

Ever since I arrived I have been worried that the bird population is decreasing. It looks like there are fewer birds now than at this time last year, but this morning I discovered many birds at Calder's Geo so I was pleased. Some of the neighbours think the birds are late coming because Shetland has had such a cold spring.

The fulmar that was a featured attraction in 'the brothel' in my book *The Last Lighthouse* is back sitting on the top of the garage. Dean calls it 'my' fulmar because he does not want to claim it. The bird does not seem to have a mate so maybe there will be no X-rated behaviour on top of the garage this year. We are not sure whether the fulmar (sort of a fat seagull with a little different colouring) mates for life or not.

The lamb injured by the hoodie crow died which was probably a blessing as it would never have been right. Lots of lambs are arriving and they are not even due to start coming until tomorrow. So far Tom has four sets of twins, which is a really good way to start. No orphans yet which is disappointing, as I want so much the experience of taking care of them. Besides it is on the list of activities I wish to present in the BBC Scotland audio diary feature.

Today I am going outside with my little DAT recorder to start the feature. Hopefully I will get some bird sounds for background to be used with the words. As soon as the link checker completes its journey through the magazine I am going to walk by the road down to Tom's house and record the sounds I hear. I still have two days until I can go near the animals or through the fields.

I finally joined a new online server that includes the price of the telephone calls so I could keep the magazine going. Having to pay for phone calls is really expensive when things like the link checker sometimes take an hour and half. I am used to being online for as long as I want in Michigan, with a dedicated line and no charge for phone calls. The constant worry of the cost of the phone calls here was driving me crazy.

May 1st

I thought I would have the honour of being the first to see the arrival in Shetland of the Arctic terns. The first person to see an Arctic tern gets mentioned on BBC Shetland radio. Walking over to Tom's I saw two terns. I was really excited since Tom said it was two weeks early for the birds. That evening I listened to BBC Shetland and two people had reported in already with sightings. Both had seen a single tern. I had seen two. Oh, well so much for my moment of glory on Shetland radio.

I was approached to write for a UK lighthouse magazine. I do not know what I will do as I have so much writing already contracted including books and two monthly magazines. I am beginning to realize a writer living at a lighthouse is much sought after because the world seems to be fascinated with lighthouses right now.

May 2nd

The wind is really strong today. It is so bad it is hard to stand up. Tom had to make a trip to Lerwick to get supplies for the sheep and I begged a ride with him. In Lerwick it was windy but maybe not as strong because it is more protected.

My big shock of the day came when I went to the fishmonger to get some haddock and it cost twice as much as it did last winter when I was here. There is big shortage of sea fish on the market. They have made some ocean areas off limits to fishing, to help replenish the supply since the seas are being over fished. It is difficult for the Shetland fishermen since they cannot fish where they have traditionally gone. Being a normal consumer I do not like the high prices but I support protecting the dwindling supply. Maybe the price will go down within the next few weeks as the fleet is being allowed out this week to begin fishing again.

Speaking of boats, the *Pharos*, the Northern Lighthouse Board's tender, was in Lerwick harbour. It is a beautiful ship and huge! I had no idea it would be so big. On one end it has a helipad and on the other end a tall crane that can reach to the top of any lighthouse tower. In the past I have been offered an opportunity to sail on it but never accepted. After seeing the beautiful ship if I get a chance when it comes in July to tend the Ve Skerry Lighthouse I will definitely take a ride.

Early tomorrow morning two amateur radio operators who will be broadcasting from Eshaness as a part of the Worldwide Lighthouse Amateur Radio Weekend in August will be here to check out reception. The open house at the lighthouse is going to be quite an event with radio broadcasting going to all parts of the world. The publicity about my books has increased the number of people who want to visit Eshaness. The open house might keep some of the tourists from disturbing us through the rest of the summer. We hope to have the lighthouse sparkling. Leslie, the Northern Lighthouse Board's attendant to the tower, is going to answer questions about the tower itself. I will be selling my books and operating a small tearoom in the generator house. All the neighbours are getting special invitations to attend.

May 3rd

It is a sunny, beautiful day at the lighthouse with gigantic surf breaking high against the rocks in the bright sunshine. It is quite a sight and should impress the radio broadcasters.

Fantastic news! My two Rugosa roses, which I thought were dead, are sprouting and the carpet roses around the sundial have new shoots. Maybe growing flowers here is not as hopeless as I thought. A storm could still come along and destroy them but at least there is a flicker of a chance in those green shoots.

Tom is about to lose another newborn lamb. He believes it is a disease they call swayback. The lamb has no co-ordination in its limbs. There is an injection for it so hopefully it can be treated. Trying to raise sheep here is difficult, with problems with weather and disease. Right now, because it has been so cold, there is a lack of food for the mothers. The reason we went to Lerwick yesterday was to get hay for the ewes.

I just e-mailed the Northern Lighthouse Board to see if the tower could be painted before the August event. Our covenant with them says we are to keep all of the other buildings to the standards of the tower. Here it is more like they need to keep the tower to the standards that Tom maintains for the other buildings. He had already started to touch up spots on our house but he now is going to wait until later in the summer so it will look stunning for August.

May 4th

How could we get so many beautiful blue days in a row in Shetland? The sky is a light pastel blue with a few puffy white clouds and the sea is a dark, glassy grey blue. I just came back from doing one of my favourite activities here – hanging up clothes. There is no more gorgeous place in the world to hang up clothes than our backyard and they smell so special afterwards.

This morning I had help. The Eshaness lighthouse nursery in the garage now has two residents. They are black caddy lambs. Caddy is the Shetland name for orphaned lambs. One, whose mother would not feed her, is three days old and the other is a tiny day-old black lamb, which was one of twins. Its mother just did not know how to cope with two babies, as they were her first lambs. They are spry and looking pretty healthy but one is so small survival is questionable. They are certainly drinking well from the bottle. I am following the directions exactly as I mix and administer the milk because the lambs can eat too much or the milk can be too strong and it can kill them. It is a scary responsibility. I will not name them until they are over a week old as the history has been for Tom to loose his lambs in the first week.

Great find yesterday – my rhubarb is coming up. I am being pleasantly surprised by what plants are still alive in the yard around the lighthouse. Yesterday one of my publishers was able to convince *Scottish Field*, a very prestigious and up market magazine, to do a story on the house and gardens here. As Dean said, 'What gardens? All we have are a few daffodils and some roses'. Seeds are coming up in trays in all the windows so we will at least have annuals that I can put in pots so if a storm comes along I can shelter them. My plan is to make an arrangement of annuals in pots and put them in old lobster creels, which I will put at each side of the front door.

The challenge with decorating at the lighthouse is keeping things simple both in the garden and the house. What I want to create is a simple elegance in tune with the environment. What I did to the bathroom is an example. I have it decorated with shells collected here. The bath mat and accessories are in a seashell motif. Simple, but fits with a lighthouse. Before *Scottish Field*'s visit I will need to do something with my office. It worries me that this is an upscale magazine. Eshaness is not an upscale place.

The meeting with the amateur radio people went well and the open house will be exciting. They will be broadcasting for two days, 24 hours a day, to lighthouses all over the world. We could use some help with serving and selling books in the tearoom so I will ask some of the neighbours. With the broadcasters and Leslie here it should be a hoot.

I had the fresh haddock for dinner last night and even though it was expensive it tasted good accompanied by a salad, baked potato and rice pudding. One thing for sure is I do eat well.

May 5th

It is a beautiful Saturday with sunshine and not much wind. As soon as I get this written I am going out to spade up a small garden right beside our garage. It is the most protected place we have. My plan is to try and make it into a salad/flower garden. The ground is rocky so I will bring some peat from Tom's house to make it a little more fertile. If we get a storm I will go to the beach and gather seaweed and put it on a sheet and so it will get rained on for a few days to wash off the salt before I dig it into the soil. Seaweed is a wonderful natural fertilizer.

I suppose I will let my two charges out to get some sunshine and exercise. The lambs can be nuisances because they get underfoot. They are growing but have developed diarrhoea, which is not a good sign. They do eat and get around really well though.

Being such a nice day I had lunch down at the Seal Rocks (known in Shetland as the Bruddans). I have a new thermos in which I can take coffee or tea in my backpack. The surf was so high I thought the seals would not be out. Surprisingly there were 18 huge seals lined up in a row taking a sunbath on one of the bigger rocks. Once in a while they would slip into the water for a swim but soon come back up for a little more sun. It was fun watching them being totally lazy. They had better start being careful as a pod of six Orcas (killer whales) has been spotted just north of us. A pilot whale was seen just south of here so the big guys are moving in and the little guys (the seals) need to take care.

Later in the day I helped Tom with some of his new lambs. A couple of times he had to turn the ewes over so I could put the lamb up to suck. The mothers just did not seem to get the hang of this feeding bit.

Tom decided I should see the fence he built during the winter. What a walk it was! It took us an hour to reach the end of the fence, which is on the north end of the Eshaness peninsula. I have never climbed such hills. Needless to say I am sore and except for spading the garden I am not doing any big exercise today, no matter what.

May 6th

It is warm enough today to have some of my plants out to get more sunshine. The garage, now called the caddy shack, door opens so the caddies can get a little fresh air. After I feed them maybe I will take some time to sit outside so they can run around the yard.

Tom offered me a plot of ground to use as a larger garden so now I have to decide what I am going to put in it. Each day I try to have what I call a 'fun activity' to keep things from becoming too repetitive. Choosing my seeds for the garden will be my fun activity this afternoon.

Three daffodils are blooming and two more are about to come out. It is so exciting. I can grow daffodils and roses so maybe I will be able to grow something else. My little salad garden is dug up and I have added some peat to it. This week I will get some fertilizer in Lerwick, as no seaweed seems to be around.

An even bigger happening was I saw a few puffins floating at the bottom of the cliffs. The large migration is not here but at least some have arrived. Hopefully we will have lots and lots.

I have a local maker of Shetland rugs coming in a few minutes to give me an estimate for a scatter rug for in front the Rayburn. I think I am going have him make me a semi-circular rug with a Viking design in brown and red to match the Rayburn and a little green to match the furniture. Maybe he would lend me some striking and unique rugs to use when *Scottish Field* is here.

May 7th

Today is a bank holiday – what ever is that? Why the country closes down to give the banks a holiday no one I have asked seems to know. This is the May Day bank holiday. Maybe they just have a holiday on the Monday after a significant day, anyway almost everything is closed. There is a major sale at the home furnishing store in Lerwick and if the buses were running or I had a car I would go but I don't so I guess I will save my money.

The man who makes Shetland rugs and his wife came yesterday. For in front of the Rayburn I am either going to have one of their standard designs or the designer wants to make a custom pattern with a picture of Eshaness lighthouse. The custom design would look a lot like the gold and diamond necklace that Dean had made for my birthday last year; shaped like the lighthouse's square tower. If he does the standard design it would be burgundy like the Rayburn with a Shetland sheep mauve background. I like the idea of a custom-made lighthouse rug but it could be too commercial.

I saw another 'line up' this morning. When I went out to feed the fuzzy black critters better known as the caddies that live in the garage, there were hordes of oystercatchers lined up on the rocks at the top of the cliffs behind the lighthouse. Shimmering black and white in the sunshine, their orange beaks and feet looked gold. The sea is calm today so I just might take a chair and read on the seaside since there is little wind. Hopefully this kind of weather might be around for a while but in Shetland you never know so you take advantage when you can. The problem with reading outside is bunches of tourists, since it is a holiday. It really spoils the atmosphere to have people walking by staring at you!

May 8th

Out checking the sheep with Tom this morning we stopped on a sloping hill with a vista of dark blue sea and a light powder blue sky. It was a spectacular sight.

This has been a strange year in Shetland since the weather has been mostly sunny with a few cold winds. According to the neighbours the weather has not been as bad as usual for lambing.

I found myself feeling empathy for the ewe as I thought back to when my daughters were born. They say mothers never forget giving birth and I definitely haven't. I wondered what it would be like to give birth in the middle of an open field with the ocean in the background. I think I prefer a nice clean hospital with a doctor on hand. We saw a ewe that seemed to be struggling so we watched for a few minutes. She was definitely in labour. It was a remarkable experience watching a new life come into the world in such a beautiful spot with sparkling sunshine to greet the newborn. It was a normal birth and the lamb was healthy and strong.

Watching the beginning of life around here makes me appreciate even more the whole process of being a mother. The two wonderful mothers of my life are gone now but they had much to do with how I turned out. My mother died many years ago so my memories are dim. My husband Dean's mom died only a few months ago and I miss her dreadfully. I guess the thing to do is focus on the blessings and wisdom they brought into my life while they were here.

May 9th

I am going to work in the garden, as it is a beautiful day. I have no patience to wait and see my photographs so I made a quick trip to Lerwick yesterday and got my latest pictures developed. The stars of this roll of film were the caddies out scampering around in the yard. The biggest one now can jump the fence out of the garage so I have to keep an eye on them even though Tom fenced the entire yard so they could have the run of the place.

It would be a horrible tragedy if one of my charges got out and fell over the cliff into the sea or Calder's Geo.

May 10th

The ladies of the light are out taking a sunbath and it is so warm I may just go and join them. I am calling the caddies the ladies of the light now since they are all female. When I am sure they are going to survive then I will give them names. Their favourite place to take their snooze is in the doorway where there is no wind and the sun has warmed the concrete. I will try and take a picture of them sleeping but it will be difficult. When they hear me coming they think it is time for a snack.

On my last trip to Lerwick I saw the most beautiful little lamb. It was spotted black and white. Big spots, not just small ones scattered around. It looked a lot like a black and white spotted Great Dane dog. I am going to buy a female lamb if the lady who owns it will sell. That will mean my flock will have three members. My strategy is to add my three to Tom's flock so when I come back from the USA they will be here.

Tom put the wee red boat in the harbour at Stenness so shellfish is now on the menu. He gave me two small lobsters that I am going to make into a lobster white sauce and put on pasta for supper tonight. It is an easy dish if the lobster is cooked and shelled. All I have to do is make the sauce and cook the pasta.

New seafood is going to be added to the lighthouse menu. Every time Tom brings up his creels they have big (and little) brown crabs in them. He takes off their claws and throws the main body back in the sea to grow new claws. Tom got three pretty good-sized claws yesterday and while I was down helping him with the sheep he boiled them for a snack. They are as good as lobster in my opinion. Since he only harvests the claws you need quite a few to make something. Searching the Internet I found some devilled crab and crab salad recipes. It sounds like I may live on crab salad sandwiches most of the summer since the source is plentiful.

I am hoping my seeds come today so I can plant vegetables in the corner of Tom's garden. I got all cold weather crops like beets, broccoli, parsnips, and cauliflower. The down side of my gardening efforts is that a storm could come along and wipe everything out just like it did in June last year.

On the flower front I planted three new Rugosa roses, one white and one pink from a nursery and some big roots from red ones in Tom's garden. I am keeping my fingers crossed they take hold.

A tourist walked by this morning and took a picture of the caddies in the sun and complimented me on my daffodils. If they only knew how much work goes into the flowers they would even be more impressed.

May 11th

Some of the best times living here are early morning and sunset. It would be inaccurate to say sunrise since the sun is up before 4:30 am and I am not. When I first get up I make myself a cup of coffee and sit at the table to watch the surf on the islands – it looks beautiful in the morning light. My brother who is an artist taught me that early morning and late afternoon light is best for photographs. It is also best for looking for at the sea.

The high point of my day is to take a book into the master bedroom after watching the evening news and just read. As the sun sets over the ocean the walls of the bedroom turn all different colours. The kaleidoscope on the walls begins with bright white light as the sun shines directly in the window then becomes more yellow before turning pink. When it starts becoming pink I spend more time staring out the window than reading. Sunsets are so exquisite here even when there are no clouds. It is the colours that make them so spectacular. Last night the sky was rosy pink and the sea was a deep purple. It stayed that way until after 11:00 pm.

Soon the summer dim will begin. Summer dim is the muted pink and purple pastel illumination that occurs during the summer when the sun never sets. I will be going to sleep before the sun sets as it gets later and later.

May 12th

Tomorrow is Mother's Day in the US. It will be a bit lonely for me as my children and grandchildren are so far away but I was here last Mother's Day so I know I will get through by keeping busy.

With the launch of the new book, *Scottish Lighthouses*, I am back in the media. The *Shetland Times* just came out with the notice of my book signing next Saturday. This will be the 'official' launch of the new book. Lots of people should be in Lerwick as BBC's *Antiques Roadshow* will be in Lerwick the same day. I hope we will have a good crowd for the signing.

I will be interviewed on a national radio program called *Out of Doors* on Saturday at 7:05 UK time. It will be a 15 minute interview recorded in BBC Shetland's studio next Wednesday. On the same day I will be recording a feature for BBC Shetland on the new book. The response to *Scottish Lighthouses* is over the top. It is mostly the beautiful pictures that sell the book but the reviews of the text have been good also. The popularity of *The Last Lighthouse* also is making people pick it up and take a look.

One of the local hotels is having a Shetland food celebration next Saturday sponsored by the Shetland Agricultural Marketing Group. They have on the menu dressed Shetland crab salad, smoked mackerel and oatcakes, Voe beef and Auld Rock ale pie, baked Scalloway haddock with prawn sauce, roast Olna duck and orange sauce all served with Ness tatties, Graven cabbage and Quendale neeps. Dessert is marmalade pudding and custard, old fashioned boozy trifle and ginger crunch ice cream. Needless to say when I mentioned it to Tom he said we had to drop by. So next Saturday will be a big day with the book signing, *Antiques Roadshow* and Shetland food.

It is brown trout season. Last Saturday a 6 lb, a 5 lb, and a 4lb 10 oz brown trout were landed in the lochs in this area. They have special rules because of foot and mouth but the fishing is going on. I saw four guys fishing at the loch down the hill from the lighthouse. When I asked how they were doing they said they had caught four pretty good-sized fish on flies.

I am off to record natural sounds from the area for the *Out of Doors* programme before the tourists arrive. Maybe I should record the tourist traffic, as that is a big part of activity around here on the weekends. The caddy lambs are becoming famous as just about every visitor takes a picture of them running around in the lighthouse yard.

May 13th

It has arrived! The lighthouse has a hedgehog. Yesterday when Tom returned home from checking the sheep he found a hedgehog right in front of his door.

Looking on the Internet for information on hedgehogs I found the Welsh Hedgehog Hospital. I wish we had found this site earlier as we had given the new arrival milk, which the site said might kill a hedgehog, but it seems okay this morning.

I am trying to think up an appropriate a name for the little guy or gal. I have had a few ideas such as Stevenson, David A, Thistle, or PC standing for Prickly Creature. A tradition at the Krauskopf house is to give pets distinguished names so that no matter what their background they have a great heritage.

Having given up hope on finding a hedgehog I am totally unprepared with no cage or food for it. I will try and make do with a cardboard box and small dishes until I can get the right stuff. The hedgehog seems happy enough eating and drinking from flowerpot saucers.

Yesterday morning I went for my first ride in the Tom's wee red boat. It was a little foggy. The motor was contrary and kept dying. It was a little distressing being out in a small boat in the fog with a motor that would not run. But then the fog cleared, the motor ran and we had a wonderful ride. Tom got three lobsters and one creel had 32 crabs in it. Only a couple of the crabs were big enough to take the claws and none big enough to harvest for eating. Lots of seals were about including one beautiful white one with a little black baby sunning on a rock.

May 14th

An upset stomach has been bothering me for the last few days so I am going to try and see a doctor today in Lerwick.

Also the littlest caddy lamb is not well. She cannot seem to get her front legs to work right, making it hard to get up or down. When she gets up she eats well and wags her tail so I believe there is still hope. I just talked to the vet and he is sending some medicine out on the bus for her. Hopefully she will be all right until then. I would hate to see her die after getting this far. I must admit I have gotten really attached to the caddies and they are a hit with the tourists.

May 15th

It is van day at the lighthouse. The fish van will appear with fresh fish later today and the library van is also coming. It is really nice when you are so far from civilization to get things brought to your front door.

My littlest caddy's health seems to have improved. Her medicine did not arrive on last night's bus but the bus company just called. They found the medicine and it will come tonight. She was very spry this morning and I am about to take her out and let her run around. Maybe she will make it after all.

I am feeling a little better. I saw the doctor yesterday and the medicine she gave me for my stomach seems to be helping. There is a possibility I have developed an ulcer so hopefully the medicine will work. I am trying to figure out what is making me so stressed out. They may want to hospitalise me in the next few weeks to have a look. I am not sure I want to go into the hospital here. I might let them do tests but nothing more. If something more needs to happen, I will wait until I get home. There I know the system better and would be working with a doctor who has been taking care of me for years.

Last night a new menace appeared in my flowers and garden. I looked out the window and there were eight big rabbits on the sea side. The garden is in the front yard but it won't take long for them to find it. We are fencing the garden but I doubt if that will keep the rabbits out. Such a struggle growing things here!

May 16th

The caddy shack, as one of my friends calls it, has a new member; a white lamb with black spots that was born yesterday. So now there are two black lambs and one white one running around in the yard. I put them out early for exercise as I am off to town to record the *Out of Doors* programme and the feature for BBC Shetland.

The littlest black lamb's medicine arrived last night on the bus. The bus driver had forgotten to give it to Bertie, our feeder bus driver, the first day. Tom gave her the first injection and she does seem better this morning but we really won't see any major change until she has had all her shots. Hopefully she will make it. The new lamb is the same size as the littlest black one, which is ten days old.

Had fresh haddock from the fish van last night for dinner. It was cheaper and better than the haddock I had purchased at the fishmonger in town. The van will be coming every Tuesday now.

The library van was fun. I could take as many books as I wanted and can keep them for a month. That is like letting me loose in a candy store. I got 35 books and am trying some new authors the librarian recommended.

The hedgehog is fine and I hope today to get it a house. I am looking for a gerbil cage or something that will allow me to watch it. I forgot to mention among the names being considered is 'Hedgie', a suggestion from our oldest grandchild, Austin. I have narrowed it down to Hedgie or Thistle. It likes to eat but only cooked food with the exception of bugs, which it absolutely adores. It is also very fond of cheese. So I have on my grocery list cheese for the hedgehog.

May 17th

I have been gardening including re-potting my petunias, which are going into the lobster creels. I am going to keep them in the house for a couple of days before putting them in the creels, which will be wrapped in clear plastic. They really make neat greenhouses. One of the tomatoes is now in a big pot so that it can be moved in and out. Tom will put two of the other four tomato plants in his garden and I will put two in the salad garden here. The first plants seeded directly in the ground are coming up in the garden. It is so dry I will have to take a bucket and water them this afternoon. Tom is building fences to keep the caddy crowd, and hopefully the rabbits, away from the garden.

Hedgie is running, or I guess it is more accurate to say he is wobbling, around his new house since he moves with sort of a shuffle. He loves his new cat food diet. He crunches on it just like he does bugs. I am thankful he runs around in the daytime and sleeps at night; just the opposite of what hedgehogs normally do.

Recording went well yesterday and Radio Shetland aired their segment last night. It was very professional and made me proud to be a part. *Out of Doors* will be on Saturday. It was a different kind of interview with a twist I did not expect – 'The Romance of Lighthouses'. *Scottish Radiance* writer, Kay Glasgow, even got mentioned on the program because I made the mistake of telling the program's host about her listening to him on the Internet and he was thrilled.

Two newspapers called and interviewed me yesterday. It looks like *Scottish Lighthouses* may be bigger than *The Last Lighthouse*.

May 18th

It is more like Shetland today with strong winds and a little rain. The caddies have been out running around but it must be hard going for the little ones with the wind so strong. They could get blown away.

Hedgie, the hedgehog, had a technical problem. He has a nest ball, which he is supposed to crawl into so he can lay down or roll around. Well, it seems Hedgie is too fat. He got only half way in and got stuck. The ball rolled and I had an upside down hedgehog with feet straight up in the air. After some work so as to not hurt his spines I removed him from the ball none the worse for the experience. He can really make a mess of his cage, worse than our guinea pig used to.

Tomorrow is the big day with the book signing, *Antiques Roadshow*, and the Shetland feast. In addition I will try to get up early enough so I can listen to the *Out of Doors* interview before I go to town.

May 19th

I got up early to listen to my interview on *Out of Doors* and was surprised it turned out very well.

It is a bright sunny day here but cold. I think it rained quite a bit last night because my garden looked really wet this morning. Hopefully that will help things grow.

Yesterday the littlest black caddy was worse, with the infection causing swelling in her joints. Maybe I let her play too long outside on a cold day. I called the vet who is continuing the antibiotic injections for five more days. Today I am only going to let her out for a short time before I go to Lerwick since I think a little exercise is good for her. The other two are running all over the place.

Hedgie is up and has a new favourite food – toast. I made the hole in its ball bigger and now that is its preferred place. Tom thinks it is because it is so cosy and the hedgehog can curl up. I took pictures of Hedgie, which I will take to Lerwick to get developed.

Today should be great fun. I think even Tom is excited. He hates crowds but he has a knife that is very old with all kinds of carving on it that he wants to take to the show so he is really geared up. The knife looks to me like it is Spanish so it might have come off of a Spanish Armada ship wreck which we have lots of around here.

May 20th

Antiques Roadshow was great fun. Tom's knife was from Ceylon, very old and worth £125. He was tickled but said he wished it had been worth £125,000. Men are never satisfied.

My book signing went well with people standing in line at times. We sold a surprising number of books. I enjoy the book signings at the *Shetland Times* bookstore as I meet so many neat people from all over the islands.

Only disappointment was by the time we got to the Shetland meal it was sold out. The owner said they were going to do it again. I will get reservations early next time so we are not disappointed. We went to Busta House in Brae instead.

The caddies are calling. They must think they are hungry. Littlest black one seems better but I would say still not out of the woods as she falls over often.

At 3:30 pm Hedgie died. He had not moved around much all day and then he just breathed his last. I am devastated. 'If only' is what I want to say to myself but I have no idea why he died so I cannot even say that. The little house beside the sea seems so empty. It was so much fun to have something to talk to, watch and play with. All of my life I have had pets and I guess I am lost without one.

I cannot stop crying. At least when Dean's mom died I talked with other people by phone and Tom stayed close by. People who say its just a pet have never lost a pet they loved. As those of us with pets know it hurts just like losing a human friend or member of the family.

Right now I am wondering if I can make it for a year here. I guess that is yet to be found out.

May 21st

I am still trying to get over losing Hedgie. It is the consensus of opinion that he might have been sick when he arrived. It is unusual to find a hedgehog on your front step. Tom has the whole neighbourhood looking for another hedgehog for me. As always when I loose a pet I do not feel I want another one right away but it did seem sad to not be able to give the end of my toast to Hedgie this morning.

After loosing Hedgie someone suggested when you live alone with little or no outside human contact you look more inside yourself. You live closer to your emotions since there are no distractions or conversations with other people to cover them up. This should make me a better writer in the long run, I hope.

The caddies are growing and it looks like the one who has been sick is finally getting well. They are pets of sorts; most of all they are fun to watch. They are also big nuisances. Yesterday when I was trying to take Hedgie's cage out to the generator house all three decided to visit inside the big house. The one that has been sick decided she wanted to take a full tour. She made it all the way to the master bedroom before I could catch her. The other two went into the living room. Sheep do not belong in the house no matter how cute they are.

It is a cold and foggy day here. It is supposed to clear and be nice later. If it does I might get some of my plants planted in the garden. Yesterday we planted the two tomato plants I grew from seed at Tom's where it is more protected than here. I have two to plant here in our only protected spot beside the garage plus the one in a big pot that I can move inside if a storm comes along. My lettuce and one row of flowers are up in the garden. Of course we have had no storms so who knows what will happen to them.

I think if it stays nasty I will do some spinning today. It will soon be time for shearing and I will get more wool. I still have some left to wash and card from last year.

May 22nd

Another cold windy day with huge surf has arrived. I have been sitting at the table by the window doing a final proofread of my Shetland and Orkney lighthouse book, *Northern Lights*, which is soon off to the publisher.

I am in a decorating mood, brought on by the *Scottish Field* visit. Last night I moved the furniture around in the Rayburn room and the new arrangement makes the room look bigger. It also allows more people to watch TV.

Today after the fish van arrives I am going to Brae to get paint samples. The only room that needed work when we moved in was my office and hopefully I can get it painted within the next two weeks. I still do not know when *Scottish Field* is coming but I want to be ready

After the trip to Brae I am going to work on the lobster creel greenhouses and put the plants in them. I should be able to get an interesting effect with low growing blue and white petunias mixed with geraniums. I got red geranium cuttings from Tom who had thrown them out. The creel idea being it will allow me to protect them with the plastic when the weather gets bad or even bring them inside.

Yesterday Tom brought me wild primroses from his neighbour's garden. They are a beautiful yellow colour with white centres. I planted them in a protected spot but I am not sure whether they will survive the wind.

An online review of *Scottish Lighthouses* from a major newspaper is a really good one. The publicity and reviews have been great. Two well-received books in a row are scaring me. Maybe the next one will be a flop.

I had bad news from Dean today. Something slaughtered some of our chickens. This is not a good weeks for animals at either of the Krauskopf homes.

May 23rd

It is a foggy, warm day so I have been outside all morning planting some of my plants grown from seed. Hopefully they will grow. It is a bit risky but I will never know if I do not try.

A rhubarb pie is in the oven. Tom showed up with his arms full of rhubarb and said, 'This should make a pie'. I call that an obvious hint. He brought enough to make six pies. If he can get the sugar in Hillswick when he goes on Friday I will begin making rhubarb and ginger jam. Never a dull moment here as I also have had two radio interviews this morning.

I have neglected writing about caddy number three. She is white with longer wool and her face is speckled with grey and black. The bottoms of her legs are black so she looks like she is wearing socks. Tom found her in the hill with no ewe in sight so he gave her colostrum and brought her to me. She is extremely active and is always the first in the door. Her size is a concern. She has not grown much since birth so she is quite small. I think she is developing now so maybe she will be okay.

All of the caddies have free run of the yard with open access to the caddy shack. They have begun to eat grass but one of them prefers the tops of the sea pinks that are just coming into bloom. I am assuming that sea pinks will not hurt lambs but there is not a whole lot I can do about it.

I am going to be interviewed on the Warren Pierce show on WJR in Detroit, Michigan for the second time this Saturday at 5:50 am US time. Thank goodness the interview is also aired later in the day so the people who sleep in can hear it.

May 24th

It is a magnificent day with the sun shining brightly and the water a beautiful light blue. I have washing in the machine and will hang out clothes today. The caddies are all lined up on the sidewalk along the generator house in the sun. They love having the freedom to run anywhere inside the fence. The sea pink flowers in the yard are quickly disappearing thanks to nibbling caddies but there are thousands getting ready to bloom outside the fence.

I only lost three of the plants transplanted yesterday to the rabbits. I will have to work on getting the garden area more rabbit-proof. I am also getting some wild primrose roots from one neighbour and a big bunch of buttercup roots from another. The wild buttercups are one of my favourite flowers because they are so bright and cheerful. Today I am going down to set some plants in my patch at Tom's.

On Sunday I am having a visitor from the States. She is coming to Shetland for a bird watching tour but she is coming here because she lives in a lighthouse, Montauk Point Lighthouse, on the end of Long Island in New York. Peter Leybourne, who is coordinating the amateur radio event, is bringing her from Sumburgh to Eshaness.

May 25th

It is a bleak day. The sun shines every once in a while but the wind is cold. A sudden gust of wind yesterday broke the two tomato plants I was going to put in the garden. I still planted them in the hope that they will come up from the roots but they look really sick this morning. The two at Tom's house are growing and the one in the pot is alive and well. It is sad when you start something from seed, tend it in the window for a month or more and you can't get them outside without being destroyed. I knew their survival was 'iffy'. Well, it looks like I was unfortunately right.

The caddies are really into eating grass so it should not be too long until they can be moved to Tom's where there is more grass and company for them. I want to keep them here as long as I can but it depends on how long the grass lasts.

Yesterday evening I was able to sit on the sea side of the lighthouse and read a book in warm sunshine. The caddies munched the grass, and my shoelaces. They are into shoelaces. I think it is more playing with them instead of eating them.

This is *Scottish Radiance* programming weekend and I have three more columns to do besides writing two book reviews so most of the weekend will be spent in front of the computer.

May 26th

It is spitting a little rain outside. The weather is helping me work. Once the Internet magazine is done it will be another reading and writing day. I will try to make the reading light and not work too much on the book since it is a weekend.

My plan had been to go looking for wild flowers today. The rain means it is a good time to get the plants but not such a good time to be out. My tomatoes are barely alive and I doubt they will make it. The light rain and mist is good for them and the wind has finally moved to another direction to give them a rest.

I feel like I am living in a rhubarb patch. Last night Tom showed up with another huge armful. Being the frugal person I am I made a pie, a big dish of rhubarb crisp for company tomorrow, and two jars of rhubarb and ginger jam. Tom wanted to bring more! Since he said he sat down and ate a whole pie in one sitting I do not expect to see him today, as he will need to stay near a bathroom. Or at least I would.

May 27th

A rainy and foggy day for the visit of the lady from Long Island. Shetland never co-operates; when you want the weather to be one way it ends up the other.

Went wild flower harvesting yesterday and found some nice plants for the yard, but a few minutes ago I saw three little caddies eating them. I hope they decide they do not like them. Sheep will eat anything.

May 28th

It is a warm misty day, one I would call soft. Just completed my daily routine of emptying the Rayburn's ashes on the rocks and feeding the starving caddies. My nose is running a little and I felt a little bit under the weather last night so I am going to take a day off and watch a Humphrey Bogart festival on BBC 2. Being a holiday weekend, they always have a movie festival on one of the BBC channels. If I had a VCR I would tape them to watch another rainy day.

My guests arrived yesterday when it was so foggy you could not see the sundial. We chatted, had tea and rhubarb crumble until it was time to feed the caddies. The lady from New York really enjoyed feeding the little ladies and said that it might be the highlight of her whole trip. She fell in love with them. I have to admit they are really cute right now but I would not say they were well behaved as they have taken to eating the marsh marigolds I planted in the yard. Hopefully the flowers will survive but I will not know until next year.

The visitors and I walked to the Bruddans in the fog, hoping the sun would come out and we could see some seals. The sun did show its shiny face just about the time we arrived and the visitors were totally awestruck. They kept saying it was too beautiful to be true. I couldn't wait until they saw the cliffs, then they would definitely think this was one of the most beautiful places in the world. They were totally enchanted. They used three rolls of film just on the cliffs and the lighthouse. We saw about forty puffins swimming off the cliffs, which was an added bonus.

We decided to drive down and see Tom's peat bank, Dore Holm, and Stenness.

By the time we arrived at Stenness the fog was back and Dore was invisible. We drove over to Tom's so they could see an original croft house. They loved the setting of Tom's house.

Speaking of Tom's house, his geese have a nest full of eggs. I hope the babies survive and maybe I will get a goose for a pet. The yard is all fenced so it would be contained. That would really send the tourists nuts.

May 29th

I am in a hurry as I am off to Lerwick to buy caddy milk. They are almost out. They are eating grass but should not be weaned for another three weeks.

Victory! My nasturtiums came up in the garden so I have them, lettuce, and a row of mixed fragrant annuals. No broccoli or cauliflower has appeared yet. The tomatoes look sick but are still alive.

May 30th

It is a beautiful day so I am going to look for bird nests. I want to start recording around the nests for the radio feature as well as take some pictures. Tom is going to act as guide as I do not know the habitat that well.

My lobster creel greenhouses are working reasonably well and the plants inside are really growing. The creels can be opened or shut as the weather dictates.

Kay Glasgow came through again and found one of my newspaper interviews on the Internet. I knew this one would have mistakes, as the reporter was very sloppy about collecting information. He did not ask good follow-up questions. One disadvantage of living here is that we receive no newspapers. Thank goodness for the Internet, at least I can read them online even though they do not put everything there. I am surprised my husband survives when he is here as he reads two newspapers from cover to cover every day in Michigan.

May 31st

Yesterday I spent all afternoon hunting bird eggs. I found three different types of nests, all of them in open ground with no camouflage. Some of the eggs were laid in rock-lined nests. I believe those are either Arctic terns or lapwings. One nest with big eggs and grass bedding was probably a seagull nest. All the eggs were a light olive green colour but the spots and shapes were different. The seagull eggs were larger with bigger dark greenish brown spots. The lapwing eggs were pear shaped with dark greenish brown squiggly spots almost like lines in places. I am going to keep watching the nests with my long-range camera lens and hopefully will get some pictures of the babies

I am searching for a book with sea birds' egg pictures in colour so I can be more accurate in my identification.

I have finally finished the programming of *Scottish Radiance* and so I will have more time to spend outside. Every time I finish uploading, I say I am going to cut back on its content but never do because of all the positive feedback from the readers.

June

June 1st

It is a sunny but cool day with lots of wind. If the wind dies I should be able to get out and try to identify some more bird eggs this afternoon. Tom had planned to paint the ceiling in the office today if it rained but I imagine he is in the boat right now.

He dropped in yesterday afternoon to check on me and to tell me he had gotten three lobsters that morning. One was too small to keep so he cooked it. Well, brazen me I invited myself to his house for supper since I never turn down a chance to eat lobster. I think he was a little afraid what he served would not be fancy enough for me but what a Shetland feast he put together. I had fresh cooked lobster and crab with wonderful bread from the Voe bakery, Orkney cheese and pickled onions. It was absolutely out of this world. A gourmet's delight. To thank Tom I just finished making him a trifle.

My broccoli and cauliflower are up so it is time to start weeding the garden. The tomatoes at Tom's are still alive and growing a little, which is a miracle.

Tomorrow or maybe today since it is nice, Tom said he would take me out in the wee red boat to look for eider duck nests. Their eggs are supposed to be huge and interesting. If we find one we will return to take pictures of the hatchlings (I think that is the right term).

I have the library and the *Shetland Times* bookstore looking for books with colour pictures of sea birds' eggs. I am finding lots of nests but have absolutely no idea what they are.

June 2nd

It is a nasty day with cold north winds and off and on heavy rain. Inside activities are the plan for the weekend. I am going to make rhubarb bread and while it is baking I will paint my office. After that I will take a bath and curl up with a good book and some music.

I have enough rhubarb to make rhubarb streusel (a delicious crumbly topping) pie for tomorrow when Tom comes up for dinner. I am trying some new recipes because in 10 days my stand-in BBC producer from Australia is coming for four days. I want to feed her Shetland things. Last night I tried baking smoked haddock in milk and then using the milk on top of a baked potato. It was really tasty.

I am hoping for better weather tomorrow so Tom can take me looking for eggs. I am really into finding birds' nests and watching the chicks of whatever bird growing up.

June 3rd

I am sitting in my redecorated office that now has dazzling aqua pearl walls that are actually sea foam green in colour. Painting this room with its eight-foot high ceiling was no easy task. It is good to have the job done and now I can start hanging all of the pictures. This is the only room that is decorated in my style as the rest of the house I have not changed. The former owners did such a good job of sprucing it up it would be a shame to alter it.

Eating is the big activity as the caddies are out nibbling grass and Tom just arrived for dinner. Sunday is definitely a day of rest around here except for food consumption.

June 4th

Civilisation is coming to the lighthouse; I just ordered a VCR. My frustration had reached the limit when there were three good movies on digital channels all at the same time. I had a terrible time making a choice. The VCR model I ordered will also play US version tapes so that is a big plus.

I have decided to fly to Foula; the island I gaze at every day. It has only 40 people and hundreds of sheep but is supposed to be one of the really spectacular places in Shetland. If I can get reservations on the plane I want to go next week before my BBC producer arrives. Tom has decided to go with me, as he has never been there. It is only a 15-minute flight and you can get back in the same day. It has some of the highest cliffs in Britain (1200 feet) and they are supposed to be full of sea birds. Keep your fingers crossed that it is a nice day, as we will have no place to go to get away from the elements.

I found a wonderful review of *Scottish Lighthouses* on the website, amazon.co.uk.

Reviews from ordinary readers mean more to me than opinions of professional reviewers for some reason.

June 5th

It is another nasty rainy windy morning at the lighthouse, but warm. Tom is going into Lerwick so I am hitching a ride. I need to get the posters of my various book signings and the covers of each book framed for the newly painted office.

Yesterday Tom found an area I have nicknamed 'the hatchery' because it has so many nests and baby birds on the far side of a small loch near his house. There are literally hundreds of regular and black-headed gulls' nests in the area. Most are small nests with three or four brownish eggs with darker spots but some have blue green eggs with spots. The hatched birds are either fluffy grey with spots or light brown with brown spots. I recorded the sounds of the young chicks. We found one on the shore of the loch that was probably just a day old. We scared it and it jumped into the water and began it swim. Tom was afraid it could not get out of the loch so he helped it back on shore. We later read that seagull chicks can swim right after they are born. I took some pictures, which I hope are in focus.

We also found rain geese, the Shetland name for red-throated divers, in the loch in the centre of the area. We watched for a long time until we spotted the female go up to her nest. After the adults had flown away I used my long-range lens to take pictures of her two dark brown eggs.

The best part of the day was recording a baby seagull that was breaking out of his shell. He was chirping even before he entered the world. It was remarkable. Also I found an oystercatcher that was only seconds old. How did I know he was an oystercatcher? He had the long beak just like his parents and his parents were having a fit.

Our trip to Foula is well timed, as I should be able to get pictures of all kinds of baby birds. Tom is due in a few minutes to go to Lerwick to get supplies for the trip to Foula and food for my BBC producer next week. I am looking forward to her visit as she is an Australian and it will be interesting to see what she thinks of Shetland.

June 6th

I have spent most of the day scanning in my latest pictures. It is costly to have so many pictures developed and then I seem to spend hours scanning them in. What

I need is a digital camera so I can save money and most of all time.

It is a beautiful but cold day and I want to play twitcher again – better known as bird watcher. Baby lapwings and Arctic terns are the desired treasure to find today.

June 7th

I have been out egg 'hunting' already this morning. Leslie Johnson, the attendant to the light and Tom's half brother, took me to see a mother eider duck sitting on her nest. She was way up in the hills among the heather. If Leslie had not known where she was I would not have seen her since their technique of protection is to sit on the nest and not move since they blend in so well with their environment. I touched her but she never stirred. Eider duck down is supposed to be the softest in the world and she was like silky gentle velvet to the touch. Leslie moved her a little and she got up. She had three green eggs one of which was starting to hatch.

This morning Tom and I left early as eider babies leave the nest right after birth. Even knowing the general area where she was located I did not see her and it took us a while to find her. Again she stayed on the nest, which allowed Tom to see her really well. He nudged her off her nest to see the eggs. One egg had the top off of it but the baby bird was not out yet. Tom will check later to see if the chicks have all hatched. We will not disturb her any more until the chicks are all hatched.

On the way back to the lighthouse we found four baby lapwings running around in the grass and I photographed them. They are black and white with the upright body of their beautiful parents. They were on the run so I will have to see how the pictures turn out.

The other exceptional find was a handsome snipe. They are so quick you hardly ever see them but this one must have had a nest as she stayed in one general area. Hopefully, using the long-range lens, I got a good picture of her.

I have yet to get good pictures of baby eider ducks, golden plovers and Arctic terns, when I do that will give me pictures of chicks of most of the birds at Eshaness. We did get some pictures of Arctic terns and golden plover nests and eggs yesterday. The terns were upset but didn't peck us.

June 8th

Tom had to make a trip to Ollaberry to see the lady who does the books for his croft. I hitched a ride as I have only been in that area once. I did not expect to find the hills covered with wild flowers. One old-fashioned croft house had the most beautiful wildflower garden in front. It was full of blues, pinks and different shades of white.

I picked a big bouquet of blue, white, and pink bluebells along the road. They are growing in great profusion in the sheltered areas. Also there were some primroses along with two light blue flowers I have not identified. It would be lovely to get some roots to plant in the yard but they probably wouldn't survive. I want to look up all of the flowers we saw in my flower book.

A new feathered friend has arrived. Pigeons are everywhere. I have never seen pigeons here before but they arrived in huge numbers in the last few days. I do not think I will waste my time by taking pictures of pigeons. They just look like pigeons I have seen in Michigan and in big cities.

June 9th

I worked in the garden for a long time this morning since it was a glorious day with a slight breeze, a full sun and a few white fluffy clouds. Things in the garden are growing slowly. One of the perennials I purchased from a nursery last fall is about to bloom. This is a major event since it will be the first flower besides daffodils to make it through the winter and *bloom*.

I transplanted the roses, which were around the sundial to a more protected place by the garage. They still had some healthy roots so they might survive. In place of the roses around the sundial I put pansies. I grew them from seed and they have been outside getting hardened off so hopefully they will live. Covering the flowers with wire mesh will make them caddy proof, I hope.

My nasturtiums have some bunny damage but are still alive. My collection of annuals is also growing because the bunnies have not yet found them. I have some volunteer potatoes coming up which I am going to leave just to see what happens. It is not much of a garden but it is all mine.

Keeping flowers successfully is not easy – the sheep ate the marsh marigolds but maybe they will come up from the roots.

Next week will be busy with the trip to Foula on Monday, the inspection team from the Northern Lighthouse Board due (hopefully to give me a helicopter ride to the Ve Skerries), and then the Australian producer will be here for three days. It all should be fun.

Submitted the *Northern Lights* book so I can relax from writing for a while. I have found a great source of videos. The British Film library is online and I am going to get some classic black and white videos from them. My first will be *At the Edge of the World* that was shot on Foula.

June 10th

I just got back from taking a ride in Tom's wee boat to Stenness Island. Tom could not get the motor started so he rowed us to the island. Thank goodness it was a sunny and extremely calm day with a smooth and glassy sea. We landed on a small beach and tied the boat to a rock. Four good-sized gull chicks met us but having never seen a human before they scurried away. The island is covered with every type of wild flower. It was a mass of green with blue, pink and yellow spots. The pink was sea pinks, the blue was miniature bluebells but it was the yellow that fascinated me. There were small yellow orchids all over the island.

We wandered all over the island but did not find one nest with birds in it. I think it is getting pretty late to see nesting birds. The gull chicks were the size of turtledoves.

Even if we did not see many birds it was a thrilling experience being in such deserted territory surrounded by the sea. I sat on a rock and just enjoyed the solitude. The island did have lots of adult birds such as cormorants, eider ducks, black-backed gulls, common gulls, oystercatchers, golden plovers, and some little larks I did not recognize.

When we got back in the boat the motor finally started so we were able to finish checking the lobster creels. No lobsters did we find. Tom fished for a little while but no luck there either, but seals surrounded us. There were so many I lost count. One big black one followed us all over the bay. I saw more seals than I have seen in any of my boat trips.

When we got between the island and the Skerry we saw hundreds, possibly thousands, of guillemots sitting on the Skerry cliffs. They look like penguins with white tummies and black dinner jackets but they have long narrow necks and heads ending in a very pointed beak. There were also loads of them in the sea.

While Tom was baiting a creel two puffins flew over into the cliffs. They must have a nest there. They were the first puffins I had seen on our end of Stenness.

Returning to the lighthouse we saw what is not a rare sight, a mass of tourists. There was a tour bus and the car park was so full you could not get one more car into it. I think I will stay in the house for the rest of the day until the tourist onslaught ends. Tom will be back to eat a pork roast that I put into the Rayburn before we left for the boat ride. He had to go home because he smelled like fish.

June 11th

It is not a happy Monday here today. Rain moved in last night along with a cold north west wind so we had to cancel our trip to Foula. It can always be done later in the summer and after the trip to Stenness Island yesterday I am sure the birds would all be out of the nests and difficult to find anyway. Also if we go later the bonxies will not be quite so aggressive since they will not have chicks. Bonxies are big birds that live off stealing other birds' eggs and babies. They are hostile and will dive-bomb an adult human with intent to do bodily harm. The largest colony of bonxies in the world is on Foula. The Foula residents are not too fond of these birds since they have driven lots of birds away from the island.

Since Tom and I were all prepared to go we have decided to go to Lerwick and get supplies. I have three rolls of film to be developed. I am hoping to make a collage and put my bird pictures in it. It would be interesting to see the different stages of bird development in one frame.

Leslie painted the trim he could reach on the tower. Everything is in readiness for the inspection by the Northern Lighthouse Board. The *Pharos* is on its way and should be in this area within the next few days. It might even be in Lerwick so I am taking my camera. I am hoping to hitch a ride in the helicopter to get some aerial shots of our lighthouse.

June 12th

I was out first thing washing the windows since it is a nice day. It is only a temporary solution. To really clean the windows the protective plastic shields have to come off so I can wash under them before the windows look truly clean. Gradually I am getting the place spick and span.

It is supposed to rain this afternoon so I am going to make this short so I can take a long walk this morning. The baby birds are growing and I want to get more pictures of them.

June 13th

Early this morning I planted three more wildflowers Tom brought me yesterday. It was a chilly job as the sun was out but the wind cold. When we have cloud cover it is cold but once the sun gets out it is usually warm. Our latitude is close to the sun and the danger of sunburn is high.

Three pieces of animal news are the main topics for today. A beautiful wild orange rabbit had been hanging around Tom's house recently. Last night, having made a trip down to check the red-throated diver nest with binoculars, we came upon the orange rabbit beside the road. It seemed to be having trouble with its hind legs. It could still move, but not well, and Tom was able to catch it. Checking it over carefully we could find no cuts or broken bones. We assumed a car had hit it but it should have shown some sign of injury on its body. We took it to the lighthouse and put it in the big hedgehog cage and gave it grass and a dish of water. I expected it would be dead when I went out this morning but it wasn't. It had drunk water and eaten all of the grass we gave it. After I finish writing I will go out and check again. Leslie came by and examined it and found no broken bones. We think it was hit on the head and has brain damage. With a bit of luck the damage is temporary and it will live. I took two carrots out this morning and hopefully it has eaten them. I am not going to get too attached to it until it gets better. The death of Hedgie still haunts me and I do not want to go through that again so soon.

Tom just arrived and the rabbit was moving a lot better than yesterday so maybe it will make it.

If the weather permits Tom is going to help Leslie by painting the yellow trim around the top of the tower. The whole place is really looking nice now with the trimming painted on the tower.

The red-throated divers we have been watching with the binoculars have two babies, which is really good.

Tom's goose is still sitting on two eggs. Maybe I will end up with a pet goose yet.

June 14th

My BBC producer, Michelle Raynor, arrives this afternoon for the weekend. I have been cooking up a storm so I won't have to bother while she is here. I have made shepherd's pie and a Shetland haddock pie, a pineapple upside down cake and rhubarb crisp. Saturday night we have reservations for another Shetland feast like the one Tom and I were unable to get into.

The bunny is doing okay. He eats, moves around, drinks water and goes to the bathroom all over his cage. I cleaned him again this morning. Because we have so many predators he would not have survived injured in the wild. He seems to be getting along fine in the cage and I am more optimistic he will survive. His back legs have more movement than when we first found him but he would need to be placed outside the cage to see if they really work. I might do that later today when Tom is here to help me. We could put the top of the hedgehog cage over him.

I am off to pick flowers for my guest's room and finish hoovering.

June 15th

Tom has taken Michelle out in the wee red boat so I have a few minutes to write.

She loves Shetland and seems to be enjoying herself immensely.

Last night after dinner we took a walk and saw a whole bunch of puffins sitting outside their burrows. It was the first time I had seen that many puffins on the lighthouse cliffs. I was relieved to know they are still here.

This morning we walked to the Houlland broch and saw a mother eider duck on a loch with her babies in tow. I did not know until later that Michelle taped the whole thing so that should be interesting. She also taped a conversation with Tom. Whether he will let her use it remains to be seen.

Tomorrow we are stopping at an estate sale in Brae and going to the Shetland feast. Michelle would like to get something to take home from Shetland and she likes old things. I am just looking for things for the house.

I am making lobster salad sandwiches for lunch that we will take as a picnic out on the rocks. It is nice to have guests as I get to do all the things I like and do not feel guilty that I am not working.

June 16th

We are about to run off to Brae with a stop so Michelle can see Tom's wee croft house. Tom is driving the pickup to the sale also so if I see anything wonderful and big I can buy it.

I have enjoyed Michelle's company and Tom really likes her because he says she is down to earth. They had great fun in the boat and brought back a whole bunch of crab claws. Tom stayed for lunch and taught us how to cook and crack the claws. Later Michelle recorded a long interview to accompany my diary recordings.

After dinner we went out and watched the puffins fly in and out. I have found a really good vantage point where, with binoculars, we can watch them close up. Two of the puffins were billing which is a kind of ritual they do which looks like fighting but is actually just a game.

Michelle is a runner and getting ready for a marathon. She ran this morning and found the wind more than she could contend with and had to walk part of the way. Maybe it is not such a good day to go to an outdoor estate sale.

June 17th

Today is Father's Day in the USA and I must call Dean so he will know I remembered.

I have been flying around Shetland in the Northern Lighthouse Board's helicopter. It was so wonderful to see our part of Shetland from the air. I took pictures of Eshaness Light and the coastline. The pilot was pleasant and I gave him a signed copy of *Scottish Lighthouses* as a thank you for the ride. He just flew back to the *Pharos*, the lighthouse board's supply ship.

Michelle is gone. I enjoyed her company immensely and after all my visitors the lighthouse seems a little bit quiet.

I am higher than a kite with excitement (or should I say I am higher than a helicopter with excitement) but also very tired so will write more tomorrow about the auction and the Shetland feast.

June 18th

To get up to date on recent activities, first the caddies are in a lot of trouble. On Friday they took it into to their heads to trim my tomato plant in the pot. It would not have been so bad but they ate the first blooms that were coming on the plant. Bad caddies!

Tonight I will be broadcasting on BBC Shetland to try to contact retired lighthouse keepers in Orkney and Shetland in preparation for my winter activity of writing a novel about a Scottish lighthouse keeper. This is the book that my agent in Los Angeles thinks he can sell to a major movie studio and already has interest.

The weather was awful on Saturday for the sale, but what fun we had. There were mostly Northmavine (northern part of the main island) people in attendance with a few antique dealers. A large soup tureen that looks like a Rhode Island Red chicken sitting on a nest with eggs became my first love. I was able to buy it for £10, which is really cheap for such a large tureen. I thought it would sit on the corner cupboards in the kitchen but is too big so it is now sitting on the counter and being used as a cookie jar. I also bought a box that had a set of eight wine glasses, a lot of glass dishes, and many wee dram glasses. The boxes are the most fun since you do not really know what you are going to get. The box of glass cost me £4. It was so cold that Michelle and I left before the sale was over. Tom stayed and tried to buy a vacuum cleaner and a beautiful light fixture for me but the seller would not let them go at the price I told him I would pay.

The Shetland meal was wonderful. I had king scallops with a tarragon sauce on spinach noodles surrounded by snow peas. It was served with rosemary bread (rosemary grows outside here as do bay trees). The soup was smoked haddock, potato, and leek – need I say anything more. For dessert we split a rhubarb tart topped with honey ice cream with a side of rhubarb and ginger sauce. The rhubarb in the tart had not been sweetened but with the ice cream it was really good. We were stuffed after eating all that.

How do I describe the helicopter ride? This is an incredibly beautiful place from the ground but from a helicopter it takes your breath away. I have never experienced such beauty. The pilot got out of the helicopter after he brought the last of the crew back from the Ve Skerries lighthouse so I took the opportunity to talk to him. He is a Scot but was trained to fly in Texas and spent many years flying on big Texas ranches rounding up cattle. He returned to Scotland because the money was so much better here for specialized helicopter flying. I told him how much I would love to see the area from the air and about 15 minutes later there was knock at the door and he asked if I would like to go for a ride. You can imagine my delight. The helicopter is bright red with the Northern Lighthouse Board emblem and the name of the owner – Bond – on it. The NLB rents it for the year as the machine itself cost over £2.5 million. The NLB has two pilots who fly for them full time. For three months in the winter they are loaned to the Scottish National Ambulance Service and the 'bird' is kept in the Inverness home of Bond. In the summer they fly crews to the lighthouses for maintenance and inspection from the NLB ship *Pharos*.

Because there were only the two of us I got to be co-pilot. I took my camera but goofed as I only had ten pictures on the roll of film in the camera but hopefully they will all turn out. The car park which is usually used as our helipad was full of tourists, so we took off from the flat area just to the east of the sundial. It was amazing. The helicopter itself had so many dials I could not look at them all. The day was a bad one with a stiff wind so I was worried about turbulence on take off but as soon as the helicopter began to climb we shot straight up. I was surprised there was no sign of bouncing. We flew north so I could take a picture of the lighthouse with the cliffs in the foreground and it was stunning. We flew by the lighthouse on the seaside. The pilot was fascinated with the sea caves so we flew low along the cliffs to look at them. To get a different perspective we flew out over Stenness, Dore Holm, St Magnus Bay and the Hillswick lighthouse. We approached our lighthouse from the east. It was all magical. The pilot said something I can relate totally to. People ask him why he flies in Scotland, one of the worst areas in the world for wind and weather, and his answer is, 'Because it is so rugged, no high rises or condos exist on the beautiful coasts. The coastline is picturesque and unspoiled'. He is so right. If I thought this was one of the most beautiful seascapes in the world before the ride, seeing it from the air I now know it is.

The pilot said from what he hears the NLB appreciates what I am doing. My books and interviews are bringing long overdue recognition to the Scottish Lighthouse Service, which is one of the best in the world. The people in Scotland knew that but partly because of my efforts the world is finding out.

The NLB maintenance crew is here so I am going to quit now and ask them in for coffee and biscuits.

June 19th

Nasty, rainy day so Tom showed up early this morning and announced we were going to Lerwick. We just got back.

Big excitement yesterday! Tom was out checking his creels for lobsters in the little red boat and off to his side was a big black fin, which pretty soon turned into a huge black and white whale. He was in the middle of a pod of four Orcas. He headed for shore so if they tipped him over he could get to safety. They are not aggressive to humans but could easily collide with a small boat and capsize it. They swam around the islands and made some splashing – probably our seal population decreasing – and then they took off for the Bruddans. I imagine the seal population there went down too. After Tom told me I watched most of the afternoon but did not see them. They swim very fast and could have been down to the south of the mainland in a couple of hours. Hopefully when the rain quits Tom will be able to go out and see how much damage they did to the seals.

June 20th

The sun has come out for the first time in a few days and I want to do a couple of things outside. I have come down with a slight cold and do not feel very well. Hopefully I will not get too far from the lighthouse if it decides to rain.

I need to see if we have any seals left after the Orcas passed through so I want to walk to the Bruddans. I have fallen in love with a little wild flower called a forget-me-not but it is different from any I have ever seen. It has a tiny blue flower with small blue petals surrounding a yellow heart. It would be nice if I could transplant some to the lighthouse before they quit blooming.

Tomorrow is the longest day of the year and we will be celebrating the midnight sun. Tom and I had planned to go to the top of Ronas Hill to read the newspaper at midnight, the traditional Shetland celebration. The weather is iffy and since I am not feeling good I think I will be sitting out on the rocks watching the puffins and reading the newspaper.

I have given up growing vegetables in the garden. What survived the wind and rain, the baby rabbits have eaten. For some reason the rabbits do not like the flowers so I still have sort of a flower garden.

The injured rabbit seems to be getting better every day. I bought food for it yesterday that it ate right away. I am hoping it will totally recover so it could be upgraded to a pet, Tom could build a raised cage so it could be outside. The problem is where to put the rabbit to shelter it from the wind.

June 21st

It is the longest day of the year and the day of the midnight sun. The rain and the mist will have to go away before anyone around here will see the sun at midnight or any other time. It is supposed to clear but not until tomorrow.

Yesterday afternoon it was sunny and warm for a short time so I decided to walk and see if I could find any of the wild orchids. It turned out to be a fun adventure as I found fields full of orchids; so many I had to be careful where I stepped. They come in all different colours and sizes. Most are small but have the typical orchid leaf. Some have spots on their leaves and some don't. I took some pictures of the most common varieties.

I moved one of each variety to the lighthouse. If it clears I'll find another field and move some more. I do not want to deplete any one area.

Tom was out fixing a fence yesterday and stumbled on a snipe nest. They are shy birds and only come out at night. They hide their nests in tall grass and the eggs are green and sort of pear shaped. I took pictures of the nest and hopefully I will be able to photograph the babies. While I was out I saw some ringed plovers only a few days old. They were fully marked and looked exactly like their parents. I have never seen a bird run so fast as those little guys. The parents would pretend to be injured to lure me away. It is sad to think they might have to give up their lives to save their babies.

June 22nd

Well, the longest day is past. I went to bed at 10:00 pm as it was cloudy and foggy. You could not see the midnight sun anywhere on Shetland. There are still three days in which the sun can be seen all night from Ronas Hill so hopefully Tom will take me up on Saturday or Sunday. I hinted many times for Tom to give me the trip to Ronas Hill as a birthday present (my birthday is next Wednesday). It is difficult for him as he has to take a night off work and diesel for the truck is so expensive. I plan on trying to pay for the diesel for the trip if he will let me.

You can drive about half way up Ronas Hill and then you have to walk the rest of the way. I have not been up there and am looking forward to it, as the hill is a rare example of artic tundra and wild flowers below the Arctic Circle. I will not try to bring any flowers back to the house, as they would not survive but I do hope to get some pictures.

The orcas showed up in a bay on the north side of the mainland not too far from here. This time it was a pod of seven. They were seen playing with the large buoys that are used to mark salmon farms. That must have been a sight, those dramatic giant black and white creatures playing with the orange balls. I am hoping they stay around the island until Dean and my youngest daughter's family arrive but that is three weeks away and they may have moved on by then.

I am trying to wean the caddies and they want no part of it. I dropped their nightly bottle but they stood in the caddy shack and yelled, then they moved up to the door of the house and screamed some more. I gave in and they are still getting a morning and evening bottle but only half as much milk as before. They seem satisfied with that as they go off and eat grass as soon as they have had their milk.

One of the joys of editing *Scottish Radiance* is reading two books a month for book reviews. I try to vary the subject so I read lots of books that I would not read just for pleasure, such as Scottish history.

June 23rd

I just got back from accompanying Tom in the little red boat on another foggy and misty day. It was a good morning for him; getting two lobsters, a bunch of crab claws, a bucket full of piltocks and two mackerel. I am boiling some of the piltocks and will have them cold on a chef's salad tonight. For lunch I am frying mackerel. There is nothing in the world better than fresh mackerel and this is truly fresh.

The seal inventory was disappointing with very few seals about. Either they were lunch for the Orcas or they are still scared. I saw a mother seal giving birth to a baby on the rocks by the water – quite a sight. There was a surprising number of tiny seals. I will have to look in my wildlife book but this seems the wrong time of year for babies.

Yesterday I went over to Tom's to weed my beets, broccoli, cauliflower and parsnips. There are gaps where the rabbits have eaten some of the vegetables but I still have quite a good stand of everything. On the way over we drove by the loch where the red-throated diver has her nest and she was in the loch swimming with the baby on her back. The diver is in the same family as the North American loon and the loon carries her baby in the same way. When the baby got off for a swim it was suddenly attacked from the air by gulls. The mother fought them off and somehow managed to get the baby back on her back. The chicks are camouflaged when on the adults back as they blend in with the colour of the mother's feathers. The male then showed up with a beak full of something. It did not look like fish but whatever it was the baby liked it as it pecked away. While the father fed the chick the mother fought off the gulls. We had witnessed a gull, which is not usually a predator, attacking baby 'number two' weeks ago. The gull dropped the chick so we had hoped it had survived, but now we know it did not.

One lesson I am learning with all of this bird watching is how harsh nature can be. The red-throated diver is a rare, protected bird but the gulls only see it as lunch. The Orcas think only of the seals as food. You really get a sense of the food chain here. I wonder what eats starfish? We caught a bunch of them in the lobster creels and it made me wonder where they fit on the food chain.

Come to think of it I am not much better than the gulls as I am off to fry my fresh mackerel. I guess we never think about how much of a predator man is until you compare our behaviour to that of other animals.

June 24th

I just got back from another great ride in the little red boat. The sea was like glass and I could see the bottom in many places. We were among thousands of birds that were floating around looking for fish. Tom caught a lot of piltocks but no mackerel today. The fresh mackerel I had yesterday for lunch was absolutely superb. Tom gave me some crab claws and they were exceptional.

Our plan was to make a run to Ronas Hill today but it is still covered with fog so I doubt if that will happen. My birthday dinner consisted of new potatoes with parsley that I grew on the windowsill, green beans, and a turkey Tom bought. I made a fabulous rhubarb cake, which we decided was the best yet. It had chunks of rhubarb in it and was dusted with icing sugar. Not a bad birthday dinner even if I had to cook it myself.

Speaking of rhubarb, I made the pineapple and rhubarb jam. It really is a good combination. My rhubarb recipes source is http://www.rhubarbinfo.com. It is a fabulous website if you have access to rhubarb.

I have to run and take a bath as I smell like fish. If the sun comes out Tom will be here to take me to Ronas Hill. I never know when he will turn up. If there is a break in the weather you take advantage right away.

June 25th

Sunshine in all its glory has come to the lighthouse. It is warm with hardly any wind. I thought it was a good omen to start the week but it did not turn out that way. When I was feeding the lambs this morning one of them (I am not sure which) decided to give me a butt, that is the normal way they start nursing.

The butt hit my nose hard and it started to bleed. With much effort I was able to get it stopped. It hurt so much I tried to call Tom but could not reach him. Looking at the swollen nose I decided I had better call the doctor. She dropped by on her way to the surgery. It was not broken, thank goodness, and with application of ice the swelling has gone down. I may have a swollen nose and black eyes for a while but otherwise no harm done. I should look wonderful for my birthday. I believe the caddies are about to be weaned off of their bottles, as it is getting dangerous.

We did make it to Ronas Hill yesterday and it was like another planet. It looks a great deal like Mars covered with red granite rocks and not much else. The views were spectacular from the top even with some fog. It was too murky to get really good pictures but I tried.

Yesterday's ride in the boat was stunning – glassy water without a wave anywhere. The big fun on the boat ride was the baby seals. I did look in the book and this is the time of year for the common seals to have their young. The babies can swim moments after they are born so the water around the islands is full of tiny heads trying to keep up with their mothers. They swim pretty well for being only days old. They are fed milk by the mothers but must go under water to reach the nipple so being able to swim is critical. I have always loved the adult seals but the babies are even more entertaining to watch in the water.

June 26th

It is only a few minutes before Tom arrives as we are off to Lerwick again. He needs fencing and sheep shears. As always I have some pictures I want developed and need a few groceries.

I will take my trowel along just in case as I see any more common flowers I would like to add to my garden. I have geraniums blooming in the lobster greenhouses from the cuttings Tom was going to throw away.

My nose is still sore and I have a little bit of a black eye. The caddies were not given an evening bottle because when I bend over my nose hurts. They were fine this morning so now they are down to one bottle.

I spent a good part of the yesterday watching a lone red-throated diver down at the loch below the lighthouse. I was hidden behind a rock so he could not see me. The bird was relaxing by just aimlessly floating in the loch.

June 27th

It is my birthday so it is raining like mad. I hope it clears up so I can get outside.

Actually the rain is a good thing as it keeps me inside so I will work on *Scottish Radiance*. The first of the month always seems to slip up on me. Too many competing activities keep me busy.

Last night I watched the seagulls starting to train their babies to fly. I am thinking of writing a book about my feathered lighthouse neighbours because watching the birds has been so much fun. My column for *Lighthouse Digest* this month will be about my neighbours, including the puffins.

Tom is disturbed as he saw gulls raiding the guillemots' nest on the end of Eshaness Skerry. We do not have a shortage of guillemots but it is still hard to watch baby birds getting killed.

Last night I made quite a spectacle of myself. A bonxie (great Arctic skua) was raiding the only colony of Arctic terns we have left in the area. The rest have left because of a lack of fish. I was so angry I went out and threw rocks and swung my stick at the bonxie. Dean reminded me later the bonxie had babies to feed too. The problem with the birds is some species are so badly depleted by the intervention of man (including the reduction in the amount of fish), that what would be normal raids could cause extinction. People who have lived here all of their lives are really worried about the decreasing bird population. The oystercatcher is the one species that has adapted to another food source; it now eats worms and grubs instead of shellfish. It hunts in the sheep fields and the wool left on the ground gets tangled around their feet and eventually cuts the foot off. It is not uncommon to see oystercatchers with only one foot. Anyway last night I was helping to save the few baby Arctic terns we have this year by fighting the battle of the bonxie.

In my most recent pictures I have one of a heath orchid that is really good. I am submitting it to the *Shetland Times* for publication. The *Shetland Times* has asked me to write for them but I do not believe I have the time right now.

June 28th

Another very foggy day in Shetland so I can continue to get *Scottish Radiance* programmed. The sun may break through this afternoon and I would like to walk down to the museum to see if they will do the tearoom for the event in August, I also want to borrow some pictures to scan in for my monthly article for *Lighthouse Digest*.

My birthday is now over and I am, as my brother so nicely put it, going on 62! I like it better if I say I am now 61. My grandson, Austin, gave me the best birthday present by successfully having his tonsils out yesterday. He is fine with a rather sore throat. Our youngest daughter, Sandy, and her family (husband,

Darren, son, Austin, and daughter, Kara) will be visiting here in just a few weeks and I am so excited. They will be the first of our children and grandchildren to experience Eshaness. It is a big occasion for me and Dean. Dean is travelling with them to London and then here. I am envious of him getting to do that.

Yesterday I did a little walking but it is hard when it is so foggy since you can get lost so easily. Later today I will go down to the loch and watch the red-throated diver since you can get closer to the bird in the fog.

The roses are just starting to bloom in all the neighbours' yards. Soon the whole area will smell like roses. Rugosa roses are the most fragrant of the roses and they do very well in the Shetland climate.

My garden is looking better every day. It is a combination of wild flowers and annuals. I think I may have finally rabbit-proofed it with plastic bags tied on all the posts to scare them away. I may just have a nice garden by the end of the summer if a big storm does not come. I have geraniums, impatiens, and a petunia (almost) blooming in the lobster creel greenhouses. I will uncover them on nice days after the lambs go to Tom's.

The lambs and the bunny will stay until our grandkids visit and then they are going back to where they came from. The bunny is pretty healthy and needs to go back to the wild. We will soon run out of grass for the caddies. Three hungry lambs can eat a lot of grass.

June 29th

Another week is almost past. How do I know? Today the *Shetland Times* (Shetland's only newspaper that comes out weekly) hits the stores and everyone lines up to get their copy. I suppose as newspapers go it is not the greatest literary journal but everyone in Shetland reads it faithfully and I am no exception. Tom reserves a copy for both of us and joins the line at the Hillswick shop to get them on Friday morning. I mostly use the classified ads to look for things for the house since most people do not take things off the island; they sell them. But I have to plead guilty to enjoying the local gossip too.

Last night I looked out the bedroom window before I closed the shutters and munching away on the sea side was a mother rabbit and five baby bunnies. All but one of the little ones had a white dot between their eyes. I wonder if the male had the white dot, as the female did not. Over in the corner the caddies were eating grass. I guess caddies and bunnies can share a yard without any difficulty.

I made fishcakes out of some small fish Tom caught. I may have put too many mashed potatoes in the recipe because they are sort of soft. Our grandkids like fish sticks so I thought while the adults ate real fish the grandkids could eat fishcakes. I will fry them tonight and see how they do. They should taste just like fish sticks but will be round and sort of squishy with too many mashed potatoes in them.

We are expecting thunder and heavy rain this afternoon so I want to get my writing done early in case I have to turn off the computer. The one thing here I am afraid of is lightning as the lighthouse has been hit three times. It is the tallest thing sticking up in the air out here.

June 30th

We have sunshine, which is great. The fog and rain have been with us for so long I forgot how beautiful sunshine could be. When the rain stopped about 8:00 pm last night and the sun broke through, I grabbed my binoculars and went out to see the puffins. They had survived flying onto the cliffs in all that fog and were sitting proudly on their ledge. I then walked down to see if the red-throated diver had made a nest in the loch down the hill from the lighthouse since it had been spending so much time there. I could not find the nest or the bird so it was a wasted trip except for being out in the beautiful sunshine.

With the sun out I got to experience summer dim at its fullest. We are four minutes shorter than the longest day but having watched a movie I went to bed at midnight. It was still light. It is hard to get used to so much daylight.

I just uploaded *Scottish Radiance* so I deserve a day off. I might take a long walk and then find a sunny spot and read a book.

Tom brought up the last of the rhubarb yesterday so I am going to make one more batch of rhubarb and pineapple jam. I think I have eight jars of jam in the cupboard and that is not bad considering I always give Tom a couple each time I make it.

July

July 1st

I had hoped to go with Tom in the boat this morning but it is too windy. Sunday is a big tourist day so after dinner Tom and I are going for a short ride in the truck to get away from them. We want to spend a good amount of time at the local museum at Tangwick Haa as I am looking for old black and white photos of Shetland.

My new toy arrived; I have a VCR. After two hours of struggle I hooked it up and it is working fine. It will record off of my digital satellite television so I can catch some movies that are on when I am busy. This place is getting to be more and more of a comfortable home.

Yesterday I spent most of the afternoon hiking and lying on the rocks reading a book. If you walk a short distance no tourists can find you. Finding a comfortable rock, I just take my book out of my backpack and read with the sound and the smell of the ocean for company.

Big quest – I am trying to find someone in Lerwick to trim my hair. I am a little nervous, as I have no idea where to go so I am just going to choose someone out of the phone book. My hair is hard to cut because it is curly and styles are different here. It is little things like getting my hair cut that can be my biggest challenge.

July 2nd

The biggest event of my writing career happened yesterday. *Scottish Lighthouses* was featured in the *Sunday Times*, the Sunday version of the London *Times*. It is like getting into the *New York Times* in the US. I checked one of the online sales rankings of the book and it was something like 8,000 yesterday and today it is 230! *The Last Lighthouse* went from 12,000 to 7,000. I was perfectly happy with the 8,000 and 12,000 since those are high rankings for a website selling millions of books, but 230 is totally unbelievable. I am sure my publisher, Appletree in Belfast, is having a celebration. *Scottish Lighthouses* is becoming one of their all time bestsellers. I often have to pinch myself to believe that these are my books, which people love so much. If Appletree keeps up the PR work on *Scottish Lighthouses* it will be a big money maker for them. Naturally they are anxious to get *Irish Lighthouses* out since it can gather momentum from *Scottish Lighthouses*.

We drove to Muckle Roe yesterday, an island community near Brae. It is a quaint and beautiful place connected to the mainland of Shetland by a bridge. It has been a little bit spoiled by lots of new houses built by personnel from the Sullom Voe Oil Terminal.

I did spend some time at the Tangwick Haa museum, which is a short distance from the lighthouse and has a good collection of local history. It was Tom's first visit and I could hardly get him out of there. I asked them to do the tearoom for the August 18–19th radio event at the lighthouse.

I've got to finish my story for *Lighthouse Digest*, as it needs to be sent tomorrow.

July 3rd

Summer has finally arrived in Shetland because I'm wearing summer clothes – a pair of jeans and a short-sleeved T-shirt. I got up early this morning and did some painting in the house since today I can open the house for ventilation.

I am going to spend the afternoon reading a book on a sunny rock since I deserve a day off. Rice pudding, macaroni and cheese, plus whatever I get from the fish van is on tonight's menu. I made the rice pudding and macaroni and cheese this morning so it will be a relaxed day all the way around.

I walked down to Tom's yesterday afternoon and got there just before a huge rainstorm. I need to be more careful before taking off for long distances since I might get absolutely soaked some day. I've been hiking farther and farther. I must be walking over seven to eight miles a day with all of my wanderings.

I feel bad that the Arctic terns have deserted their nests but it is nice not have to carry my tern stick to protect my head.

Tomorrow is the 4th July. I will have to do something special since that is what Americans do.

July 4th

It doesn't feel like the 4th July because it is cool and foggy today. Usually the 4th July in the American Midwest is hot and humid. Picnics and swimming is what the 4th means. I was not sure anyone would remember but BBC Shetland called to wish me a happy 4th and then asked if I would do an interview tonight about what the 4th would be like if I was back in the States. I'll tell them about fireworks and lightning bugs. I was able to give them a soundbite on how the birds are disappearing as they were off to Sumburgh Head to talk about the bird decline there. It is not just a west coast issue but a critical issue everywhere in Shetland.

This American will celebrate the holiday by taking some time off and maybe reading outside. I tried yesterday around 2:30 pm to do exactly that and it rained. There are two good movies on Digital TV appropriate for the day – *Born on the 4th of July* and *Yankee Doodle Dandy*. I may watch them both.

I got really upset last night watching a BBC documentary about how the British government handled the foot and mouth disease outbreak. What an all time disaster! There was so much tragedy caused by the disease itself but to have it compounded by the failures of the bureaucracy – I am still upset. All we can hope is they have it under control now and farming can get back on track.

I just took a fish pie made with potatoes, peas and cod from the oven. I love fish pie. The last one I made was when my BBC producer was here and she loved it. Last night I had fresh herring and it was wonderful. The fish van is really a joy in my life since back in Michigan we only can get 'jet fresh' sea fish.

It seems a little strange celebrating July 4th in the country from which the US broke free many years ago.

July 5th

I am off to Lerwick to get my hair trimmed. The last time I got my hair cut I had eight years growth of hair sheared. It was down to my waist. Now my short hair is shaggy so it only needs a trim.

I found the 4th July a hard day. I missed Michigan and the USA desperately and was badly homesick for the first time. It may have been the fog. The whole island is going crazy as we have had heavy fog almost every day for two and half weeks. It gets to you after a while since you cannot do much walking or enjoy the scenery.

The BBC Shetland report on the birds was sad. Birds all over the island are starving. The parents are gone too long in an attempt to find food and the baby chicks die from hunger, cold and exposure. The number of puffins is down to a dangerous level. I believe we have about half the number of puffins we had last year. Even the gull population is down. The expert who spoke on the radio was not sure the population would be able to recover unless something was done about the low numbers of sand eels. We have a partial ban on sand eel fishing and I expect there may be a complete ban before too long.

I've got to go because Tom is always early. I have not seen much of him lately so it will be fun to catch up during the ride to Lerwick.

July 6th

Last night was total chaos around here. Lerwick has a new cash and carry furniture store with really good quality things so I bought a new bookcase. The old one's top shelf was bending under the weight of the TV, VCR and digital box. When I got home I tried to put it together. I must be getting better at assembling furniture as I had no problems reading the instructions, did not have to take anything apart, and it is very sturdy.

I had just finished putting all the things on the new shelf when Tom arrived to give me a hand putting it together – great timing. Two seconds later the electrician arrived to start putting in the storage heater in my office. I guess repair people in Shetland come when they can and hardly ever give you warning. The storage heater is now safely hung on the wall and its socket put in. On Saturday he will return to run 45 metres of cable to the generator house. The cost is going to be around £160, which is a big difference from the £800 the other electricians were going to charge me. The man doing the work is a local who works for Hydro Electric (our electric supplier) and does this kind of thing at night.

I got the galleys for my next book, *Irish Lighthouses*. The book is beautiful but in my opinion not as gorgeous as *Scottish Lighthouses*. I think the Irish lighthouses as a whole are not as pretty as the Scottish ones. The Scottish ones are some of the classiest in the world because of who built them and the rugged scenery where they are set. I am not complaining as the Irish book is magnificent and I am happy with it.

We have a sort of clearing day so I washed sheets and will be off to walk to Tom's to weed my garden and see if I can beg a ride in the wee red boat to see the puffins at Dore Holm. The puffins leave the first of August so I have to do it soon.

July 7th

Today it is supposed to rain. Yesterday in spite of the fog I went for a long walk to Tom's house with some diversions along the way. I saw two red-throated diver couples, each with two chicks, swimming in two different lochs. What a thrill that was. Any young chicks which are surviving are welcome here. We seem to have a lot of eider duck chicks, that is another piece of good news. The hatchery area is full of pretty good-sized baby seagulls of all kinds so we will not have a shortage of them.

Today I have to stay close to home in case the electrician needs anything. If it does not rain and Tom comes to work with the electrician I am off to dig some plants for my garden. I have identified some beautiful wild thyme, which is plentiful and can be used just like the real stuff. The flowers are bright purple and really pretty. I bought two perennials from a Shetland nursery last fall and the nursery woman said they would grow anywhere but then realizing where I lived, she corrected herself and said *almost* anywhere. Well, one is in flower but I will have to wait until it comes completely out before I can identify it. This is a big victory since it is the first plant to winter over and bloom except for the daffodils.

I received some great pictures of the Montauk Lighthouse the Long Island lady took when she was here. One actually shows I really am in Shetland. All of the other photographs I'm not in the picture because I took them. Another shows how tiny and cute the caddies were.

July 8th

It is a rainy and extremely foggy day at the lighthouse. Since it is Sunday Tom and I are going to see a local antique dealer. I am looking for old black and white photographs and one old, large Shetland picture.

Yesterday I weeded my garden at Tom's and the bunnies had eaten all of the cauliflower and broccoli. The rabbits evidently do not like beets or parsnips, as they are growing fine. We have been eating delicious lettuce out of Tom's garden. This climate is perfect for lettuce with cool and wet days. I had some of the best romaine lettuce I have ever tasted last year out of Tom's garden so I am ordering some more romaine seeds this morning.

The electrician was on call yesterday and lightning hit a pole on the south end of the island so he had to leave. He may be back today as he has very little to finish. Everything is finally falling into place in my little lighthouse home. The house is getting pretty well decorated but the walls are still bare and I need more pictures.

A beef roast will cook in the Rayburn while we make the trip to look at the antiques. I have gotten into the good Scottish habit of having a roast of some kind every Sunday.

Next Saturday Dean, Sandy, Darren, Austin and Kara (youngest daughter and family) arrive in London. They will be here the following Tuesday and I am so excited. Tom is going to take a couple of nights off so he can give boat rides to let the kids fish, show them the animals on his croft, and play checkers with Austin. Austin has been practising so Tom is a little worried my grandson will beat him.

July 9th

Sunshine has returned to Shetland. It seems so nice after all the fog.

The fog sort of ruined our trip to the antique place, which is in a part of Shetland I had not seen before. Actually I still have not seen it, as all we saw was fog. The antique store was a disappointment since it had more junk then anything else. I found a miniature hand powered sewing machine, which will work as soon as a small bolt is replaced. I did not find any black and white pictures of Shetland but our electrician brought me a whole book full. I am going to scan six or eight pictures from the 1800s into the computer so I can enlarge them for framing. Today I am off to look for some yellow iris and wild thyme for the flower garden. The garden is looking pretty good considering it is growing in rocks. I added some caddy droppings to it this morning so it is getting fertilizer. Everything on an island gets recycled.

The rhubarb pie in the oven will be the last made from fresh rhubarb this year as the plants are going to seed. I put some in the freezer so I could bake a couple of pies for the family when they are here.

Summer is in full swing so most gardens are really exquisite. Lupin in all colours grows bigger on Shetland than any other place I have been. The rugosa roses are blooming everywhere so it looks quite lovely with the green fields and all the flowers.

The lighthouse garden is not much in comparison to the more sheltered areas but at least it is growing.

July 10th

It is spitting a little rain outside so I am doing inside things. My website has been neglected lately so I am making a few technical corrections. It is amazing how little I look at the website when I am in Scotland. Its true value, of course, is to be close to Scotland when you are far away.

Yesterday I moved yellow iris and Shetland thyme into the garden. I walked a long way to get them but it was worth it since it was such a nice day. On the walk I saw lots of baby oystercatchers, which look almost exactly like their parents except they are more fuzzy or downy. The oystercatchers are starting to flock up just like blackbirds do in the fall in Michigan. It is hard to believe it will soon be migration time for some of the birds. The puffins will be the first to leave around the first of August.

Since it was clear I went to check on the lighthouse puffins. It is too dangerous to go near their cliffs in fog. They were sitting on their ledge and I think I saw a chick sticking his head out of a crack. The chicks are black so they blend in really well with the rocks and burrows. If the weather stays clear I will spend more time out on the cliffs trying to watch the parents bringing in food. The sand eel population is so low the adults have to go a long way to find food so they are not around much.

I scanned in some fantastic black and white pictures by George Washington Wilson, a famous Scottish photographer, from the book the electrician brought. They will be framed and displayed up and down the hall in the lighthouse. I wish I could buy some originals but they just are not available.

July 11th

Tom and I found a hedgehog crossing the road last night on the way to drop off a letter at the mailbox. We stopped and picked it up so I now have Hedgie II. He is smaller and according to information I found on the Internet might be about 5–8 weeks old.

With the bunny in the hedgehog cage, a big problem is housing the new arrival. As a temporary measure we put him in one of the baskets Tom uses to carry peat. We dug up five earthworms and the little guy ate them all.

I put the basket in the corner in the Rayburn room where it is warm and went to bed. When I got up this morning the basket was still there but no Hedgie. He had climbed out. I had read that they were excellent climbers but this was a huge climb for a small hedgehog. After a frantic search I found it under the couch. Now it is in the basket with my laundry basket on top. Tonight I will tie a lid on the basket or Hedgie will be out roaming around the house again.

To top off my morning I went out and the wind had blown part of the plastic off the lobster creel greenhouses. The petunias are having a struggle anyway. They are about to bloom or I should say *were* about to bloom as the lambs had some for lunch. They could only graze the tops so the plants look peculiar.

Running the lighthouse zoo is getting to be a bit much. After the grandkids are here the caddies are off to be with Tom's other sheep. They need to get used to being in a big pasture before the weather gets bad. The caddies have always had their caddy shack for shelter and must get used to being outside all the time.

As soon as the bunny can walk properly I am going to let it go. It seems to be healed but I have not really had it outside the cage to check. Then it will only be Hedgie and myself left to manage the lighthouse. I am getting an outside cage for Hedgie so he can live a more normal existence along with a used fish tank that would work nicely in the house during the winter. All the animals that live here must be able to be returned to their natural environment, as there will not be someone here all the time to take care of them.

July 12th

Well, my bunny, known as 'Bun Bun', has gone back to the wild. Yesterday we decided to make it an outside cage so Hedgie II could have the bigger cage in the house. We put up a temporary fence and put the bunny in. Tears came to my eyes when I saw that it could hop like a normal bunny since its back legs were totally useless when we found it. As we were tightening the fence it went right under it. The last I saw of it was it was running toward the hill with the World War II bunker. It was a time for extremely mixed emotions. I really wanted to keep it until Austin and Kara visited, as I don't know if they had ever seen a wild orange rabbit. My heart smiled because the bunny had healed while he was here and could now use his legs. My mind told me he should go back to the wild as he was happier there than in a cage. But when I went out to the feed the caddies this morning I missed feeding and talking to the bunny. One good thing about the escape is he had not been in captivity so long he forgot the wild ways. I hope a tourist does not hit him. We are asking all the neighbours not to shoot him since rabbits are real nuisances and some times they do shoot them. 'Bun Bun' might be less afraid of humans then other rabbits so he might be an easy target. All in all I'm happy we saved the bunny's life and he is free again.

Hedgie II is rather boring. Since he has gotten his cage he spends most of his time sleeping in a ball. They are nocturnal animals but Hedgie I was more active. I am off to Lerwick and hope to get Hedgie a toy to play with and some low calorie cat food to eat. Hedgehogs have a tendency to overeat and get fat in captivity.

July 13th

This is definitely Friday the 13th. I do not believe in bad luck on Friday 13th but it is starting out to be nothing but bad news around Eshaness.

Hedgie II died this morning. He had not been eating or drinking since we moved him into the big cage. I talked to the vet and tried to hand feed him water as the vet felt he might be dehydrated. I had no eyedropper so I tried to drip water with a little sugar into its mouth with a spoon. I did that for about an hour but he finally just stopped breathing. The vet thought maybe some fumes from the Rayburn poisoned him. This hedgehog was really healthy, we put his cage near the Rayburn so he could be kept warm and he died quickly. I feel really bad I killed two hedgehogs but no one knew (not even the vet) that the Rayburn would give off fumes so toxic to them. I will not bring another hedgehog into this house. Living here will just have to be without pets and I will just have to accept it. I buried him deep out by the garden and put a flower on this grave.

It makes me feel a little bit better that at least we got the bunny healed and it is back in the wild.

The caddies are fine and about to get tags put in their ears. EU rules dictate they must have identification tags in their ears. I will not watch while Tom puts them in because it must hurt at least a little.

Tom's little white truck won't run. He says there is oil all over the road under it, which does not sound good. This morning he is having new brake pads put on the big pickup. Once that is done I suppose he will try to find out what is wrong with the little white truck. Leslie has something wrong with the transmission on his car so he is adding to the bad things today. I am glad I do not have a car to worry about.

Yesterday Dean and Sandy's family missed their plane to London. They all thought the tickets were for today but they were for yesterday. How it happened I do not know but they were able to re-book and leave tonight.

I think I will go to bed for the rest of the day so nothing else bad can happen.

July 14th

We just got back from going fishing in the wee red boat. There were lots of seals and even more gannets. Next to the puffins the gannets are my favourite birds. They are so graceful with their bright yellow head, long narrow white bodies, and black tipped wings. They are great fun to watch as they skim along the water and then dive headfirst into it with hardly a splash. Graceful is the best word to describe these birds.

Tom caught lots of piltocks, one lobster, and a big dogfish that looks like an eel but is only good for bait. He seemed satisfied that it was a good day.

It is fairly warm today so I am waiting for the Rayburn to cool so I can touch up some spots where the black paint has come off. The Rayburn has not gone out for weeks but I can still remember the days it went out three or four times a day. Now I have trouble getting it to cool down. Things sure do change over time.

I talked to my daughter Sandy at their hotel in London. They arrived without a problem. The grandkids were really good on the flight since it was one of the new 747s with each coach seat having a TV screen. I had not realized they have an all cartoon channel for kids. Everyone was tired and it was raining so she was not sure what their first day in London would involve.

July 15th

I just got back from visiting Dore Holm. I had been told that the puffins were out there away from people and it was definitely true. They were floating in the water and fishing contentedly until they saw the wee red boat then they took to the air. The air was just black when they took flight. It was an amazing sight. I believe there were some juveniles in the flock as they were not as brightly coloured and had a lot of trouble taking off. But puffins are not great flyers so they could have just been awkward adults.

I have the only gold trimmed lambs in Eshaness. Yesterday afternoon I did a little touching up on the lighthouse trimming. All the Scottish lighthouses are trimmed in gold. Well, it seems the caddies discovered me and had to come and investigate. Austin, the big one, has a gold ear; Kara, the middle one, has streaks down her face and Alyssa, the tiny white one, has a gold nose. They are a sight. I was afraid it would make them sick but they seem to be fine today and not the least bit worried about their funny appearance.

I heard from the London crowd and they seem to be having a great time. Today I think they are going to the changing of the guard, the Tower of London and Harrods. I had a message from Kara on my answering machine, which was a nice surprise. I cannot wait until they get here.

July 16th

One day until my family arrives, I am counting the minutes. They seem to be having a good time. Being at the lighthouse will seem awfully quiet after London. We have a good weather forecast so they should be able to go out in the wee red boat, go fishing and see the seals.

I am busy cooking things ahead of time so I won't have to do much cooking while they are here. Tomorrow we are having codfish pie, Shetland coleslaw, and a rhubarb cake, all of which can be prepared ahead of time so I can just enjoy Sandy and family's first impressions of the lighthouse. Dean will probably be disappointed that we are not having rhubarb pie and lobster but that is on Wednesday's menu.

I was out weeding the garden last night and I found the first flower grown from seed to bloom in the lighthouse garden. It is not very big but it is one of the most beautiful flowers I have ever seen. I also discovered that some of the plants the rabbits had eaten off are coming up from the roots so I might still have broccoli and cauliflower. I thought they were dead so the foliage is coming up in a row of flowers that I planted to fill in that area. The garden is kind of mixed up but things are growing.

Yesterday Tom took me to the Brae Building Centre to get a special light bulb for the spare bedroom. We drove over to Sullom Voe so I could see the tugs and pilot boats that bring the big tankers into the oil terminal. The tugs are gigantic and we were lucky enough to see one leave to meet a tanker. The pilot boat and tug must meet every tanker brought into the area. A pilot actually gets on the tanker and steers it in. The rules are very strict to avoid accidents or oil spills.

July 17th

Dean just called and the family is in Shetland. I have been worried for weeks that the weather would be bad for their visit. But Shetland is showing its most beautiful side today with light blue skies, bright blue water, hardly any wind, and just spectacular visibility. It is one of those ideal Shetland days. The temperature is cool but when you are in the sun it is not cold. I do hope they like our island.

I have the two grandchildren counting Shetland ponies on the way so we will see which one spots the most. We have hundreds of ponies running wild in the north of Shetland so it should be great fun for them.

One of the biggest thrills I have had in a long time was when a car drove up beside the library van and Dean, Sandy, Darren, Austin and Kara got out. I was totally over the top with excitement.

July 18th

The weather behaved on the first day of my family's visit except for the wind becoming stronger later in the day and one shower while we were out walking.

Darren and Dean, whom I have renamed the Daredevils, decided to climb down to the ocean on the cliffs over by Moo Stack. This is not an easy thing to do and also dangerous but they did it anyway and were very proud of their accomplishment.

The caddies are getting lots of exercise as the grandchildren have been herding them. The grandcherubs (our pet name for our grandchildren) are not allowed outside the lighthouse fence without an adult but they can play inside the fence as much as they want so the caddies have become their biggest entertainment.

The agenda for today includes Tom taking people fishing and seal watching in the wee red boat if the bay is calm. Also Austin and Tom have a checkers tournament going. They have played one game so far and Tom won, but not by much. We are not sure whether he intentionally didn't play his best or whether Austin is actually a good checker player. Kara gave Tom a big hug and it was a joy to see his face.

Tomorrow is shopping. Sandy is a real shopper and she has souvenirs to buy for friends and a piece of Celtic jewellery for herself.

I hear the pitter-patter of little feet so I guess it is breakfast time for the grandchildren and then they want to help feed the caddies.

July 19th

The weather stayed really windy and cold yesterday so outside activities were limited. They tried the boat but the bay was too rough. Kara did get to pick up shells and she enjoyed that.

The highlight of the day was Austin and Kara feeding the lambs in the morning. I am waiting for them to get up so we can feed them again this morning. I had to hold Alyssa lamb so Kara and Austin could feed their namesakes without having to fight off a hungry Alyssa.

We had a magnificent boiled lobster meal last night. It was so good. I served it as a typical Shetland meal except we had macaroni and cheese instead of tatties (potatoes). The grandcherubs love macaroni and cheese.

Today we go to the big city of Lerwick to see the sights and so Sandy can shop. There is so much to do in the short time they are here.

July 20th

The family is gone and it seems unbelievably deserted at the lighthouse. It is always nice to have people visit but I miss them after they leave or at least until I fall into the routine again. Naturally it turned sunny today but still windy. They would have liked to stay here because back in Michigan it is really hot and humid while it is cool in Shetland.

I have a couple from Arizona coming for coffee this afternoon. They are *Scottish Radiance* readers and asked if they could drop in and say hello. It will be interesting to meet them because they too have fallen in love with Shetland.

Yesterday Sandy and Darren got me a small sterling silver hedgehog pin as a thank you gift. Shetland Jewellery made it and I had always wanted one of their pieces. They brought me a cuddly stuffed hedgehog toy when they came and now this one; they must think that is the only kinds of hedgehogs I can keep. They are probably right.

Hopefully tomorrow I can take the new digital camera Dean brought out in Tom's boat and see how it does taking pictures of seals, etc. Darren got a good picture of the lighthouse puffins. The odd thing is his picture was taken in the middle of the day when the puffins are usually out to sea.

July 21st

I made a quick trip to Lerwick this morning. I had coffee at a local restaurant while Tom had his truck MOTed. It passed. The wee white truck is getting a new motor so Tom's vehicles will all soon be in service.

I bought a picture of red-throated divers (yes, I know I have enough of my own). The picture is probably illegal but a reputable firm was selling it and the picture was exceptional so I had to have it. I have seen so many red-throated divers I thought it time I had a good picture of one. It is illegal to photograph them up close and personal so this professional photo is the only way I can get a good picture.

The lambs are now big caddies and will be moved to Tom's this week, maybe even tomorrow if the weather is good. The grass is running out at the lighthouse and it is not good pasture for them anyway. It is hard for me to think they are no longer going to greet me in the morning but I must admit I will not miss cleaning up their droppings on the sidewalk.

I am going to go watch the British Open for a while as a Scot is leading, or was. I usually do not watch golf but somehow it becomes more important when you are in the home of golf.

July 22nd

I tried my new digital camera and surprisingly some of the pictures taken from the wee red boat in a severe fog turned out.

Big trauma for me today as the caddies are moving to Tom's house. I will take pictures of the momentous event. I feel a little like when my children first went to school; proud that they were old and responsible enough to go but sad they would not be here to keep me company.

It looks like the fog has moved in for the entire day so I guess there won't be a Sunday trip in the car. I will spend today watching the Open, moving caddies and cooking a pork roast.

July 23rd

The weather is supposed to be good on Wednesday so I am arranging a trip to Fair Isle. I want to interview the ex-lighthouse keepers who live there and to have lunch with a weatherman who just happens to be an ex-occasional keeper. I have yet to get the seats on the plane (Tom is going with me). The weatherman has guaranteed me the weather will be good that day. Nice to have a weatherman involved.

The nest is empty at the lighthouse as the caddies are now living at Tom's. I did a pictorial story of the caddies' big trip using my new digital camera. I will eventually read the instruction manual and learn how to use it properly, but the camera has done an exceptional job on the pictures so far. Probably its biggest advantage is saving money, as I do not have to buy film or pay for developing it, which was getting to be a huge expense.

July 24th

I have much to do on the computer but after the fish van arrives I am taking a long walk since it is a beautiful sunny day. The wind is quite strong out of the south but warm. One lesson I have learned in my three months here is to take advantage of every good day. I pay a lot of attention to the weather, as it is critical to my enjoyment and safety.

I made a fool of myself in front of some tourists today. I was struggling to hang up washing in a strong wind and a sock got away from me. It was on its way to the USA or Greenland (not sure which). Chasing it before it got through the fence and into the ocean, I slipped on the wet grass and ended up on my bottom. The tourists stood in the car park and watched. I am sure they were impressed with my agility. The most important part of this tale is the sock was rescued so no one who wanders the beach on the Atlantic Ocean will find a red sock as flotsam.

The trip to Fair Isle is all arranged for tomorrow and the weather forecast is good. Tom and I are being met by an ex-lighthouse keeper when we get in at 10:30 am and will be seeing ex-keepers till noon. Then we are spending time with the weatherman who was or is a lighthouse keeper, coast guard captain, and fireman at the airport. Every time I talk to him he seems to be involved in something else.

The trip should be fun.

July 25th

I am in a panic. I knew *Scottish Field* was coming to do a feature on the house but had just kept putting off thinking about it. Well, I can put it off no more as they will be here on August 7th. *Scottish Field* is such an upscale magazine with their magnificent spreads and beautiful photography. It is a big honour to be featured in their magazine and a little scary as this is a nice house but not elegant like their usual castles and estates. However all of the outside shots they take will be so beautiful that they will make up for the simple inside.

The house has never looked better and has some neat touches like the photo gallery of black and white historic pictures in the hall, the lobster creel greenhouses that would have blooms in them if the caddies had not eaten them off, and my display of book covers and book signing posters in my office. I guess it is not so plain on the inside after all.

July 26th

Big disappointment yesterday, when we arrived at the airport the plane had been sent on an ambulance run and so we could not get to Fair Isle. The day turned out to be so beautiful and would have made perfect pictures. Tom and I went to Lerwick shopping since we were so close. I will not have to make another trip this week I hope. Somehow it did not soften the disappointment of not seeing Fair Isle.

My friends wanted to know what the inside of the house looks like so I took some pictures using the digital camera and put them on the Internet. The rooms are small with bright windows so pictures are hard to take but they turned out okay.

July 27th

I just got back from a boat ride with Tom to check the lobster creels. It was a good day with four nice lobsters caught. The seals are looking a little ratty, part white and part their usual colour, as they are moulting. I tried to get pictures of them but they went under water each time I took out the camera.

Last evening the Northern Lighthouse Board boat, *Pharos*, was in St Magnus Bay and it sailed right by the lighthouse. It still gives me goose bumps when I think about the light on top of my house and what it means to the ships. The appearance of the NLB always brings that to mind. By the time I dug out my camera the ship was quite a distance off but I still got a picture What it did was get me outside for the most beautiful sunset since I have been here.

It is that time again. I am working on August's issue of *Scottish Radiance*. I do not know where the time goes but it seems only days since I was programming last month's issue of the magazine.

July 28th

A foggy summer morning at the lighthouse can be an enjoyable experience. A light breeze makes the mist roll in sheets across the hills. I am partial to mornings like this, as they have a soft and gentle feeling. After I got the Rayburn tended and disposed of the ashes I decided to go for a long walk. In foggy weather you can only go where you know the terrain well and you can keep a familiar landmark in sight.

I wandered slowly toward the Bruddans area so I could enjoy the softness and quiet of the mist. Once there I sat on a rock for a long time. Many seals were swimming and a few were trying to sunbathe. I guess they failed to notice there was no sun. The most interesting sight was the gannets, with their bright yellow heads and black tips on their wings, flying gracefully above the ocean until they spotted a fish or some delicacy that would make them a good lunch. Without a moment's hesitation they dive full force headfirst straight into the water. What ever they catch must be small as in the mist I could not make out what it was.

I could have spent hours and hours watching them but the damp of the fog creeps inside your jacket and right into your bones if you sit too long. So up and walking again I headed for the lochs to see if any red-throated divers were around. Sometimes in misty conditions you can get closer to them than otherwise.

This morning was lucky as I found a mother and her young in the loch just down the hill from the lighthouse. Moving gradually toward the loch's edge I was able to get as close as I have ever been to these magnificent birds. I found another rock on which to sit and watch them glide across the water.

The most thrilling part of the experience was every few minutes the adult would send out a call of incredible volume with a strange eeriness to its sound. The youngster which was lost in the fog would answer with a sound not as loud as the adult but similar in tone. It reminded me of the sheep in the hills calling their lambs and the lambs always answering back. It was an experience spending time with these beautiful birds but once again the damp and cold of the mist drove me back to the lighthouse.

July 29th

What a change in the weather from yesterday when it was foggy and quiet. Today the winds are force seven coming out of the south east and the sea is in torment. Since I now have the digital camera I can capture these special moments and put them on the Internet.

I am learning what the force numbers mean in relation to wind speed. Actually my learning what that means in the forecast has a lot to with my being adequately prepared for whatever the weather has to dish out. Today we are at force seven winds with large waves crashing on the rocks at the cliffs. It is difficult to walk but the ocean is not throwing rocks or boulders.

Good news! Leslie saw the orange bunny down at his croft, which is just down the hill from the lighthouse. That is the direction the rabbit ran when it got loose. Some evening I will have to walk down and see if I can see it.

Today I am cooking a leg of lamb with rosemary and garlic. It is not Shetland lamb but Scottish; my friend Robert would have my head if I bought anything else. I found out why the Shetlander eats mutton instead of lamb. The lambs are too small here to make a family meal so they eat mutton. Most of us think of mutton as old sheep but in Shetland it is just a year or two old. The butcher told me that being heather fed, the mutton here has a really good flavour.

We are all waiting to see if the marts will open this fall or stay closed because of the foot and mouth epidemic. It is looking more and more like they won't be open. That means that over 80,000 sheep (50,000 lambs and 30,000 ewes) will have to be killed on Shetland. The farmers cannot afford to buy feed for them and there is not enough grass. My caddies are safe, as Tom has promised he will keep them.

The caddies still come running when I call them even when they are among the other sheep. It makes me feel so good that they still remember. I know it has only been a week but they are big sheep now and they will forget some time.

July 30th

This is a busy place with *Scottish Radiance* being uploaded tomorrow, three guests from Michigan arriving tomorrow night and cleaning and decorating continuing for the visit of *Scottish Field* a week from tomorrow. I will be working on the magazine this morning hoping that the wind will die so I can get outside to do some cleaning up around the buildings. The windows on ocean side still need to be washed on the outside

Yesterday, as the wind grew in strength, Tom decided the wee red boat was in danger anchored in the bay at Stenness. So being the only 'body' available to help him, I got selected to help bring the boat out of danger. I put on my wellies along with jacket and scarf and off to the beach we went. The boat was bouncing all over the place and could have been easily driven onto the rocks. Tom hauled it to shore by the guideline, and then I held it on shore while he tied the rope to the winch. Needless to say the surf was so high I got soaked to my waist and water in my wellies. Tom cranked the winch and I pushed and steadied the boat. We got it up on the grass where it was protected by the rocks and well out of reach of the seething sea. Wet all over and aching in every bone of my body, I felt superb. Life is hard here but it is a kind of hard that gives you a feeling of great satisfaction. Today I have a big bruise on my leg where the surf tossed the boat and it hit me in the thigh but it will go away.

It had been pouring with rain and the wind was howling but the sun managed to come out for a few minutes. I saw part of a rainbow in a dark and ominous sky. This is an amazing place with its fast changing weather.

July 31st

The sun is trying to peek though the clouds. If it succeeds it will be a warm, glorious day for Connie and friends' arrival. Connie Harper used to be the assistant librarian at the Parma library. I use the library constantly when I am in the States. When she retired, she decided to visit the lighthouse and convinced her friends Chris and John to come with her since it was her first trip to Europe.

I walked down to the Bruddans and got pictures of the sun breaking through the clouds. The sea is probably as beautiful after a storm as at any other time. The surf is as high as it is during the storm itself but with sunshine on it. This time it was a spectacular combination of the light and significant waves.

My caddies are getting more independent each day. Yesterday they would not come when I called but if I walked up to them they would let me pet them. This is to be expected but I still wish they would come when I call. They always slept on cement at the lighthouse so they have to find rocks that are just sticking out of the ground to sleep on so you can usually find them sleeping on a rock in the pasture while the other sheep choose nice soft grass. Weird caddies I raised.

August

August 1st

Connie Harper and her two friends arrived yesterday without a problem. Connie loves water and fishing so she is going to be happy here.

We stayed up until 1:00 am talking so I got up late. This is going to be short so we can go to the Bruddans to see the seals, as it is a nice day.

The fish van didn't stop yesterday for some reason so we are going to Busta House (a local hotel with a gourmet restaurant) for supper tonight. Since I don't have two good double beds Chris and John are staying at the hotel.

August 2nd

A misty start to the day but I believe it is going to clear later. Chris, John, Connie and I are off to the big city of Lerwick to shop. I need to get two enlargements of pictures of the lighthouse from the air matted and pick up a few more things for the *Scottish Field* visit next Monday. There really is not a whole lot more I can do to the house at this point except wash the windows before they come. Tom is painting a little more of the trim, which has rusted. The tower still has streaks of rust on the sea side and the lighthouse board will not paint it.

Chris and John played golf at the Lerwick Golf Club, an 18 hole links course. They said it was difficult and the hills that you had to climb were terrible. It was so bad they didn't even keep score. There is a heather course on the island of Whalsay and so they are going to try that next.

Tomorrow and Saturday the visitors are sight-seeing so I will stay here and work on washing windows etc. We are having a big lobster feed on Sunday since Chris and John have to leave for the airport hotel on Monday.

John brought his pole so everyone went trout fishing yesterday. Their only bait was a plastic worm they brought from home. They saw lots of fish jumping and Connie saw a big one just below the surface of the water but I guess the fish didn't like American plastic worms. Today we are going to the fishing store in Lerwick to buy a pole for the lighthouse that Connie can use and get advice on lures and bait. Connie wants to fish a lot after Chris and John leave.

The dinner at Busta House was scrumptious. I had cream of tomato and herb soup, prawn cocktail, scallops and sticky toffee pudding for dessert. You don't count calories when eating that kind of a meal. Connie, Chris and John were quite taken with sticky toffee pudding.

Tom has the boat back in the water and brought us some crab claws and mackerel but since we were going out he took them back and ate them himself. He will probably be doing tour guide/captain of the boat duty for everyone in the next few days.

August 3rd

We were all tired last night when we got home from Lerwick so everyone was going to have a quiet evening and go to bed early but Connie decided to put together the new fishing pole we bought in Lerwick. She began to have some technical difficulties so we called Tom for advice but she still couldn't get it to work. I then phoned Leslie Johnson who tried to talk Connie through it but even after his instructions Connie still couldn't get it together and was frustrated. She muttered something like 'If I don't get this to cast I will just cry'. She struggled until about 10:00 pm when there was a quiet knock at the front door and there was Leslie. Within a few minutes he had it working fine. They were trying to cast in the living room and were catching carpet squares.

Chris and John left before the fishing pole incident to drive back to Busta House but today they told us they were mugged on the way. The herd of wild Shetland ponies that live near the lighthouse surrounded their car so they had to stop. They decided to feed them. It seems ponies like salt and vinegar crisps. Tom told us because the tourists feed them all the time the ponies come right up to cars that slow down and it's a big problem.

Chris and John are out in the wee red boat with Tom right now. I have to finish my *Lighthouse Digest* article. Hopefully I will get to use the new fishing rod this afternoon and catch the first trout. Tomorrow Connie is going to try first thing in the morning while on Sunday it is Chris and John's turn. We got some special lures recommended by the tackle store chap. Leslie said they were the best type so I am sure we will catch a fish this time.

August 4th

Connie is out with Tom catching lobsters. I am about to go out and wash windows and do some touching up on the paint. It is a little windy but dry and bright.

Chris and John saw dolphins while they were in the little red boat yesterday. I was so jealous as I have not seen dolphins from the boat yet. They also saw lots of seals and caught one lobster. I practised with the new fishing pole while my visitors were gone. It works great but I am not good at casting. I dug some worms in Tom's garden to be used for catching trout, then went with Tom to the fish factory to see if I could see my caddies who are in a field behind it by the ocean. I did not see them and am more than a little worried about them.

The guests are going to stay around here today as the trip to Unst tired them out. Chris and John are playing golf this morning while Connie goes out in the boat. They still want to go to Whalsay where the course is mostly heather but Connie thought they were too tired for that today.

Great sunset last night and a full moon tomorrow night so there are many photo opportunities.

I have got to get the windows washed and the painting started before the weather changes. I haven't started because I am having such a good time with the guests – or maybe it is a case of creative avoidance.

August 5th

Today is lobster day. Connie is helping Tom catch them in the wee red boat while Chris and John are on their way to catch brown trout in the loch. If they get lucky we will have trout for supper also. There really are a lot of trout jumping around in the lochs so their chances might be good.

The planned dinner is lobster, clapshot (mashed rutabaga and potatoes), and baked beans, tossed salad with lettuce from Tom's garden and a chocolate and Michigan dried cherry cake with real whipped cream. I would not be surprised if Tom and Connie bring crab claws so we might have fresh crab too.

Connie and I painted the west side of the lighthouse. Later Tom came up and touched up where we could not reach. It looks first-class. I finished washing the windows so all that is left to do is to clean the inside.

Connie is in charge of collecting bouquets of flowers for decoration when *Scottish Field* is here. We will probably convince Tom to take us in his truck to collect them.

I am about to take a book out and sit in the sunshine to dry my hair until everyone gets back.

August 6th

Both Connie and I just got back from a ride in the wee red boat. We took the fishing rod with us and Connie caught lots of mackerel and piltocks.

Yesterday's lobster meal was out of this world, particularly the clapshot. John does not like unusual things so we told him it was mashed potatoes. He loved it and only later did we tell him it also had rutabaga in it.

I am cleaning the house from top to bottom for *Scottish Field*. Later we are walking down to Tom's because he is cooking crab claws and Connie's mackerel. I am bringing dessert and clapshot. I'm not going to cook fish in the lighthouse until after *Scottish Field*'s visit tomorrow because of the smell.

Connie is going to write a marathon e-mail to tell the story of catching each fish plus two days of being a tourist. That should give me plenty of time to get the dusting done.

August 7th

I only have a couple of minutes before the people from *Scottish Field* arrive. It could not be a better day for their visit with a blue, blue ocean and light blue skies. They will get some great photographs. The house looks beautiful and is full of Connie's bouquets.

Forgot to mention that we took the wee red boat under Dore Holm's neck yesterday. It was a momentous event and something I have wanted to do forever.

August 8th

Dragging a little today from the nerves and rush to get ready for *Scottish Field's* visit. The house looked really nice with Connie's beautiful flower arrangements and each room sparkling. The photographer and the writer stayed for over 3½ hours so I guess they enjoyed it. I would have liked to follow the photographer around to see what he shot but I was busy being interviewed. He took lots of pictures of Connie's arrangement of a lobster, a whole whiting and home grown lettuce. The article should be in the November issue but of course they never tell you for sure.

We took the *Scottish Field* writer and photographer over to take a picture of Tom's house and found a herd of wild Shetland ponies. I would not be surprised to see a picture of a Shetland pony in *Scottish Field* since they posed beautifully and we did not even have any salt and vinegar crisps!

Today I began work on the radio lighthouse weekend. I sent a press release to the *Shetland Times* and some hand-written invitations. We are going to Lerwick this afternoon and I will buy some of the food that I can stock ahead like cookies, tea and coffee. Connie worked up a good menu and we will start making ahead what we can. We have about ten days to get ready.

The reason for the trip to Lerwick is we are going to an auction. Tom is taking us in his pickup but I will have to ride in the bed of his pickup in the sofa bed chair. It may be the most uncomfortable ride I will ever have to Lerwick but the auction should be fun. We have had rain off and on so I hope Tom's truck bed cover is waterproof or I will be one wet rider.

August 9th

Rather cold and windy so inside activities today are at the top of my agenda.

The sofa chair bed in the back of the pick up was actually pretty comfortable for the trip to the sale in Lerwick. The back of the pickup cover was open so I got cold riding back after the sale, but it worked.

The sale was super. Connie and I both found a teapot we liked so we were off and running, or should I say spending. The thing I needed for the house was a good vacuum cleaner. They had one just like what I was looking for and I got it for £15 and was pleased. Needless to say many things came along we just could not resist so our purchases were more than expected. I also got a wool winder to use with my spinning wheel, a beautiful bowl with gold rim and flowers painted on the inside, a salad bowl set with six bowls and a clothes hamper. I wanted a teapot shaped like a duck and a wonderful china piggy bank but an antique dealer out-bid me on those.

We were quite pleased when we got home with everything except the vacuum cleaner. The motor runs but it does not vacuum. Connie seems to think it is a belt so hopefully I will find someone in Lerwick that can get me another belt or fix it. I am upset; as that was the one thing I went to the sale looking for. The rest of the things were just impulse additions.

I am off to the kitchen to make fish stew for supper. We eat pretty well around here with lobster salad for lunch yesterday.

August 10th

Because of the radio weekend, faxes and telephone calls are coming in right and left. The *Shetland Times* article was published today in the newspaper and on the web. It had some mistakes in it, which is par for the course but the headline was really good.

Connie and I still have to clean the generator house workshop where they will be broadcasting and the little office in the generator house that will be the tearoom.

Luath Press, publisher of *The Last Lighthouse*, is doing posters that I will distribute by mail to various places in Shetland.

The fish stew I made last night was fantastic. It was tomato based and had the greatest flavour. We finally figured out it was the parsnips that made it so good. I wonder if you would get the same result with beef. Today I am making a kedgeree (smoked fish, hard boiled eggs and rice in a cream sauce) and a pie with bananas, toffee and whipped cream. Tom is coming up to eat at 3:30 pm and then Connie and I are going to walk to see the caddies, the Grinds of Navir and back to Tom's house.

Connie is out fishing for trout that we will have for dinner tomorrow or so she says.

August 11th

Just got back from a wee red boat ride and it was big time rough. I actually got scared since the waves were huge and we really rocked about. Connie and I both were glad when the ride was over. It will probably be Connie's last ride as the wind is getting worse every minute. Have to clean out the generator house today to get ready for next weekend so I hope the few drops we are having do not turn into heavy rain.

Yesterday Connie and I walked to see my caddies. They were at the top of an enormous hill that meant we had to climb the steepest hill out there. But when we got close I called them and they came. They are still pretty tame as they allowed Connie to pet them and they had never seen her before. Kara gave me a kiss on the nose and Connie took a picture that I am hoping will be good. It was nice to see them and I realize I miss them a great deal.

We have not caught a trout yet so yesterday afternoon Connie went out and fished alone. She caught a bobber. Yes, I said a bobber. Her bobber and lure broke off in the middle of the loch so being resourceful she cast another bobber and line after it and it bit. She fought to bring it in against the wind. It's not easy landing a bobber. So, after becoming an expert bobber catcher she will probably catch a trout or maybe next time it will be the whole fishing pole. Who knows?

August 12th

The sun is out but the wind is blowing at almost gale force with huge surf and a little spray. We may have to move the wee red boat onshore as wind from the west is dangerous in Stenness Bay because it can drive the boat onto the beach. We will check after dinner.

Yesterday after the scary boat ride Connie and I just hung out in the house and read books. To be honest we tried to read but both of us fell asleep and had a wonderful nap. Last night it rained really hard so we spent the evening watching movies. *American Beauty* was shown for the first time on UK television so we watched that. What a depressing story.

Today the plan is to have roast pork, stovies (potato dish), crab salad, and rhubarb bread pudding with custard sauce for dinner. It is already starting to smell good. Tom may take us to Brae so Connie can get another throwaway camera as she is out and still has a few days to go.

August 13th

Yesterday's pork and rhubarb bread and butter pudding were good but not as exciting as the stovies and crab salad, which were superb. After dinner we all climbed in Tom's truck and went to Brae to get Connie two more throwaway cameras. After we got the cameras we drove around Muckle Roe so she could take pictures. She finished one camera and is working on the second.

The head keeper (me) is a little under the weather today. I must be coming down with a cold or something. Last night I was chilling and aching; today I have a slight runny nose but that could be a result of going out in the boat.

The wind and rain stopped for a short time this morning so we went out in the wee red boat. It was rough at first. Then it calmed and got murky and rainy, which isn't so good for someone coming down with a cold. Connie and Tom bought a new line at Brae Building centre with three sea fishing flies on it. It really worked as Connie caught 19 piltocks. We were hoping for 20 but the last strike was either a really big one or maybe three fish at the same time as the line broke and she lost the flies and weight. She loved catching so many fish. Tom got two lobsters so it was worth the trip.

I am going to curl up on the couch with a book, as I am not feeling well and it is really misty and foggy outside. Connie is going after one of those elusive trout this afternoon.

I am currently bidding for a fish finder for Tom's wee red boat on ebay.com. The fish won't have a chance. I lost one bidding contest yesterday because I felt too bad to stay up and monitor the bids. Today bids close at 5:00 pm our time so I should be able to stay with it.

August 15th

For the first time I did not write yesterday. The telephone went out and we had to get that fixed and after that, I got an e-mail from Connie's husband that turned out to have been hacked off her hard drive and sent with a virus. Now that same malicious virus is sending files out to people. I warned everyone if they got an e-mail from me with a document attached they should not open it. I have cleaned the hard drive and talked to my server and there is no contamination on this computer. Hopefully this will be the end of it as Connie thinks she knows who might want to mess up her e-mail.

We went fishing early in the morning at Houlland Loch. There were lots of trout jumping all over the place and each of us got two bites but we failed to catch even one. I guess I do not know how to set the hook when they bite.

After the telephone and virus problems we took off for the Bruddans to a place where we see a man sea fishing almost every day. He caught 40 piltocks and some mackerel yesterday. It is possible to fish the sea from the shore at the Bruddans with the right equipment.

We went to the loch by Tom's house to fish for trout but it was too weedy. It was a beautiful afternoon, so we enjoyed being out even if we couldn't fish. Tom gave us a lift home and we saw lots of trout jumping at the loch down by the cemetery so we decided to give it a try. There is nothing more frustrating than to have a trout jump right by your line and not take. That happens a lot around here. The midges were out and attacked us in swarms but another fisherman joined us and gave us a stick of cream that repels midges. It worked for a while but we got frustrated with the midges buzzing around our heads and the trout not biting so we started up the lighthouse hill. Tired, eaten alive and discouraged with trout fishing we were rescued by Leslie. He picked us up and brought us home so we did not have to trudge up the huge lighthouse hill.

Connie was thrilled when Leslie took her up into the tower to see one of the most beautiful sunsets of the summer. Leslie came in for a scotch and we talked until midnight.

Connie left on the early 7:15 am bus. There is no later bus on Wednesday because it is half day when most stores close at noon. It is raining and I keep thinking about her in Lerwick in the wet. She is staying at the Sumburgh Hotel tonight so she can catch the early flight tomorrow.

I am trying to wash and clean a little bit, as this weekend is the big radio event. I am going to town with Tom on Friday to look for paper cups for serving hot drinks in the tearoom. The trip to Lerwick on Friday means all the cleaning must be done today and tomorrow. I have washing drying all over the house since it's a rainy day. It is supposed to clear this afternoon so hopefully the wash will then go outside.

August 16th

Tom moved the tables and chairs into the generator house tearoom and I will begin making the sandwich fillings this afternoon. Tomorrow night I will make up the sandwiches. Tonight I am doing a major interview about the weekend on BBC Shetland so that should help bring a few people.

Yesterday I spent 3½ hours getting the virus off of my computer. Norton has directions for removal of major viruses on their website and without that help I would have been dead as the virus had become imbedded in Windows. I had to reinstall Windows because Norton deleted an operating file while trying to remove the bug but even after reinstalling Windows I still had the virus. Finally about 8:30 pm I got it. My computer is virus free again so I can relax. It was my first virus and a frightening thing for someone who does so much work on the Web. We found how the virus got on Connie's computer. Hopefully she will be able to get it off her machine without the trauma I went through.

I am feeling really bad with aches all over my body and it is a mystery, as I do not have any cough, sore throat, or stomach problems. Maybe I am just tired. This is the last day I can rest for a couple of days. Rest is what I am going to do for the remainder of the afternoon after I make egg salad and tuna salad for sandwiches.

It's warm but the fog is so thick it is hard to see very far which makes it a cosy day to stay inside and rest.

August 17th

Tom is coming to get me for a rushed trip to Lerwick to get rid of his wool and get the last minute things for the weekend.

I am better, not 100%, but I should make it through the weekend. My stomach is sore and a little upset so it must have been a kind of flu. The broadcasters start moving in tonight and it will be chaos from about 5:00 pm on. Leslie and Tom will be here to help and keep an eye on things. Most of the activity will be in the generator house where they will set up their radios. One antenna will be free standing and the other will be attached to the tallest flagpole. They will be sleeping in shifts in the guest bedroom. I plan to go to bed early and just let them do their thing.

All the sandwich fillings are made and I am getting sliced ham and cheese in town. I will get up early tomorrow and make the sandwiches.

I hope we get lots of visitors, as this thing has been a lot of work.

August 18th

It is 5:00 am and I am up to monitor a bid on a fish finder on ebay.com. I hope to go back to bed when the bidding is over.

The radio people are all set up and when I went to bed at 10:30 pm they were talking to Puerto Rico. The lighthouse event had not started yet so it was just someone who was on the air. The Amateur Lighthouse Society event started officially at 1:00 am our time. The broadcasters have put a big map on the wall where they will flag all the stations they talk to. I am dying to know which ones they have reached so far but if I go out there I will not be able to go back to sleep. It looks like it will be a long day as we even had visitors last night while they were setting up.

Three broadcasters are sleeping in the house in the spare bedroom while there are two caravans in the car park and a tent in the yard. It really looks like something is happening around here. We are only in the first hours of the big weekend and I know I will be glad to have my peace and quiet back.

Later today I will put a web page on *Scottish Radiance* and send a notice out to my readers list to let them know where they can see pictures of all the activity.

I am still the highest bidder on the fish finder but I need to spend all of my time on ebay.com for the last five minutes to make sure I get it.

August 19th

It is cloudy and supposed to rain so I am not sure we will have much of a crowd for the open house. Yesterday was one of the most beautiful days I have seen in Shetland. It was warm, almost hot, with a light breeze to keep the midges away. Everyone except me got sunburned. I was too busy in the house making sandwiches and in the tearoom signing books to go outside much.

Probably over 200 people visited and I think most of them were local. We realized early on that there is a whole generation in Shetland who have never been in a working lighthouse. Leslie and a former NLB staff member were on the go all day leading trips up the tower. I bet they are sore today.

The tearoom was a huge success and I am actually making money on a 'donation only' payment for the food. In all probability I made about £50 yesterday after expenses. Everyone says a permanent tearoom at the lighthouse would make money especially in the summer and yesterday proved they were right. My books are selling well but I have not had time to count how many I sold because I have just been too busy.

We all finished the day by watching the sunset, which was beautiful. All in all it could not have been more successful. I hope the weather doesn't get too bad today so we will have more visitors.

I am tired but feel really good that we opened up the tower so the younger generation could experience being in a working lighthouse.

August 20th

Well, the big weekend is over and by all criteria it was a huge success. No one has any idea how many people attended but around 200 signed the lighthouse guest book. I am sure the number is double that or more as the guest book was in an out of the way place where most people probably missed it. Yesterday was an awful day with wind and rain but people still came and climbed the tower. We expected some people to come and spend time in the broadcast room and the tearoom but not climb the tower. We were wrong.

The radio operators had hundreds of contacts. It was so busy the broadcasters could only handle the microphone for a half hour at a time and then they had to change operators because they got so tired. They never got to talk to hundreds of people that were lined up. The plan was to stay on the air until midnight last night but a storm moved in with gale force winds and the antenna began to look like it was going to blow away. Leslie, Tom and the three broadcasters were able to get it down and lash it to the fence so it would not be damaged or lost. John, our broadcasting visitor from Louisiana, could not believe how horrific the storm was. It got so bad the three broadcasters stayed all night and left early this morning. When John got up he was amazed as the wind was calm. He was fascinated with the Shetland weather and how fast it can change.

Everyone wants to do the event again next year but I am a little reluctant as I had a hard time keeping up with the tearoom and signing the books that I sold. If I could get help with the tearoom I would be positive about doing it again. I made about £100 on the tearoom and sold over £450 worth of books so it was a good weekend for me financially, but a lot of work.

The best part of the weekend was not related to any of the above. Tom has never seen his grandchildren nor met his three children's spouses as a result of a nasty divorce many years ago. I issued special invitations to attend this weekend's event to all of Tom's children without Tom knowing. He would have been so disappointed if they did not come and nervous all weekend so I kept it a secret. One invitation got returned in the mail so I knew that daughter would not come but the two invitations to the children who live in Lerwick did not get returned. Late yesterday afternoon I saw Paul, Tom's son, in the crowd and my heart stopped since I wanted so badly for Paul to have the entire family with him and he did. Tom met his son's wife and got to spend a good bit of time with two of his grandchildren. He took them down to his house and I have never seen him so happy. I had to tell him what I had done as he kept wondering why Paul had come. I was scared that he would be mad at me but he just laughed. He tried to make me promise I would not connive behind his back again but I wouldn't because I want to help him see the rest of his grandchildren, which he wants more than anything else in the world. Anything I do will probably be done without his knowledge, as it would hurt him too much if I failed. The important point is Tom has now met one of his children's family and he is so happy. Both of his grandchildren (the girl is 12 and the boy 14) are taller then Tom. I wanted to take their picture all together but I had to go sign books. Next time I will make sure photographs are taken.

An added bonus to the weekend was we had three retired lighthouse keepers attend. I got to interview all of them on tape for an upcoming book. Also the son of Willie Gifford, the last keeper at Eshaness, came. It was interesting to hear all of his stories. He stayed all afternoon with his family and every minute I could spare I spent with him.

The Northern Lighthouse Board engineers are here laying cables in the lighthouse so I am going to serve them tea and if it stops raining I am going trout fishing for the rest of the day.

August 21st

It is sunny and fairly warm but the winds are really blowing, up to gale force eight later today, so I am focusing on inside activities.

A new sighting was an otter running across a boggy field down the road from the lighthouse yesterday afternoon. We have not seen an otter since Dean scared the one at the Bruddans. In case you didn't read *The Last Lighthouse*, it seems the otter was curious about Dean climbing around on the rocks and got just a little too close. Not being sure what the otter would do Dean shooed it away. We have not seen an otter down there since.

Speaking of the Bruddans, I saw a gigantic lobster claw on the rocks there. It was as long as the distance from the tip of my fingers to my elbow. Gigantic! I cannot imagine what size the entire lobster would have been.

Last night the man who co-ordinated the broadcasting last weekend was on Radio Shetland telling about how many contacts we made, but the official statistics are not done so his numbers were just estimates. I am really anxious to know what the real numbers are.

I have made my plans to return to the US for Christmas. I will be flying home just before Thanksgiving and coming back the day after Christmas. This means I will celebrate Christmas at the lighthouse after Christmas but my documentary editor says that is okay as long as there is a holiday celebration.

August 22nd

It is a sunny, windy day. The wind is not gale force so I was able to hang clothes outside and finish washing the bedding from the weekend.

I have added a new activity to my morning chores. I go trout fishing every nice morning. This morning I went for about an hour but I did not catch anything. I forgot to take the worm container so I used lures and a fly I made out of a bird feather I found on the shore. I did not see any fish but it was nice to stand by the shimmering lake with the blue sky above.

Last night I was reading in the bedroom, as it is quieter when the wind is in the south. Looking out the window I saw the clouds magically clearing. In a few seconds we went from a dark cloudy sky to a bright pastel horizon as the sunset had begun. It really was stunning. I watched for about 15 minutes until the clouds returned.

I am off to a complete house auction tonight as they have a freezer for sale. I would like to have a bigger freezer so I could buy half a pig and split it with Tom. That would guarantee I would have meat all the time. I love going to the auctions because I am fascinated with all the Shetland things that are new to me. Speaking of auctions, I fixed the vacuum cleaner. I replaced all the belts and it works fine now.

August 23rd

It is another sunny but breezy day. Tom is going to put the wee red boat back in the bay so lobster tending and fishing can begin again. Yesterday, when we went to Lerwick, Tom helped me buy some trout flies so I could catch one of those blasted fish. Dean is coming over on the 17th September and staying through the 2nd October so I want to catch a trout before he gets here to prove women are better and all that!

The auction last night had tons of people and the prices on dishes were particularly high. I got a small teapot that looks like a goose, some baking pans and a small pendulum clock, which took some fiddling to get started but it is now hanging over the Rayburn and keeping good time. I also got a beautiful and comfortable shaker type rocker (I know it is comfortable as I sat in it during the auction) and a large mirror with a gold scrolling for the spare bedroom for £10. My biggest purchase was a chest type freezer for which I paid £30. I cleaned it and put it in the generator house. It seems to be working fine as it has been on for only a little over an hour and has frozen a small block of ice. It has a few scratches but being outside in the generator house it does not matter, as no one will see it. I will not put anything in it until I have made sure it is working okay. I wish I had a freezer thermometer to check it.

I talked to a man who will sell us half a pig, cut, wrapped and delivered for £60. That would only be £30 for me so I probably will do it.

Tom fell twice last night. First trying to put up my pendulum clock and then getting some stuff out of his pickup at home. He is sore but nothing major seems to be wrong. He finally admitted he tries to hurry too much and takes too many chances. He is the most impatient person I have ever met and does have a tendency to hurry too much.

Tom is taking me to a sheltered loch this afternoon to try out my new trout flies. He has gotten into the trout fishing just as I have.

Until we leave I am working on *Scottish Radiance* and *Lighthouse Digest* stories plus trimming wool. I am going to begin to wash the fleeces I have so they can be clean and ready to card when winter comes. Spinning and carding are great activities for the long winter nights.

August 24th

I just got back from trout fishing at the lighthouse loch on a foggy and windy but warm Shetland morning. I saw some trout jumping but I still have not caught one. Yesterday I put trout flies on the fishing line hoping that would work better than worms. I am not sure anything would have enticed them today, as the water was so bumpy from the wind.

I washed four fleeces last night and have a bunch of washed Shetland wool hanging in a mesh bag on the fence. I hope to wash four more tonight. I must have 35 fleeces in the garage to wash. I need to get them dry before the winter storms. I do not like to dry them inside as they make the house smell like wet sheep.

Speaking of sheep, Tom has a lamb that went blind. He went to the vet and got some medicine to clear up the blindness. The vet warned Tom the lamb's ears would fall off. We thought the lamb had avoided that atrocious occurrence but the fleece on his face started to fall off about a week ago and yesterday his ears fell off. The poor thing is so sad looking but he is spry and seems happy eating away in a protected field of good grass. I have no idea how he will heal and whether his ears will grow back or not. I do hope they do, as a lamb without ears looks strange indeed.

My caddies will be coming home from the hills within the next few days. I have not seen them since Connie and I walked out there but Tom saw them just a few days ago. I will be so glad to have the caddies where I can see them every few days. I hope they remember me.

August 25th

I just got back from going for a ride in the wee red boat, as it is a beautiful sunny day here. It was bumpy with big surf. Since we have had no storms and little wind I cannot figure out why the sea was so rough. I was uncomfortable and worried for a while.

I did join the illustrious club of Shetland anglers by catching two pretty good-sized piltock on the fishing rod. Mackerel would have been better but we saw none this morning. I will be eating my fish with a salad for dinner.

The caddies are home from the hills and look really good. They knew me and let me give them a good rub.

Today I have to finish reading a book for a review (as good an excuse as I can think of for reading a book) so I think I will take it out in the sun and enjoy the day while I read it.

August 26th

Finally success, a trout has been landed. Tom drove me to Gluss Water Loch this morning, which a neighbour said had trout and he was right. I brought the trout home and we had it for the appetiser for dinner today. The meal also included a salad made out of the first lettuce out of *my* garden, which was a big event. The rest of the meal was roast beef, stovies, cooked carrots, and a banana toffee pie.

Tom is going to try to check the lobster creels, as it was way too rough this morning. That is why we went trout fishing so early. The whole day has been turned around but that is okay as living way out here no one cares in which order you do things.

Tonight I may walk to Houlland Loch to try for trout there. I have seen more trout jumping there than anywhere else. Hopefully I will have good luck.

August 27th

It is Monday, the day I put the garbage out for the council truck to pick up. It is a bank holiday here so I am taking part of a day off to go trout fishing – what else. Actually going trout fishing twice a day gives me a good excuse to get outside for some exercise.

Last night I went fishing at the two connected lochs south of the lighthouse by the Bruddans. It was a wonderful sunny evening with a few fluffy clouds passing by every once in a while. The wind was strong but if you were in the right place it carried your cast a long distance. It was so peaceful watching the cloud designs on the water and the ripples when the wind gusted up. Fishing is just an excuse for being outside, I think. I did not catch anything but I saw two of the biggest trout jumping that I have seen in Shetland. They made huge splashes. That seems strange, as those lochs are some of the smaller lochs around here. Maybe it is because they are away from the beaten track and are not fished much.

Fishing might seem to be all I do but that is not true. It is just the most fun to talk about. I am working on *Scottish Radiance*'s September issue, writing my article for *Lighthouse Digest* and looking for an agent for my novel. I have neglected trying to sell my novel as my non-fiction books are selling so well. So the pattern for today and most days is to fish morning and night then I can work at the computer the rest of the day. Whoops, forgot I am also washing wool every night so it will be dry by winter when the nights are long and I can spin.

August 28th

It is another partly cloudy day with a pretty stiff wind. I went out fishing for a while this morning but had to call it a day, as I needed to finish *Scottish Radiance*. Every day I see beautiful trout jumping in the lochs but so far the only one caught was at Gluss Water, which is a long way from here.

Gerdie Loch, which I often refer to as the split loch, has big trout jumping every day. The biggest I have seen has been on the east side of the loch. I fished there this morning and saw a lot of activity in the west side. Those trout really get around.

The loch of Framgord is what I call the lighthouse loch and it has been a few days since I have seen a fish in that one. I think it has been over-fished since it is so near the road.

Houlland Loch always has trout jumping but it is a huge loch so it is hard to tell where to fish. Yesterday I saw only one fish on the south side while on the other side of the small island with the broch there were many.

Ganderhouse Loch has lots jumping and I have spotted many fish in the water but it is farther from the lighthouse and I do not get down there much. The biggest problem is you must climb the lighthouse hill to get back home.

I have not tried West Loch, Muckla Water, or Black Loch but Muckla Water has produced a lot of small trout for Tom's neighbour. Maybe this afternoon when I get the magazine done I will give it a try.

The fishing is more about being outdoors then catching fish but it really is annoying when the fish jump right in front of you but do not bite. I keep alternating worms and flies but so far the only trout caught was taken on a fly.

Tom saw the orange rabbit down by Ganderhouse last night when he was checking on the boat. I am so glad it is still alive.

August 29th

It is a rainy, misty day so I may have to do inside things all day. That means writing and cleaning up the house a little. The house is always neat but the Rayburn sprays dust all over when I clean it every morning so I have to clean that room about twice a week.

Tom caught a large brown trout yesterday in Houlland Loch. It was over a pound and fourteen inches long. I was trying but it was his turn. He cleaned it and put in my new freezer. We will have a trout dinner when Dean arrives. That is if I catch any more.

Speaking of the freezer, Tom and I did decide to split one half of a pig. It is Shetland born, raised and butchered. We will pick it up from the farmer next Tuesday. The major cuts are put in big bags that we will have to divide and put whatever each of us wants in separate smaller bags. There is a meat company here that sells various packages of beef so I may get one of those on my next trip to Lerwick. With both pork and beef in the freezer plus a supply of bread I would be fine out here for a month without going to town.

The Internet magazine is almost done so I will be able to goof off this weekend. I might take the bus into town Saturday, as Tom is not planning a trip to Lerwick this week. It would give me time at the library – when I go with Tom he just rushes from one place to another.

August 30th

A sunny day in Shetland has brought a bunch of tourists. It seems I cannot win. On sunny days tourists make working outside difficult by constantly coming up to me and asking questions, and on bad days I cannot get outside. I did fish for a while this morning. I saw a few trout but did not catch any.

I watched four huge bonxies chasing one juvenile seagull. They kept diving at the poor gull. But as they went over the hill the baby seagull was still out-smarting them. I am glad I did not see the end result. Four against one is pretty bad odds and the seagull was a baby.

When I got back to the lighthouse I moved my wool outside to air some more as it is still damp around the edges. As I went into the garage a black and white spotted kitty ran out and went into one of the open generator house doors. I put food in with it and closed the door. When Tom makes his daily check on me I will try to catch it. It looked only about half grown. We have lots of wild cats on the cliffs and this must be one of the babies. I would like to have it continue visiting by putting food out but Tom does not like cats so I cannot make it a permanent resident.

I may get two chickens though and keep them in the garage. There is a crofter who has all kinds of rare breed chickens. Tom would take the chickens to his croft when I am not at the lighthouse. Also I am used to fresh eggs from the chickens in Michigan. Nothing is better than fresh eggs.

August 31st

It is a rainy and warm day. The rain is helping me stay inside to finish up the September issue of *Scottish Radiance*.

A precious moment in an author's life is when they come face to face with a reader who has been touched by their work. That happened yesterday. Tom went to a funeral at the nearby cemetery and he stopped at the lighthouse to see if everything was okay before he went home. When he was getting in his truck a young man came up to him and asked if he was 'Mr Tom'. Tom did not know what to say so he sort of stumbled around until the young man told him he had read *The Last Lighthouse*. I was just going back inside and overheard the conversation so I went out to rescue Tom. The gentleman was Italian and had come to visit Eshaness because he had read my book. He wanted to know where the seal rocks were and if the Rayburn was finally working. He said reading my book had changed his life and made him actively pursue his dream of knowing more about his Scottish ancestors. He began his search by coming to Eshaness to see if it was real and was even more excited after meeting Tom and seeing the things described in the book. He told me he was even more convinced most things you want are possible if you try hard enough. I was totally flabbergasted. I have met many people who *The Last Lighthouse* had affected in that way. We had always thought the market for the book was lighthouse people but it has turned out to be more for people who want to chase an elusive dream. What was so moving about this young man was that he was way out here by himself chasing his dream because of my book. It was a special moment and one I will treasure for a long time. I know from the Shetland Tourist Board that the book was bringing people to Eshaness but this was the first one I had met who had travelled so far. It made me glad that we published that book. *Scottish Lighthouses* is outselling *The Last Lighthouse* but I think I am more proud of *The Last Lighthouse* and how it is being received.

September

September 1st

I woke early this morning. The hills are starting to turn brown as the grass dries out and there is a feel of fall in the air. It is a lovely day but the air definitely has a nip in it. A cold north wind is blowing but the sun is shining brightly, bathing the area in a warm golden radiance. The colour may not be special as the sun is rising later and I am seeing the normal sunrise colour for a change. We are expecting gales before the day is over so I think I will go fishing in a few minutes. I will need extra layers of clothing if I am going to be outside.

September 2nd

The sun keeps trying to shine but big black clouds interrupt, bringing huge amounts of rain every once in a while. It was sunny when I got up so I went fishing early this morning but I didn't catch anything.

Sunday dinner is cooking – roast chicken, mashed potatoes, garlic bread, cream of celery soup, sliced tomatoes, and chocolate cake with ice cream and toffee sauce. I am getting a little short of supplies, as I have not been to Lerwick for a week and half. A trip to Brae helped but the store didn't have everything I needed.

Big sighting yesterday when I went for a ride in the wee red boat to Dore Holm. Tom said it would probably be the last day it would be calm enough to go out in the boat this year. No puffins, but something even better since it was a first. A dolphin was swimming around mischievously. It scared me at first when I saw the fin. I thought it was a shark but it was definitely a playful dolphin. That was my first close sighting of a fin in the water from the wee red boat. Because it looked like rain I did not take the camera, a huge mistake. I am still hoping to see an Orca but it is getting pretty late in the season for them.

The other big news is Tom now has his fish finder. Dean and I bought it on the Internet for him as an early Christmas present. It is just the right size for Tom' s boat. After we put batteries in it the lights came on and everything seemed to be working. Tom went to check the lobster creels and I would not be the least surprised if he tried it while he was out in the boat. It was too rough for me and besides it was pouring with rain. It will be fun to map the bottom of Stenness Bay along with finding fish.

Tom caught a ling, a four foot long fish that lives on the sea bottom, which looks like an enormous eel. Actually I thought it quite ugly but they say they are real good eating.

Last night's sunset was remarkable, containing every shade of pastel. I took pictures of our two flags waving in the wind during the height of the colour. Taking sunset photographs is addictive and I do not believe I will ever tire of it.

September 3rd

A bad day with heavy rain and the gales moving in, making it difficult to walk so Tom decided to go to Lerwick. We just got back. I imagine it will be my last time in town until Dean comes.

I got a supply of meat for my freezer from a Lerwick butcher and found he sends a van to our area every Monday. The van does not come as far as the lighthouse but I could order meat and have it brought to the end of the Eshaness road. That really does not help, as I still have to ask Tom to go and get it. The butcher gave me a price list. I got roast beef and some sausage to try the quality before ordering more. I have my quarter of pig so I am set for a while.

I went to the library for a few minutes and realized how much I miss going to a library. I always went once a week back in the USA. The van only comes once a month to the lighthouse unless I go to Lerwick. I might take the bus into town just to go to the library once a week. With Dean coming I will have transportation for a couple of weeks of library visits.

The highlight of the Lerwick trip was Tom going to one of the big fishing boats from Whalsay to get a bucket of herring to salt. I got out of the car and inspected the marvellous ship. The ship was huge and cost £6,800,000. It was in perfect condition and so clean you could give it the white glove test. For some reason the Whalsay fishermen had the courage to borrow the money to purchase seven of these big ships, and all are doing very well. They probably could do better if there were more fish around but one boat just changed owners and each of the original partners had a profit of £1,800,000.

I've got to watch *Ready Steady Cook*, my favourite TV programme, and then I probably will curl up with a new book for the evening, as television does not have much to offer.

September 4th

I am about to go out and put my wool on the wire dryer I have strung across the fence. Sunshine has returned to Shetland but the wind is still with us. Let's hope it does not blow my wool to Iceland or some place like that.

Today I am working on my recordings as my producer gets back from Australia next week and wants to launch into the editing of what I have done. They are short of tape recorders so I will have to send my recorder back while Dean is here so they can use it for another feature. You would think the BBC would have lots of recorders but it seems not. I know they are expensive but everyone in the country who has a television pays a TV licence, which supports the BBC. That should be enough to buy a few recorders.

I just finished my story for this month's *Lighthouse Digest*, which included all the statistics from the radio weekend.

The radio broadcasting was popular and we had to set up chairs for all the people who wanted to listen. I was fascinated with the number of countries they were reaching. We had a total of 555 radio contacts over the weekend in 48 countries and they talked to 43 lighthouses in 21 countries. The most distant lighthouse was Galinhos lighthouse in Brazil. Here is the list of lighthouse contacts.

Country	Location
Belgium	Blankenberge
Belgium	Nieuwport
Brazil	Galinhos
Canada	Call Signal Can43; location unknown
Croatia	Sestrice
Denmark	Lightship Fyrskib xxi
England	Light Vessel Trinity
England	Glasson Dock
England	Hunstanton L/H
England	Lamp Rock

England	Souter
England	Withernsea
England	Anvil Point Light
England	The Lizard
England	Trinity Buoy Wharf, London
England	Shoreham
Finland	Ulkokalla L/H
France	Dieppe
Germany	Campen
Germany	Norderney
Germany	Dornbusch
Ireland	Old Head of Kinsale
Israel	Acco
Italy	La Lanterna, Genova
Italy	Vittoria
Lithuania	Cape Vente
Lithuania	Sventoji
Lithuania	Juodkrante L/H
Netherlands	Lightship Texel
Netherlands	de Ven L/H Enkhuizen
Netherlands	Noord Hinder Lightship
N. Ireland	Blackhead, Co. Antrim
N. Ireland	St Johns, Co. Down
Poland	Czolpino L/H ?
Scotland	Corran Point
Scotland	Little Cumbrae
Scotland	Hoy High, Orkney
Slovenia	Piran-Punta
South Africa	Green Point
Sweden	Gasoren
USA	Marquette Harbour (located in my home state)
USA	Ponce de Leon Inlet
USA	Ocracoke Island

September 5th

It is a sunny but windy day here and I am at the computer working on publishing type things. A major breakthrough for me is I now have an editor at Macmillan Pan (the overall umbrella for all the Macmillan divisions) who wants me to submit book proposals and my novel after October 1st. This is no small event in a writer's career since like all writers I dream of having one of the world's largest publishers publishing my work. I am the most excited about the interest in my novel which I have rewritten a couple of times but haven't spent any effort marketing.

The smaller publishers that currently I work with don't have a lot of resources to promote my work but have been doing pretty well with what they have. A big outfit has the capital and the staff to really sell your work and I am keeping my fingers and toes crossed that this submission will succeed. It will be a slow process, and probably I will not know any thing for six months, but if I succeed with a big publisher I will be able to start the next book, that I hope is destined for a movie, in January.

I am also trying to get a bigger UK publisher interested in *Northern Lights*, the book about Shetland and Orkney lighthouses. I have three small local publishers interested but none of them have signed a contract so why not try a big publisher.

Most writers would be delighted to be in my shoes with so much interest in their writing but it is frustrating having to do your own marketing as well as the writing. I have been looking for a UK agent to take over marketing my writing but if I can do it myself then I get the extra 10 or 15%. So if Macmillan comes through then I can just settle down and write.

September 6th

Yikes, the wind is blowing so hard it just might blow the tails off the sheep, which would make a great story line for a children's book. My day will be spent working on the novel, carding wool (a most repetitive and difficult job), and doing a little fishing.

I went down to the loch early this morning to see if any troot (Shetland pronunciation) were about because I was not sure if it was going to rain. I fished for about an hour until it looked like rain any second, then I hiked back to the lighthouse. It was tough walking against the wind but at least I could stand up which is better than sometimes and of course it did not rain.

Tonight one of my favourite Scottish mystery writers, Ian Rankin, has his main character, Inspector Rebus, brought to TV in a series. This is a major event for me. I like Rankin's work. His plots are great and his character is believable, if not exactly likeable. Some people do not like Rankin because he deals with the dark and dirty side of life. The city is Edinburgh but it is the Edinburgh most of us will never see.

Another miracle has occurred at the lighthouse. I stuck two lemon seeds in a pot and a month and half later I have two lemon plants growing. I do not know how many times I had tried this in Michigan and it just did not work but here on the windowsill the seeds sprouted. Who knows why plants do what they do? My husband is supposed to know those kinds of things so I guess I will have to ask him why my lemon seeds sprouted here and not in Michigan.

September 7th

The day started off normally enough with my going fishing but then it turned weird. All of a sudden great big snowflakes started falling while I was fishing. I thought I must was seeing things, as it was relatively warm but in fact it was big particles of sea spray. When the winds get high foam collects around the shore and then every once in a while blows inland. I was at a loch quite a distance from the sea so it really does move around. This again emphasises how the area is battered by sea. I did not catch a trout.

I forgot to write earlier because I was trying to spin wool. My spinning wheel seems not to be able to hold the right tension even though I had the worn parts replaced. It is kind of like computer programs – you just have to keep using the blasted things until you finally figure out how they work.

The sun is all pink, as it is getting ready to set and the wind is out of the north so the office is cold. I will sign off for now and write tomorrow.

September 8th

The wind is howling out of the north this morning so it is cold. I was out rearranging the caddy shack, formerly known as the garage, as it soon will become home to chickens. When we went to the antique dealer some Sundays ago we passed a farm that had many rare breeds of chickens and I had been trying to contact the owner to see if he would sell me some laying hens. Yesterday I finally reached him and he is going to sell me some of his chickens. I am thinking three or four but that is yet to be decided. He has so many different types I have no idea what kinds I will end up with. We have some rare breeds on the farm in Michigan so it would be fun to get something different here. I will talk to Dean and see if he has any preferences for colour or type. I wanted to wait until Dean came to get them but the man may be gone while Dean is here.

Tom is making nests out of fish boxes and going to give me some straw to put on the floor of the garage. He is excited about the chickens and is talking about building a chicken house for them when I go back to the States. He doesn't care what kind I get as long as they lay eggs.

Because the wind is so strong I think I will stay inside most of the day and spin and card wool while listening to Radio 4. I have found my spinning time goes faster when I have the radio on. I have a lot of wool to card and spin so it will keep me out of mischief at least today.

September 9th

Another Sunday has arrived – time seems to move rapidly here, just like the wind. The wind is gale force again. There are huge white caps on the sea and there isn't a cloud in the sky right now so everything is sparkling. I am taking all the cameras with me when I go to collect the chickens, as there should be some spectacular shots.

I talked to the chicken man again last night and he has various colours of Light Sussex, Cochin, and Black Rocks. I did a search to find examples of all of these on the Internet so I could show Dean. Dean likes the Light Sussex and the Black Rocks but is concerned that the Cochin might have trouble with mud and wet because they have feathers on their feet.

Tom made the cutest nests out of fish boxes. Each fish box has two nests in it. We made perches for them and a feeder box out of some wood that was here. The caddy shack will make a nice little chicken house

Good news! The Aberdeen Mart opened and P&O Ferries is soon to begin to take sheep to be sold. The Shetland Mart has had two lamb sales so at least the Shetland lambs are getting sold. What price the crofters will be able to get is another story. Foot and mouth has really destroyed so much, it is a relief to know that the crofters might get to sell the lambs instead of having them killed. Being remote helps sometimes.

September 10th

It is windy and cold so the new chickens cannot go outside to check their yard. I have been out a couple of times to inspect them and they seem to be doing well.

I cannot remember the breed of one of the chickens so I am calling it 'unknown' until I can find out the correct name from the man who raised them. It is probably the most beautiful of the whole bunch and I think it is a Maran but I am not sure, as none of the Maran pictures seem to have birds with fuzzy feet.

My next task will be to name them. I have asked for suggestions from my Internet friends and I put pictures on the Internet so they could consider their appearance in choosing a name.

No eggs have appeared but the crofter said they all had been laying. The chickens are nervous after their move so it might be a while until I get any eggs. I am keeping a close eye on them for the first few days. I heard a cackle like one had laid an egg when I was putting the garbage out but I did not find any.

September 11th

I think it is morning since it is so foggy I cannot really tell whether the sun is out or not. I am writing very early because we are going to Lerwick today. I need food, woodchips, laying mash and a water dispenser for the chickens and I am buying some lamb treats so I can bribe the caddies to come see me as soon as they hear my voice

The pork was delivered last night. I have not eaten any yet, but it looks good. I put the meat in my little £30 freezer late last night and it has already frozen. I will try and cook some pork tomorrow. With the trip to Lerwick I am too worn out to do it tonight.

Good news! The new residents are earning their keep. I found two eggs this morning; one in a nest, the other on the floor, so one chicken must be mixed up on where to lay. I have no idea which chickens are laying. They are settling in really well and I am amazed at the places they have found in the garage to roost. You never know where you will find them. I suppose I will distress them again when I spread the wood chips and get no eggs for another day or so.

I just remembered I have to buy supplies for the upcoming visit of the Laird, better known as Dean, my husband. That means beer and crisps. Strange trip to Lerwick when I have to buy supplies for a husband and chickens both. I will not comment on which is more important.

September 12th

I do not know where to begin after what happened in the US yesterday. Everyone will always remember how they heard what happened on September 11th 2002 just like they did on the day Pearl Harbour was bombed or John Kennedy was killed. It is not surprising that I found out via computer. Returning from Lerwick

I checked my e-mail and I noticed a whole string of e-mail alerts from CNN. My first reaction to the title 'America Under Attack' was that it was some kind of virus or scam. I opened one and could not believe what it said. Rushing to the second one I was convinced it was a cruel joke. To prove to myself it was a hoax I turned on CNN and sat in a state of shock and started to cry as I saw the pictures of the destruction of the World Trade Centre and the Pentagon on the television. Even with the pictures I felt like it was a novel or a movie and not actually happening. My first reaction was to call Dean as it was early in the US and more planes could be involved. I screamed 'Oh, my God, please let nothing happen in or near Detroit'. Now, it seems selfish but I imagine everyone with friends and relatives far away felt something similar.

The international telephone connections were so busy a recording came on saying 'We cannot accept your call right now'. It was not until 10:00 pm British time that I finally reached my husband. Our family was fortunate that no one was involved in any of the destruction but many other families were not so lucky. My heart goes out to them as they wait hoping that their loved ones are okay.

I stayed up late last night but got to the point that I could not stand any more pictures of the horror so I went to bed. When I woke this morning I turned on the TV, which is totally out of character for me. Usually the television is not on during the day as I am busy writing or working on *Scottish Radiance*. I just had to find out if there was any new information. The only thing new seemed to be people panicking and buying gasoline so the price had shot up. I turned the TV off and am trying to have a normal day. Struggling is a better word. As long as I stay away from the TV I might be able to do something constructive but whether I will be successful has yet to be seen.

How do I feel about all that has happened? I suppose my reactions are much the same as most Americans – shock, anger, disbelief and a hope that the projected numbers of those killed are lower than thousands.

I have an additional problem. I am a pacifist and have been all of my life. There no doubt will be some aggressive action by the US government when they find out who is responsible which I am sure most people will want and support. But what does someone who believes in pacifism do in a situation like this? I really do not know but more than likely I will be against retaliation. Friends might even be angry with me for feeling the way I do but I believe that what makes America great is we can all have different beliefs and they are accepted. A question which is always fired at me is 'What would you do? Just let them go on killing Americans?' My only answer and probably not a good one is 'Will killing more people change what happened yesterday and is there a chance it might escalate into something even more horrible?' As I said before, it makes very little difference what I think, as the government will do what they think is right. I do believe that some kind of military action will be taken.

The media on this side of the ocean has been very supportive of the US, as have all the governments, which is some consolation.

The fire in the Rayburn went out as I got so involved with what was going on in the outside world I didn't pay any attention to it. The first time in four months by neglect – the only other time I put it out so I could clean it. It is now burning brightly again.

September 13th

The sun is shining so I spent two hours trying to catch an elusive trout. I saw so many I thought for sure I would finally get one. I am making a decided effort to do normal things and am trying to stay away from TV as it just upsets me. Last night I broke down and cried for a long time, probably as a result of a news report from the BBC saying that most Americans on UK soil were having serious emotional problems because of the events in the US. I guess all I had to be told was that others were experiencing the same kind of feelings to finally let all of what was going on inside me spill out. After many e-mails from the States I do not think it is just those of us on foreign soil that are having problems coping but most Americans. It is not the best time to be alone in an isolated spot. Staying very busy seems to keep me little calmer but watching TV does not really help. Maybe it will be better today.

I just checked the status of airports, as Dean is to fly over here on Sunday. The security at Heathrow is so tight he will never be able to make it in one day. The big if is whether he can get out of the US. Some people have said they would not get on a plane right now but it might be the safest time in history. I flew over here two days after the Lockerbie bombing and even though it was slow and security unbelievable, we made it without any problems.

The BA flight from Detroit to London is cancelled again today. I would imagine if the US airports open later today that the flight from London to the US might go on Friday. It seems international flights will be the slowest to come back into service. We will just have to wait and see what happens.

One piece of good news is the BBC started an absolutely spectacular new series called *The Blue Planet* last night. It was the only non-news program they ran. It is the story of the oceans and the name comes from the fact that most of the Earth is covered by ocean – thus the blue planet. It was one of the best programs I have ever seen. I taped it so Dean can see the first segment, as he should be here to see the next two segments.

September 14th

On this day of mourning around the world I did what I could. I picked one of the few flowers in my garden, took it to the Bruddans and floated it gently into the sea with a prayer for all the dead and the misery of the families who have lost a loved one. The flower looked sad and so tiny in the big sea but it was precious to me so it was an important gesture.

Many of our friends have been asking whether Dean will make it to the lighthouse next week. It did not come as a surprise that he will not be coming on Monday. There are still no flights between Detroit and London so he made a reservation for the following Monday. I am trying to convince him not to come as he can only stay a week due to work commitments. It will be a two-day journey, as the restrictions at London Heathrow require all international luggage to come off and be searched before anyone can continue on so he will miss the connections into Aberdeen and Shetland. If you take four days out for travel it would leave him only three days here. I have not heard from him to see what he has decided.

We tried Tom's new fish finder in the sea today and it works great. It was fun to see the depth of the water change as we went around the bay. The only fish we found were a huge bunch of sillocks, which you could actually see just below the surface. Most fish seem to have disappeared for now, maybe it is because the sea is so turbulent. Yesterday afternoon I spent three hours down at the Bruddans watching gigantic waves, beautiful green surf and immense rollovers. It was a nice escape from the world crisis.

My brother and sister-in-law called me last night. They are in Maine where they spent a large period of time watching the same ocean except on the other side. They also felt it was a perfect escape from the horror of September 11th.

Life must go on, but it is so difficult to keep my mind focused on anything but the carnage of the day.

September 15th

Another off and on rainy day so I am doing things indoors. I did try to catch a trout this morning before it rained and I may try a little later in Houlland Loch for a change if the rain stops.

I am going to make pizza this afternoon from scratch – a first for here. I hope it turns out okay but it will be fun just to try.

With rain outside and chaos in the world I escaped for a couple of hours by going through my pictures and putting together a web page of Shetland beauty.

http://www.eshanesslight.shetland.co.uk/beauty.htm.

September 16th

I am trying to find a little peace on the first Sunday after the terrorist attack. Everyone needs to relax and appreciate the good things of this world after last week. It is a little difficult to be peaceful here as there is a roaring, and I mean roaring, north wind. For the first time this trip I had trouble going to sleep because of the wind making so much racket in the tower

Tom is due in a little bit. We are going to see if we can find a used tyre for his big tractor as he has been looking for the last year for a replacement. I am taking my camera and hope to get pictures of the tormented ocean and BIG surf. When we return we are having a beef rib roast from the new butcher, mashed potatoes (Tom always has to have some kind of potatoes), dill carrots, and a salad with a devilled egg in the centre (thanks to the new chickens) and another Dundee cake. I really liked last week's Dundee cake so I made another one.

Tom may have to go to Lerwick tomorrow to get an application for a licence to sell his sheep. Moving sheep is one of the biggest bureaucratic nightmares I have seen in a long time. The sheep are very slowly being taken off the island and sold while the smaller lambs are being culled at £10 each. This will help the crofters, as the shipping to Aberdeen is over £8 on the small lambs. They sell for almost nothing so last year everyone lost money on the small lambs. The culling includes shipping so the crofter is actually making money on it even though £10 sounds like nothing.

If Tom goes to Lerwick I will probably ride along and spend time in the library. I am a little blue since Dean was supposed to arrive tomorrow but next week he should be here. He really wants to come if only for a short time and I will be awfully glad to see him.

Not a very exciting day but I need the peace and quiet.

September 17th

When I put out the garbage and emptied the Rayburn's ashes there was a rainbow over the lighthouse. I have decided that is a sign it's going to be a good week. The rainbow's arch went all the way from the ocean on one side to the other. I ran for my camera but by the time I got back out it was too late and the rainbow was gone.

Some nice things happened during my trip to Lerwick. Edna, who runs the *Shetland Times* bookstore, came up and gave me a big hug and said she had been thinking about me. A couple of people approached me when they heard me talking and said their thoughts were with the Americans. It made me realize again how much people are thinking and praying for us.

Tom still wants a car. This is the third time we have gone to Lerwick and he stopped at each dealer to look. They talk about women not making up their minds. I do not know if he will ever decide about this car. He would like to have a new one but they do not have the model he likes in Shetland and cannot get one for three months. In the last few days he has decided he would like a Ford because Sheila (our post lady) got a used one and she really likes it.

Tom found out he could not get his licence for the sheep to go to Aberdeen until he knows when they are going to travel. He thinks it will be Sunday when they leave Eshaness for the boat but P&O usually calls the night before to confirm the pickup and the blasted office for the licence is not open on weekends. He is really frustrated. He was going to call P&O and try to get a firm date but does not think they will do it.

It is a nice day and I cannot accomplish a lot in the writing area this late in the afternoon. I got some new wellies in town so I think I will take them for a trial run by going down to the loch and try to get a trout.

September 18th

A sunny and misty day finds me running to Lerwick again with Tom, as he had to take in his licence application. I wanted to stop at the Oxfam shop in Brae. They had a hairdryer for 50p. Even with my short hair it takes a while to dry so 50p seemed like a bargain.

The chickens do not want to come out of their house. Their door was open all day yesterday and not once did I see them out. So far today they have not come out either. They are still blessing me with two hen fruit a day, which is plenty for one person. Just saw the Black Rock out in the yard so maybe they are getting the idea.

I am busy working on *Scottish Radiance*, as I do not want to have to do it while Dean is here. My publisher is arranging a book signing for me in Inverness the week after Dean leaves. I hope to be able to fly to Aberdeen with Dean and then take the train to Inverness. Going away means I need to get caught up on everything before he gets here.

I have beef stew on the Rayburn made out of leftovers from the roast on Sunday. The fish van will soon arrive and I will probably have fish tonight and the stew tomorrow. Stew is always better after it sets.

September 19th

I have been wandering around outside. It is a pretty cold day with a strong northeast wind but it was quite a delightful morning to be out. I headed for

Houlland Loch to fish and saw a whole bunch jumping but did they jump onto my hook – no way. Since the loch was sheltered from the wind I walked all the way around it. Then I decided to take an old peat road (road built to reach peat banks) and found myself in new territory. Nothing significant about the area but it was fun to be someplace new. After a while I came back to the main road to the lighthouse and walked for another hour to get back home. I am a little tired but probably the big problem tomorrow will be sore feet. My new wellies fit well and I am much more secure on my feet than I was in the old ones, which were too big and clumsy.

Dean says I am saving all the big trout for him. I may be doing that but believe me, it is not intentional.

My trip to mainland Scotland is all arranged. I will leave here with Dean on the 2nd and go to the Scottish Lighthouse Museum to pick out pictures for my *Northern Lights* book. Then I'll stay with the Macdonalds whom I have not seen for a while. I fly back to Shetland on October 8th. It will be a nice break and will help me adjust to Dean's departure.

I moved my tomato plant inside and it is on a table at an east window in the living room. I wonder how many people have tomatoes growing in their living rooms? It has buds so I am hopeful. It is one of the new grape type tomatoes that I grew from seed.

My windowsill is full of herbs but I have ordered some more. It is great fun to have fresh herbs to experiment with when you have a limited variety of food.

September 20th

Tom put me in charge of the fish finder in the wee red boat this morning and it was a huge success. It is an amazing gadget. We were able to spot three fish with it and since fish are so scarce in the bay right now, that was a major accomplishment.

It is amazing how things are changing as fall advances. The seals seem to have departed and the only sea birds left are the cormorants. The colours of the hills are turning brown and much redder.

Two chickens are moving around outside. The Light Sussex and the Black Rock have found their way out the door. The Light Sussex jumps up on the bar that is across the width of the garage to support the bottom of the garage doors then outside. The Black Rock just goes under the bar, which is the most logical way. Now the unknown is thinking about coming out. Couchin likes to stay inside. I am worried that they will eat coal since I saw them pecking at the little pieces near the coal bin. Coal cannot be good for chickens.

I am finishing the last episodes of the BBC feature to be aired in December and have to send them to the producer. I may take the recorder and tapes to the offices of BBC Shetland tomorrow, as Tom has to go in to Lerwick to get another licence for his lambs. P&O pick the lambs up on Saturday and they will be sold on Tuesday in Aberdeen. A Shetland crofter sees the sale of the lambs as the beginning of winter, which begins the slowest time of year until the sheep have to be fed in December.

Back to working on *Scottish Radiance* so I can spin more wool. Sitting at my spinning wheel watching the sun go down through the office window is really fun.

September 21st

It is a rainy and foggy morning. I got my recordings edited so I can turn them in and send the equipment back so someone else can use it. I drop everything off at the BBC Shetland studio and then it goes by inter-office mail to Glasgow. It seems strange when inter-office mail goes across the North Sea.

Last night I went fishing for about an hour and a half at Gerdie Loch. It was a cloudy night so the lighthouse switched on early. It was the gentle sweep of the beam of the light and myself in the emptiness. It was the first time I had been out in the hills at dusk when the light was on. I was a little afraid but after a while it became an exceptionally peaceful moment. I did not want to return as the loveliness and splendour of it all settled in on me. When it got so dark I could no longer see my bobber I got concerned about my walk back to the lighthouse. Not getting lost, as that was impossible with the light sweeping the hills, but tripping in a hole or stumbling on a rock. It will be nice when Dean gets here. Then we can fish in the evening together.

Surprise in my e-mail this morning was a letter from a big UK agent who may be willing to negotiate a deal for *Northern Lights*, my book on the Shetland and Orkney lighthouses. When I get back from Lerwick I will send them the information and we will see what happens.

September 22nd

Another chicken has learned how to come outdoors. The unknown took the plunge this morning after six tries. I hope she does not have as much trouble getting back in. A sunny and warm day like today is a good time for a chicken to take a stroll. There is hardly any wind at all so I hope to be able to spend some significant time outside. I cannot take off until after I do an interview on the Warren Pierce show on WJR in Detroit. The interview is aired at 5:30 am US Eastern Daylight

Time. Thank goodness we are five hours ahead of Detroit so I do not have to get up that early. It will be replayed during his show on Sunday so my family and friends can hear it without ruining sleeping in on a Saturday.

My trip to the Lighthouse Museum has been confirmed so I will finally get to pick out my pictures for *Northern Lights*. Rob Blackwell, who will do the layout, is going to try and meet me there. It will be fun spending a whole day at the museum. They had to lay off half of their staff so I will also be discussing helping them to raise funds. They have two keepers who I will interview while I am there for my next novel so I will have plenty to do.

Appletree Press e-mailed me that a copy of my new book, *Irish Lighthouses*, is on it way via snail mail. It is always exciting to finally see a copy of a book that you wrote so long ago in print. Rob Blackwell has seen it and says it is magnificent. I can't wait.

September 23

A grey but warm day. The weekly forecast for Shetland was in my e-mail and it looks like Dean will have pretty good weather while he is here. Somehow there was some miscommunication and Dean arrives Tuesday not Monday. All I care is that he gets here safely.

The most active creatures around here today are the chickens. They have all now braved the world beyond the caddy shack but so far they have not wandered to the west side of the house by the sea. I am a little concerned a gust of wind could blow them over the cliff. The fence should stop them but who knows with the wind around here.

Yesterday I completed a cycle. When I first arrived I spent most of my time helping Tom with the lambing. Those lambs went off in the blue and white P&O lorry yesterday on their way to Aberdeen to be sold on Tuesday. Only 50 were sent with the rest going next weekend. Thank goodness my caddies are all ladies so they will be staying at Bordigarth, Tom's croft.

After my radio broadcast yesterday I walked as fast as I could trying to get to Tom's before the lorry showed up. I need not have hurried as I met the lorry coming down the road. He was lost and had missed his turn. I got in and directed him to Tom's.

The sheep were loaded without a problem but then the blasted truck got stuck, really stuck. Tom, the driver, and Tom's neighbour Bertie Sanderson did everything they could to get it out including Tom pulling it with his four wheel drive pickup. They put rock and stones under the wheels but the tires just dug in further. Not wanting to say anything but feeling I knew how to get it out I finally told the driver to have Tom pull at an angle. First try – out it came. The driver was most appreciative but I think Tom and Bertie were not too sure they wanted to acknowledge a woman had solved the problem. Most of the crofters around here are chauvinists. I hear 'men should do men's work and women should do women's work' a lot. I think getting a lorry out of a deep hole is men's work, but it was the woman who saved the day.

September 24th

This is the story I put in *Scottish Radiance* this month about September 11th, entitled *An Every Day Hero*. It helped me struggle with my super-charged feelings about the terrorist attack.

> As most of you know an American firm owns Scottish Radiance and I am an American. The magazine is about 'all things Scottish', so some might think that my writing about my feelings in relation to what happened to America on September 11, 2001 might be a little out of line, but what occurred on that horrible day is a world issue and as such a Scottish one also.
>
> Right now I am living at our lighthouse in Scotland writing a book and doing a BBC documentary. Everyone is asking me how I found out about the terrorist attack and how am I coping. The first question is easy to answer. Returning home from a day in Lerwick I went to check my e-mail and there was list of maybe eight news alerts from CNN. As I opened up one e-mail after another I thought it was some kind of 'spam' or gigantic joke so just to make sure I turned on the TV to check. As the whole world now knows it was no hoax. How I wish it had been.
>
> My first reaction, like many others, was disbelief and absolute panic. I rushed for the telephone and placed a call to my husband in the US. At first the phone rang busy, then I started to get messages that all routes were engaged and finally the most frightening message, 'Your telephone call cannot be completed'. I sat down on the floor and sobbed as I continued to monitor the events on the television. Most of the rest of the day I spent crying and placing one phone call after another. Deciding the phone situation was hopeless I sent an e-mail to my husband telling him where I could be reached, and went to a neighbour's so I would not be alone. Dean and I finally reached each other five hours later.
>
> The second question, 'How am I surviving so far away from home?' is not so easy to answer. Like everyone else I have gone through many stages. My first and probably still most difficult issue was an obsession to get closer to my family. I wanted to go home. It just so happened my husband was due to fly to Shetland the weekend after the attack so at least I was not going to be separated from all of my family. As it turned out his flight was cancelled. It was during the time the planes were not flying that I suffered the most depression and desire to go home. Just the fact that I could not go was a shattering feeling.

Knowing that it would do neither me nor anyone else any good to dwell on my futile desire to go home, I took the tack that staying busy was the best approach. So I occupied my days with all the things that make up my life at the lighthouse. I wrote scores of pages, fished for hours, walked for miles and cooked many new dishes. Little by little it began to work, except when I stopped and watched television, the unhappiness and depression would return. I was constantly drawn toward the television but knowing it was detrimental for me to watch too much, I kept it off most of the time and relied on my e-mail news bulletins for anything new.

As the days have dragged by, I have thought for many hours about what I should do about all of this. I did some minor things – on the day the world remembered I walked two miles to Stenness beach with one of the few flowers I had been able to grow in my garden and laid this precious bloom gently in the sea and watched it float out with tears streaming down my face as I remembered. Not having a US flag my Shetland flag flew at half-mast during the US time of mourning. It was visible sign to the tourists and to myself that I cared, was American and was remembering.

Last night as I watched the BBC re-run of the US entertainment industry telethon, I realized what I should do in the future. Getting on a plane to the US to be near my family sounds like the way out of my pain but it is not; the answer lies in being an every day hero. What does that mean? It means I must go on and live my life and meet my commitments with additional effort to do it better than ever before. Like most people I am not in a position to do anything about the bigger picture. Whatever each of us does, we should make an extra effort to do it well. Never forgetting what happened and is yet to happen, but doing our small part in a heroic manner. For me it means writing the best words I can. For others it may mean helping getting the economy going again or teaching a child.

It also means turning my longing and worry for my family into a special dedication filled with love that will help me get by as I fill my commitments until Thanksgiving and Christmas when I return to the States. My husband is due to arrive here tomorrow and that will be a great joy and will help my healing continue.

The answer for what someone should do now is as different as each of us. But, for me, the answer is to become an every day hero by doing what I do with greater intensity and meeting my commitments with more devotion and energy. That will be doing my little part in what is yet to come.

September 25th

Dean is half way here. He called from Heathrow while waiting for his Aberdeen plane. Security was tight but the procedure in Heathrow had not changed. He had no trouble changing from Terminal 4 to Terminal 1. I find this a little unsettling as the security should have been a lot tighter but the search at Detroit Metro was very thorough and detailed. If the fog does not keep him in London he will arrive without a problem as we have a cloudy and warm day with no wind. If I get the magazine done I will walk down and have a go at the trout before he gets here.

I made a big pot of fish stew from the recipe I tried when Connie was here. It is absolutely wonderful and the key is the one parsnip in the stew. Dean's favourite food in the whole world is lemon meringue pie so I baked one this morning. The eggs were too fresh so the meringue does not have peaks like it should but I am sure it will taste good.

Tom went to Lerwick to buy a car. Dean is renting a car so Tom wants us to run him in to pick up his new car. I have no idea what he is going to get. He keeps fluctuating from buying a new Kia to a used Ford. I am betting he does not make up his mind today either.

The chickens are getting braver and braver as I saw them down by the tower when I went to hang out clothes. I do not like them being on the sea side but hopefully on a windy day I will have them shut up.

September 26th

Dean is here. In fact right now he is lying in bed and will not get up. I even gave him a cup of coffee in bed and he still won't get up. That is the last cup of coffee he gets in bed! His trip was totally uneventful with only a two-hour delay in London for fog.

We are going to take Tom into town this morning to pick up his new car. He decided on a used Ford Mondeo. The first thing he told me was I could not get into it with dirty oilskins or boiler suits. As if I was the one who wears dirty oilskins and boiler suits! He was so happy and proud when he told us. It is blue grey and has 25,000 miles on it.

The weather is cloudy but still not much wind and a little bit colder. You can definitely tell it is fall here. The ocean is still so Tom and Dean hope to get back and fish before any bad weather moves in.

We are having monkfish tail tonight for supper. I had the fish stew last night and I asked Dean if he would get tired of fish and he said no, so fish it is. We will probably have fish and chips in town too. Hopefully they will catch some mackerel when they are fishing so Dean can taste fresh mackerel before he leaves.

I've got to run so we can get Tom into town to pick up his car. He is always early when he picks me up so I do not want to be late picking him up. But, first I have to get Dean out of bed.

September 27th

The sun is trying to come out but there is still a little bit of mist so I have put my load of clothes on the inside drying rack instead of trying the clothes line outside. The sun will come out soon I am sure and then I will at least be able to move the sheets outside.

The fishermen have already gone out in the wee red boat. They had a great time yesterday with Dean catching 19 and touching two piltocks. (Touching means he lost them over the side as he was trying to take them off the hook.) If you count touching, he beat Connie's record of 19. Her problem was she had so many big ones on the line it broke. Connie is ahead of Dean in the mackerel department, as he has caught none. Tom got a 21 inch saithe, which is a truly big fish.

Needless to say we had piltocks for dinner last night and I just made a big pot of fish chowder for the guys when they get back from fishing.

This afternoon Dean wants to go trout fishing so I will probably stay here and work on my magazine and my submission for Macmillan since we only have one fishing pole. We planned to get another one when we took Tom in yesterday to get his car but the tackle shop was closed.

Tom's new car is beautiful. It is a grey colour that in the sun looks more blue purple. It is a four door with a wonderful stereo. He is so proud. Riding from Brae to Eshaness it was obvious the new car rides much better than his pickup. He was worrying what a crofter was doing with three cars. The wee white truck really is not safe and he does not drive it much so technically he has only a pickup and a car. I tried to tell him lots of farmers have that.

His lambs sold for £21 each, which was less than last year. You have to take off £8 for shipping so he only made £13 per lamb, which isn't much for a whole year's work. He has another bunch to go and hopefully he will get more for them.

September 28th

I just made the most wonderful dish; sliced turnips with cheese sauce. Tom brought over this gigantic turnip and I boiled the slices and then put on the sauce. It is to go with pork for dinner tonight.

The fishermen did not stay out in the wee red boat very long as the winds are building up. Tom had Dean help him bring it up onto the beach. The winds should be up to gale force before the day is over so Dean may get to see a good storm. I cooked kippers and fresh eggs for Tom and Dean's lunch. Kippers are smoked and salted herring that is often served for breakfast. I am not fond of kippers so I had an egg sandwich. The chickens are overloading the refrigerator with eggs so I will have to start using more of them.

This afternoon Dean and I are going over to Tom's to see the caddies and my garden. I am sure Dean will have something negative to say about the garden. We will probably go to Houlland Loch and try to fish unless the wind is too high. Tom wants to show Dean how an otter board works.

I had quite a scare this morning. My BBC producer is back from Australia and he cannot find any sound on the last tape I sent him. The tape was fine when it left here. Hopefully it will play on another recorder.

Tom will be waiting impatiently so I better get my act in gear as Dean so nicely put it a few minutes ago.

September 29th

Dean and I just got back from Lerwick where we did a little shopping. He got a beautiful Shetland wool vest, I got a new houseplant and we went to the grocery store. It was not the most comfortable trip because the wind was blowing like mad and it was raining hard and then it turned foggy on the way back.

I just made a frozen rhubarb pie for Sunday dinner and Dean is watching it in the oven while I finish the magazine that goes up tomorrow.

Dean has not been any luckier than I have in catching trout. He did catch fish in the sea so that makes him an official Shetland angler.

The weather is supposed to continue to deteriorate and we are to get some furious gales in the next couple of days. Up to force eight for sure and maybe force nine so fishing may be over for Dean this trip.

We are hoping the storm leaves Shetland before we are to fly on Tuesday morning. The little plane would not take off in that kind of wind.

I think Dean and I will just read a book in front of the Rayburn with a nice chunk of peat in it to make it smell good. If the wind goes as high as it is supposed to, the electricity will probably go out but we have everything here to be really cosy. There are kerosene lamps to read by, the Rayburn to cook food and give us hot water, and a supplementary propane gas heater for the bedroom. We could even sleep on the sofa bed in the living room if we had to. Dean shut the chickens up and we are just going to stay inside.

Speaking of chickens, they blessed us with three eggs in one nest yesterday. That is the first time we have had three eggs at once – a record day for the cluck brigade. My refrigerator is overwhelmed with eggs but I will give Tom some tomorrow.

September 30th

It's Sunday and the sun has come out but the wind is still pretty strong. Dean has decided to air out the entryway and so it is freezing in here with all the draughts. I hope he will close the door soon.

I am cooking a big pork roast. Clapshot, Shetland cabbage, devilled eggs, and rhubarb pie completes the menu. Tom is going to take Dean to some of the places he has not seen before dinner so I am in a real rush this morning.

Scottish Radiance's Halloween issue was just uploaded and I really like the page design I used. I complain a lot about the Internet magazine but it does give me a feeling of satisfaction when it is completed.

October

October 1st

I have been hassling with my laptop all morning and my frustration level is beyond belief. It seems that my laptop cannot communicate with AOL because the laptop software has my old user name and there is no way to change it so I will not be using AOL for e-mail while I am gone for the week. It is annoying as I have unlimited time and phone calls on AOL. Using all of the different Internet Service Providers (ISPs) is a pain. I was able to pick up my e-mail with another ISP server on the laptop so I might (?) be able to send and receive e-mail while I am on the Scottish mainland.

It was supposed to be a nasty day but it has turned out windy and sunny. It really is pretty. Dean is going for a long walk this afternoon while I write my *Lighthouse Digest* story. I would have had the story done this morning but the laptop struggle took too long.

When we went for our Sunday ride we stopped to see the crofter who raised the chickens. The unknown is now known. It is a dark Brahma. So the names of the chickens are Cochin, Rock, Sussex, and Brahma. Their breed names sound nice and are easy to remember.

Our Shetland feast yesterday was grand. Dean really liked Shetland cabbage and clapshot and the rhubarb pie turned out perfectly. Dean is fond of all kinds of pie so he was totally pleased. Tom has had everything before but he ate really well so I guess he was satisfied.

I need to write my story for *Lighthouse Digest* so I'll make this entry short. Hopefully I will be able to keep this journal going while I am gone next week since the blanky-blank laptop is being so contrary.

October 2nd

This is being written in a rush as I am getting ready to travel to the Scottish Lighthouse Museum to pick out pictures for the new book.

Dean ate the only trout we had in the freezer for dinner tonight and said it was wonderful. I baked it whole with lemon slices in the oven of the Rayburn. It makes me sad these lovely fish end up being eaten but what do I expect since I am always out there trying to catch them. I haven't caught any lately so I don't know if I would take it home or put it back.

We have a beautiful full moon over the ocean and it will be gorgeous in an hour if the clouds don't spoil it. I would go outside to look at it but I just washed my hair. I do not need a cold when I am getting ready to be gone for a week.

October 3rd

I am at Castle Grant Home Farm visiting our friends Robert, Margaret, Sarah and Jenny Macdonald. It feels so strange to be on the Scottish mainland again. It looks different from Shetland with all the trees and the big sheep. The sheep are twice the size of the ones in Shetland. You do not realize how small the Shetland sheep are until you can compare them with others.

I spent yesterday at the Scottish Lighthouse Museum picking out pictures for the book on Shetland and Orkney lighthouses. They did not have all of the pictures I needed but I found most of them. The museum's director is going to find the rest from a large group of un-catalogued pictures they have. The museum is in financial difficulty but while I was there yesterday they had about 15 visitors and it was off-season. Maybe with foot and mouth over the number of visitors will pick up.

The bus ride over was enjoyable as this is some of the richest farming land in Scotland and it is exquisite. The lush farms go right down to the sea, which is quite a sight.

The big news here is Sarah and Jenny are coming to visit the lighthouse. They will fly up on Oct 20th and return on the 28th. They do not know yet that they are going for sure. I get to tell them when they come home from school. They were excited at the possibility and now it is really happening.

There is bright sunshine on the Cairngorms across the beautiful Spey valley, which unfolds in front of the house. I think this is one of the prettier places in mainland Scotland with its trees and mountains.

October 4th

It is another fine day at Castle Grant Home Farm. The sun is shining brightly with just a few puffy clouds over the mountains. After my hair dries I am going to walk down to see the castle and maybe the walled garden. The walled garden dates back to the late 1600s and there is a plaque on the steading (barn) with the date 1638 (I think). Castle Grant was the ancestral home of the Grant Clan. Like most Scottish estates it has been sold off in pieces with one person owning the castle and the farm being run by a bigger estate. They have pheasant hunts. You see the most beautiful birds running in the fields.

Yesterday when I went for a walk I met a big group of beef cows and calves coming up the road. Assuming Robert and Roddie were shifting the cattle I just got out of the way so they could pass. As the end of the long line of cows got closer I realized there was no one moving them so I immediately went to find one of the guys. I could not find anyone so the cattle kept coming and were soon in the house yard. Finally Robbie and Robert arrived and the cows were turned around and sent back to their field. I played cowgirl for a little while by walking behind the cows. I doubt if my help was needed since Robert was in front of me with the quad and the dogs but I felt useful.

We got the airline tickets for Sarah and Jenny to come and spend a week at the lighthouse. Robert and Margaret will put them on the plane but they will fly all by themselves from Inverness to Sumburgh. Tom has agreed to take me to the airport to collect them. I hope the weather will be good.

Tonight I have a book signing in Inverness, the first one in that city. The girls and Margaret are going with me. We are going out to eat afterwards or maybe before depending on timing. I have no idea how many people will be there but with two books doing well it might be a good crowd.

October 5th

I am really having trouble with laptop so I am going to try and make this short as the computer keeps crashing.

Another beautiful day in the mountains of northern Scotland with bright sunshine that casts long shadows behind the dark green trees creating a superb day. I will probably talk about the beautiful pines the entire time I am here. Not because they are beautiful pines, which they are, but because trees are a novelty after being in Shetland where there are so few.

The attendance was low at my book signing at James Thin's in Inverness but the people who came asked lots of questions. They bought copies of *The*

Last Lighthouse and *Scottish Lighthouses* so that meant the bookstore made good money.

Margaret, the girls and I had a great gourmet dinner at McDonald's before going to the book signing. Since I have been in Shetland over five months, going to McDonalds was a big treat. I had a Big Mac and all the trimmings. After the signing we went to McDonalds again and got a McFlurry for dessert. All in all it was quite an acceptable night on the town.

The bookstore gave me two new books, which I am going to read today.

One of the neatest things I have done during this visit was watch Robert gather the lambs with his dogs. The dogs are amazing. They are quick and always seem to be able to out-smart the sheep. Robert trains his own dogs and they are exceptional.

October 7th

The weather forecast is rain with gale or strong gale force winds but it is another beautiful fall day in the mountains. I got up early to write. No one else has gotten out of bed and I can hear the larks signing outside. It is lovely.

Robert and Margaret went to a wedding reception last night so it was just the girls and I. When Margaret and I went to town earlier in the day we saw one of Robert's cows looking for a place to hide to have her calf. The girls and I were given the responsibility of going down and checking her to see if she was in fact having her baby while Robert and Margaret were gone. I was more than a little concerned what I would do if she did go into labour. The plan was to use the mobile phone and call Robert if the cow was having difficulty.

The moon was so bright it made long shadows on the fields and we could walk without a torch. As we got near the field, a car came up the road and it was Robert. Thank goodness, since the calf was half born (two feet and a nose out) but caught in the birth canal. Robert had to change his clothes and birth the large healthy bull calf.

I was certainly glad Robert came back as I am not sure I would have been strong enough to pull the calf out. Anyway it was a beautiful night to be out with the moon over the mountains, leaves crunching under our feet and the changing shapes of the tree shadows.

Today Robert sends his small lambs to the cull. It is sad to think the smallest sheep are the ones who will be killed but that is the way the system works. Robert is sending 61 and will be paid £10 each. It is something we don't like talking about as it took a lot of effort to raise those lambs for £10.

October 9th

I am back at the lighthouse sitting at the computer with an almost still ocean outside.

The trip home was fairly uneventful except I had caught a terrible cold and felt lousy. Security was tight with armed guards at Aberdeen airport. There is a great deal of concern in Britain about terrorists striking the oil production or transport since the UK derives so much income from oil. Aberdeen airport is the largest helicopter port in the world and most are going to oilrigs. That also makes Sullom Voe a big target, as it is the largest oil terminal in Europe. I do not think anything will happen but the idea is a little unsettling since Sullom Voe is close to the lighthouse.

All is fine at Eshaness lighthouse. The chickens were glad to get out and run around again. While I was gone Tom opened the caddy shack door, but always put the wire barricade across it since there was no one here to look for trouble.

I spent about an hour this morning transplanting my herbs and sowing some more seeds. Most of the plants are inside now except the petunias from the lobster creel greenhouses. I have taken them out of the creels and hope to find a place near a window where I will be able to keep them blooming.

This is fish van day so I can have monkfish tails tonight as a welcome home to Shetland and I picked a little lettuce from the garden.

October 10th

I have changed ISPs again since I cannot put up with AOL. It is just too slow and too busy. It was a nightmare on the laptop while I was gone and is not a whole lot better at the lighthouse. My new server is £8 cheaper than AOL and three times faster. I can start using it tomorrow. The ISPs in the USA are cheaper and more reliable than the ones in the UK. Actually my free one, shetland.co.uk, is great except I had to pay for the telephone calls and that makes my telephone bill too high. It really is my bad habits caused by unlimited access in the US that is the problem, not the servers.

A huge setback occurred this morning. The BBC cannot retrieve the sound from the last DAT tape I sent them. That means months and months of recording is lost. They can detect sound on the tape but they cannot retrieve it. I am devastated. It weakens the documentary significantly but my producer Mark says we will find a way to make it okay. I imagine I will have to rerecord from this journal and other stories. It will not be the same because we will have lost the birth of the baby bird and the recording of the broadcasters during the radio weekend.

Tom seems afraid to come into the house because I have a cold. I never realized he was so apprehensive about catching a cold. We all try to stay away from germs but he seems worse than most people I know. You would think I had the plague! I now realize I am more vulnerable than I thought because the person I count on for help is afraid of catching whatever I have.

Tom needed to bring his wee red boat up before gales started big time and guess who was the one to help him? So with a cold and fever I was out standing in the mud and wind. My plants fell off the west side windowsill this morning as the window was vibrating so hard from the force of the wind. It was only force eight and the wind is supposed to go up to force nine tonight so I will move all my plants out of the windows.

I think Tom will soon take the wee red boat up for the winter, as the forecast is not good for the rest of the week. He has been able to keep it in longer than usual but storing the boat really signals the beginning of winter.

It has been a bad day losing all of the recorded information, the smashing of my precious plants and Tom's fear of my cold. Part of the problem is that not feeling well makes it harder to cope. My greatest fear has always been being sick.

Right this second I would chuck it all in and go back to the States but I am sure that will pass.

October 11th

The winds are still blowing but it is sunny and I have clothes on the line. They are really going to smell nice when they come in. We are supposed to have gale force nine winds tonight so there will be another big surf tomorrow.

My cold is a little bit better. I walked down to the Bruddans to take surf pictures. It is difficult to catch a picture of surf, which rolls over in huge emerald green waves or climbs the cliffs in gigantic white foaming clouds like we have today. So much of the excitement is sound and smell. Maybe over the weekend I can put some of the digital pictures on the www.

Tom invited me down for dinner tonight but I am not sure I am going to go, as my stomach is upset and I ache all over. I think he is feeling bad for being afraid of the sickly lighthouse keeper. At least he said he was sorry.

The new ISP notified me they couldn't process a US credit card so I guess I am stuck with AOL or I will have to get a UK credit card. I think I will apply for a UK credit card. It would be handy although I've had no serious problems with my US cards up to this point.

Tonight I will finish up the package I am putting together for Macmillan and hopefully send it off tomorrow or Saturday. Tom wants to go to Lerwick tomorrow so I would like to mail it then.

I am off to the kitchen to warm up some chicken soup for lunch. They say chicken soup is the best thing for a cold so I made a big pot yesterday.

October 12th

Many of my friends who get my daily e-mails have sent me encouragement to hang in there and it really helped. I am feeling better but my cold is still with me. I had a wonderful time at Tom's as he cooked while I just sat and watched TV. I still think he went a little overboard about being afraid of the cold. I sure hope he does not catch it but he has not been within two feet of me so it should be okay.

My caddies are now in the byre for the winter or at least until the gales pass. Alyssa was so glad to see me she nipped my fingers and chewed on my jacket strings. The nip did not hurt. The gentle bite was either a sign of affection or maybe she wanted fed. I am going to Lerwick to get a few groceries, as Tom has to take the new car in for service. Hopefully the vet will give me an idea of a treat I could give the caddies by hand. I know it is spoiling them but Tom will have to deal with them not me when I leave.

Last night I did not sleep very well as the wind made so much noise. Hopefully it will slow down later today. Now it is gale force nine so I could barely stand up when I went out to feed and water the chickens. No hiking in the hills today for sure. I read the shipping forecast every day to be prepared for the winds.

While Tom is getting the car serviced I am going to the library and stay inside where it is warm. It has been a few weeks since I have had library time.

I got an e-mail from my BBC producer yesterday and he may come to Shetland. They feel bad about losing the material and he thinks he could recreate what he wants and save both of us a lot of time.

October 17th

It is a peaceful Sunday and a duck basted in orange sauce is roasting in the Rayburn. I made a potato salad to use up some of the hen fruit and we are having peas and carrots along with a sponge cake filled with homemade jam. Not a bad meal for the small lighthouse surrounded by nothing but birds and waves.

Our lost lamb has been rescued. All summer long the tourists have been telling anyone they could catch that a lamb was trapped on a ledge in Calder's. The coastguard had tried to rescue it but failed many times because of the steep sides of the Geo and the lamb being scared and running away. Its rescue made the *Shetland Times* with a picture entitled *Woolly Jumper*. The lamb, wearing a hard hat, was shown being brought up by rope. The hard hat was to protect its little head from hitting the rock sides of the Geo.

I went to the sheep sale at the Shetland Mart with Tom. Everyone had to dress in white plastic coats and walk through disinfectant. It was a disappointing trip for Tom as the prices were so poor that none of the rams put forward sold. He did meet a farmer who might rent him a ram since he could not get one.

We also went to the Shetland farmers' market, which was packed with people but not many vendors. I got some wonderful orange, ginger and jasmine Shetland soap made by a company called Smoorikens, which means kiss in Shetland dialect. The cakes of soap are done in Celtic designs and packaged in scallop shells. A group of ladies from one small village are known for their doughnuts. I bought a pack of six. I tried one and they were out of this world and Tom of course ate the rest. The Shetland pork man was there and I got some of his sausages. They were last night's dinner and are luscious. Tom bought me a bannock filled with Shetland lamb for lunch and it was scrumptious. All in all I enjoyed the market immensely.

After returning home I ran the Hoover as wood chips from the chickens are being tracked in. I am giving myself a weekend off from writing since I felt the package sent to Macmillan was impressive. The parcel was difficult to put together because it contained so many different types of writing. I said a little prayer when I posted it and will keep my fingers crossed. I probably will not hear anything for weeks or even months. I would like most for them to accept the novel.

October 15th

Monday arrived with rain and more wind. We also have dense fog, which does not seem to blow away with the strong winds. The forecast is for heavier rain so I just ran out and got a bucket of coal for the Rayburn. This means I am set for the night even though it is midday but that is how you have to prepare.

The duck I baked in the Rayburn was a gourmet delight. I was not sure the Rayburn was hot enough for the duck to get crispy but it did. Tom delivered a small birthday cake I made for his neighbour who was 89 this week. The bigger cake I gave to Tom, which has probably already been eaten.

Scottish Radiance is finally getting some restructuring and maintenance. The restructuring helps the search engines do a more complete job of indexing and takes me hours and hours as well as being very tedious. That makes it a good task for a nasty weather day.

I am going to finish this computer stuff then I plan on spinning wool. My 1847 spinning wheel I bought from the Isle of Lewis does a superior job of changing the neighbour's cast-off Shetland wool into yarn. I have some projects I want to finish before I go back to the States in a little over a month. Boredom never is a problem at the lighthouse with so many things to do.

I am still trying to take it easy and drink lots of fluids to get rid of this cold, which turned into a cough. I had to go get some cough medicine yesterday. Today is our oldest daughter's birthday and I sent her an e-mail card. It sure makes it a lot easier to have a computer when you are this far away. I would have never thought when she was born in rural Indiana that one day I would be a successful author living at a lighthouse in Scotland and sending cards by computer.

October 16th

It is a day for Shetland fun. The sun rose in a clear blue sky accompanied by a slight breeze making a perfect Shetland day. The sea is still stirred up from all of the gales so when you are out in the bright sunshine the roar of the waves breaking on the cliffs surrounds you. As soon as I got the Rayburn cleaned and the ashes emptied I headed for the split loch down the hill from the lighthouse to see if there were any trout around. The sun was making gigantic silver and gold bands across the loch's blue grey water. The stripes of colour were interrupted when one trout after another jumped into the air with their silver tummies bright in the sun. One small one jumped only a matter of inches from my bobber but I didn't catch any. I only stayed a wee while as today is busy with the library van and the fish van both due.

Tom is coming over after the vans have gone and we are going to try again to catch one of those elusive trout. After that we are going down to Eshaness Pier to see if we can catch some piltocks. With winter coming on we need to take advantage of such a beautiful day.

I have been invited to submit a story to *Scots Magazine* so I want to start a draft and pick some pictures to go with what I write. I want to have the story on its way by the end of the week since next week I will have Sarah and Jenny visiting. I hope we have a day like today while the girls are here so they can get out in the hills with the Shetland ponies and see the seals at the Bruddans.

October 17th

A little late beginning to write this journal as I have been writing the story for *Scots Magazine* and working on *Scottish Radiance*. I realized yesterday that I would have to get most of the magazine done this week because I will have company next week and a web page for the new *Irish Lighthouses* book needs to be created also.

It is a beautiful day and I cannot resist a little play. Tom took me down to Eshaness Pier to fish for piltocks and sillocks. I got three good-sized piltocks and seven sillocks. A sillock is a very young saithe and a piltock is a two year old saithe. I was hoping a mackerel would come by but the only other visitor was a seal that was feasting on some of the fish I wanted to catch.

It is hard to stay in on a day like today but if I am going to get my work done I must. I hope it will start raining tonight so it will be easier to stay in the house.

For dinner tonight I am having monkfish (my favourite), home grown parsnips and a salad made with the last of my lettuce. My parsnips did really well in Tom's garden.

October 18th

I just got back from fishing at Eshaness Pier. I caught a big one but it broke my line. The fishing pole has line for trout not sea fish so this gigantic (?) one got away. I did not see it but it sure put up a big fight. A trip to Brae or Lerwick is needed to get new fishing tackle to be used in the sea. The easiest answer might be to buy a rod for fishing specifically in the sea. I will have to think about that.

The weather is not especially nice today with lots of wind and it seems to be getting colder. I was going to hang my clothes outside but gave up and have them on the line above the Rayburn. I have often thought of getting an electric clothes dryer and putting it out in the generator house. Maybe a cheap one at a Harry Hay sale would be the answer. I hate to, as electricity is so expensive here.

Most of the day will be spent at the computer working on my story for *Scots Magazine* and the next issue of *Scottish Radiance*. I got the web page up for the Irish lighthouse book. I am not real happy with it because it is so plain but it will have to do. Designing web pages is one of the most creative things I do but it takes time and *Irish Lighthouses* did not get the time it deserved.

It is raining outside so I will have to stay at the computer and work. It could not be better timed.

October 19th

Rain is coming down in sheets through a heavy fog. I will be working on my computer for the rest of the day if the rain persists. My story for *Scots Magazine* is in draft form and I will send if off to a few people to proof and then in it goes.

If it sells I want to buy a big storage heater for the hall. Since storage heaters run at night when the electricity rates are the lowest and then radiate heat from the bricks inside for the rest of the day they keep the whole house warm even when I am not here. I would also like an original black and white photo by Rattar. He is a famous Shetland photographer and his pictures can cost as much as £100.

Something new might be on the horizon for me. Another BBC producer has contacted me who is doing a series called *A Sense of Place*. It will be six half-hour programmes broadcast in the spring on Radio Scotland and will focus on what makes somebody feel they belong in a certain area or place. What is a sense of place: a memory, a network of relationships, and/or a physical place? If I get involved it will only be for one segment and would not change my return time to the States. I am doing a lot of radio over here but that is fine since it sells books. I will talk to the producer and see what transpires.

A Harry Hay sale is scheduled this week. Harry Hay is the local auctioneer who sells items on consignment or does estate auctions. I have attended many of his sales recently. I will have to talk to the girls to see if they want to go. If they would not enjoy it I can wait until the next one since I am only looking for small stuff anyway.

I need to get back to working on *Scottish Radiance* but I want to bake a cake for Tom. I have been slack in my baking for him with all the work on the computer and writing so he will get a dried cherry and chocolate cake today.

October 20th

It is so foggy here you cannot see the sundial. That is really foggy even by Shetland standards. I have been cleaning the house a little. That is a usual weekend task as I try to stay away from writing. I will be doing some *Scottish Radiance* magazine work but that is not considered writing.

It is difficult to contain myself and not write since I have had an e-mail from Macmillan and they are interested in my books. In fact the upcoming lighthouse books have gone to the appropriate editor to begin the processing. The most exciting thing is they want a synopsis of the novel because they like my writing style. I just have to take it one step at a time and always be prepared for a rejection.

I had a long telephone conversation with the BBC producer who is doing the *Sense of Place* series. It definitely looks like I will be involved in one segment but it might be recorded while I am in the US. I will need to find some equipment but maybe WJR, Dean's radio station, can help. I broadcast for WJR without pay so maybe they might let Dean and I have a recorder for a few days. I suggested Dean could be involved to the BBC producer and he seemed to like the idea.

It is usually peaceful at the lighthouse on foggy days but I am so excited that I am flying around here today.

Tomorrow Sarah and Jenny are coming for a week's stay during their potato holiday. The fall potato holiday began when the children were needed at home to help harvest the annual tattie crop. I have always been very close to Sarah and Jenny. I am looking forward to seeing them.

October 21st

A foggy and misty Sunday but I do not think it is heavy enough now to prevent Sarah and Jenny's plane from getting in but the wind has died and that means the fog will build up. I checked with British Midland airlines. The plane is still scheduled for an on time arrival. But it is not a very nice day to come to Shetland for the first time since you can't see a thing.

I will put a chicken in the Rayburn and hopefully it will not be burned to a crisp by the time we get back from the airport.

This morning I was asked to do another radio interview in the States. This pleases me, as my books need a marketing push in the USA because the publishers have done nothing with them.

Tom just arrived. He is always early and I know he is worried about the girls getting in. I will write more about getting Sarah and Jenny tomorrow.

October 22nd

The weather has improved and I have a few clothes hanging on the clothes line. The wind is blowing but not at gale force, the sun is not shining but it is not raining. It is amazing how your attitude changes depending on what you are used to. An appropriate saying for this is 'everything is relative'.

Sarah and Jenny's flight was rough as we still had high winds so they were both a little travel-sick. They slept in the car and by the time we reached Brae they were back to normal. Today we are going to walk to the Bruddans and maybe go fishing at the pier. Right now the girls are playing draughts (checkers in the USA).

I put a half frozen roasting chicken in the Rayburn yesterday and we had the best roast chicken when we got back from the airport. Any time I am gone for a long time and want a meal when I get back that is what I will do. After a roast on

Sunday there will be curry for tea tonight. It is getting to be a lighthouse tradition as we usually have meat left after Sunday dinner. The girls like curry so that will work out fine.

Ever since we began coming to Scotland I have wanted a big aluminium kettle like the one the Macdonalds had on their Rayburn on their Skye farm. I think they are especially made for cook stoves. I have tried to steal Tom's but he won't let me have it. I kept hoping one would come up at the sales but none ever did. The new ones are not only expensive but also flimsy. Sarah and Jenny brought me their kettle and it looks just right sitting on my Rayburn. It heats faster than my cheap one as it has a big flat base. It is perfect and brings back all those great memories of the kitchen at Orbost Farm.

October 23rd

It is dripping a little rain and windy but the sun is trying to break through. I hope it turns sunny, as the girls want to go fishing. Tom made them each an old-fashioned pole without a reel. The reason for the enthusiasm is we had a hugely successful fishing trip yesterday morning to Eshaness Pier. Tom caught the first fish (a tiny one) but then things started to really happen. Sarah got the next one, a pretty good size piltock. Then I got one that was really tiny. Tom then took over my pole since the girls were using his and got two really good-sized piltocks. I got my pole back and caught some more really tiny sillocks. Jenny then used my pole and caught a big piltock. My pole was doing well but I certainly was not. The girls thought it was great they caught big fish.

After fishing we went over to Tom's so the girls could meet my caddies. The two littlest caddies were friendly but Austin was aloof again. Tom's dog Jill got along better with the girls then with me. I have been trying for two years to get that dog to like me. She will only take a treat out of my hand but not let me touch her.

The hill ponies were near the road when we left Tom's so we stopped. Some of ponies would let the girls stroke them so they had a ball. The ponies thought they were going to get a free lunch but we had nothing to feed them. The whole day was a huge success.

A lesson learned is never to leave the house without appropriate supplies. It would help to have a little bread to draw fish to our lines and of course the ponies will eat almost anything.

I am getting ready to submit my *Scots Magazine* article. I have a feeling they will turn it down but that is just part of writing.

October 24th

I think winter has arrived. The wind is blowing fiercely and it was pouring down rain. There is no sign of sunshine. It bothers me the weather is not better for the girls' visit but we shouldn't complain, as we have been able to go fishing both Monday and Tuesday.

Yesterday's fishing was not as successful as Monday's. It was gusty and I do not think the fish could see the flies in the turbulent water but we caught twelve fish with Jenny catching two. I once again caught only four little, tiny ones. Sarah did not get any and Tom got the rest. When we got back to the house Tom cleaned the fish and I made fish cakes for Sarah and me. Jenny does not like fish so she had chicken Kiev.

We saw the ponies on the hills and the girls were able to take their pictures with a little walking. They are really having fun with their throwaway cameras. Who knows how the pictures will turn out? Connie got good pictures with her throwaway cameras.

Today is a big day as we are off to Lerwick to shop in the afternoon followed by a Harry Hay sale tonight. I love the sales and hope he has lots of neat stuff. The girls are excited about going to Lerwick and the sale. With the bad weather we cannot do much outside. Hopefully the rain will cease while we shop in Lerwick.

I submitted my story to *Scots Magazine*. Now I just wait. I do not know why I feel that this one is going to be turned down. I write for two magazines every month so I should not be uncomfortable about submitting a magazine story but I just am.

October 25th

I am more than a little upset. My feelings about the *Scots Magazine* article were correct. They are not going to publish the story. Not because of the way it was written, as they were ready to go with it. They received their copy of *Scottish Field*, in which I feature prominently. Their policy is not to use anything covering the same material as *Scottish Field* so they will not be using my story. They hoped I would not be disappointed.

How can I not be disappointed? Because of a fantastic spread in *Scottish Field* my *Scots Magazine* article is not going to be run. I have written asking them if I could write another article at a later date. Hopefully they will say yes.

The sale last night was fun as always. I bought Sarah a junk box and Tom bought Jenny one. They got lots of nifty stuff such as old-fashioned games and knick-knacks. I got some dishes and some Christmas presents. Tom did not get anything. He just had fun with the girls. His comment was 'the girls are really special and they can come to visit me any time'. Robert and Margaret may want to take him up on that.

It is a pretty nice day so I am going to make this short. The girls want to go trout fishing this morning. I have been bugging Tom to get a physical so he is at the doctor's but said he will take us to the pier this afternoon to sea fish.

The *Shetland Times* bookstore manager is encouraging me to write a children's story about a Shetland pony that takes place in Shetland. There are plenty of books about Shetland ponies but none set in Shetland, which is weird. I would like the story to be illustrated with photographs of real Shetland ponies.

October 26th

I am a little late writing as we had a long stay at the pier. We caught some fish but it would have been nice to get some more. Sarah caught one. I got two big ones on one line and almost broke the pole. Then the biggest one of the day twisted free as I lifted it out of the water. It was a disappointment for all of us. Tom caught the rest of them.

I have chicken pieces cooking in tomato and basil sauce which we will have over pasta for supper. Desert is orange layer pudding. Tomorrow Jenny is cooking a big meal for everyone including Tom. I hope she hasn't selected too many complicated things and gets frustrated.

Sarah is outside looking at the glorious surf. Jenny is glued to the TV. I have tried everything to get her outside but have had no luck. I am going to join Sarah and see if I can get some pictures. We have bright sunshine and high surf so the cliffs should make some spectacular pictures.

The *Scottish Field* article was good with only a few mistakes, which is surprising for a four page article. The pictures were superb. Even a full-page picture of me by the sundial isn't bad, at least that's what everyone says. I do not think it is so great but I guess you never like your own pictures.

Tom's little sheep go to the cull tomorrow so he ran to Lerwick today to get his licence. These sheep movement licences are such a pain.

It is almost time for *Ready Steady Cook*, which is my favourite TV programme. I like the people involved and learn many quick and easy recipes that I can use with my limited supplies.

October 27th

Sarah and Jenny are in the kitchen cooking dinner so I am sort of on vacation today. They have baked a cake and the pork chops are marinating. The cake fell a little but once the icing is on no one will know the difference. They are making potato cheese skins for a starter but haven't begun that yet. I have put the *Scottish Field* article on the Internet. Every once in a while I am thankful for my webmaster skills. Maybe all of those hours becoming a top webmaster were worthwhile. Dean wanted to make sure the text could be read easily so the page is very big and will take a long time for anyone to download.

I forgot to write that Ronnie, the local fisherman, came down to the pier while we were fishing and showed the girls his lobsters. Some of them are gigantic and the girls got to hold one of the biggest. I would say he had over 250 lobsters in his tanks.

October 28th

Tom and I took Sarah and Jenny to the airport. We made a stop in Lerwick at the Co-op for a few groceries and to see if we could find any more copies of *Scottish Field*. Tom bought the girls each a plastic candy cane full of chocolate for Christmas. Next we went to the newspaper shop in Lerwick to look for copies of *Scottish Field*. They were out as there had been a big rush on them.

We got to the airport in time to have a snack. While in the gift shop we found copies of *Scottish Field* of all things. We had looked all over Lerwick and found none.

The plane was on time and so the girls should have arrived in Inverness without a problem.

October 29th

I am in for the day. The wind is going to be gale force nine out of the west so the lighthouse will be covered with spray. Hopefully the power will stay on and I can work on the computer.

There are three Christmas cakes baking in the Rayburn. I got the recipe from Margaret Macdonald and the cakes are full of all kinds of fruit, lots of spices, and brandy. They will take almost the entire morning to bake but they will be really moist. After they come out I will put some more brandy in them and store them in the back room where it is cold. Before I leave for the States I will put marzipan on them. I am leaving a small one for Tom, taking one back to the States, and keeping one to share with the neighbours at New Year.

My December article for *Lighthouse Digest* will be about Christmas at the lighthouse. That means this afternoon after I finish *Scottish Radiance* I am putting up my Christmas tree. It will be a great picture with the Christmas tree in front of the window and a gale blowing outside. It is too early for the tree to be up so I will hide it in the closet after I take the pictures for the article. *Lighthouse Digest* has asked me to write their Christmas story again and I have to think up a subject. It will probably about be about spending a Christmas isolated by a gale, as that is what is going on today.

Sarah and Jenny arrived home without incident. It is a good thing they did not have to go today because they would not have made it out. I think they really had a good time but who knows about teenagers.

Well, the electricity is still on so I will finish the magazine before I decorate for Christmas. Also I have to get busy on my homemade Christmas presents since I have less than a month until I return to the States and I want to take them with me.

October 30th

It is looks like Christmas around here. The little tree is pretty and I got some good pictures for my article. I will be taking it down tomorrow or the next day, as it is just too early for Christmas.

A big problem in the caddy shack is causing major problems for the hens. Brahma has gone broody and is setting on the nest that all the hens lay in. I keep evicting her but she climbs right back in. This morning when I went out to feed them she was sitting in the nest and there were two hens waiting to get into the nest to lay their eggs. I mean they were actually standing in line. I am looking for a stone shaped like an egg to put in another nest so Brahma can sit on it and the other hens can use the laying nest. Since I do not have a rooster the eggs are not fertile so Brahma is wasting her time sitting on them.

The weather has taken a turn for the better and I have clothes out on the line. They are flapping in a gentle breeze so they should dry fast. The storm moved out as fast as it came in. Shetland weather is funny like that. We have great surf today so if I can get my writing done I will go for a walk and take pictures.

October 31st

I guess it is a good thing that Halloween is not a big thing here as the wind is so strong out of the north that it would blow any trick or treaters away. It is very cold in my office and for the first time since I have had the storage heater I have to supplement it with the Dimplex wall heater. The Rayburn is going full force and it is at least comfortable in the front room.

Tom is here building shelves in the windows for my plants. I have lots of plants in pots, which need sunlight. I guess this house is a little lighthouse greenhouse.

My broody chicken is happy sitting on a stone egg that I borrowed from Tom. I thought she might notice the difference but she hasn't. This leaves the nest where all the chickens lay open for the other hens so things are back to normal. One of the hens poked her head out this morning, immediately turned around and went back in. There is too much wind for a little chicken to get around today.

I am working on my Christmas story for *Lighthouse Digest*. I have been doing this for a few years so I might eventually run out of ideas but I have a good concept for this year so it should be fun. My first story ever published was a Christmas story and I always enjoy writing them.

It's time for a bowl of homemade chicken soup and a cup of tea, as I will do anything to keep warm while working at this computer.

November/December

November 1st

It is a rainy, cold day so inside activities are on the agenda. I'm ready to submit my Lighthouse Reflections column to *Lighthouse Digest* along with a Christmas story entitled 'Santa's Wee Red Boat'. It actually turned out pretty well for a rush job.

 The last segment of *The Blue Planet* aired last night. I have dearly loved this series because it taught me so much about the ocean that I am surrounded by. I found the last segment hideous. They filmed Orcas killing baby seals and you could even hear the baby seals scream as the Orcas grabbed them. The killer whales take the seals and play with them by tossing them in the air while they are still alive and even continue to throw the seals into the air after they are dead. I hated every minute of the Orca scenes. If I had not been taping for Tom and could have put it on automatic I would have stopped watching completely. I did leave the room but the producers were so proud of the killing scenes they finished the program by showing how they were taken so I saw all the scenes. It made me cry and have nightmares. I know what was shown is true, as Tom has seen the Orcas do the same thing here with the seals. It seems so cruel to me.

November 2nd

I am off to Lerwick, as Tom has to go in and sign some papers. We have gale force eight winds that are going up to gale force nine. I am not sure I will be able to stand up to get to the car unless I'm careful to stay protected by the building most of the way.

The big news is Eshaness Lighthouse is going to be a part of a big screen film being produced in Shetland. It is called *Devil's Gate* and is directed by a British director. The film is to be released world-wide so everyone should be able to see it. I got a telephone call last night asking if it would cause any inconvenience if they shot some scenes around the cliffs. They are talking about only one day but it is a major undertaking. Since they want to do it in January I said no problem, as there are few tourists up here then. As the conversation progressed he asked if they could use the house to keep the lead actors out of the weather and I immediately said no problem again. The main roles are not cast yet but they are negotiating with people who have starred in films before. I cannot tell you who they are as it is to be kept quiet until they sign. The producer, director, and art director will visit Eshaness in a week to check everything out. If they like the look of the lighthouse it will be an inn that turns away the leading lady, who in confusion and desperation runs to the cliffs. They are hoping for bad weather so the waves will be violent. The have rented the Eshaness Hall for the cast and crewmembers to eat and hang out. It sounds like fun being a part of something like this and I am excited. The representative was extremely careful to explain all of the details since they had a problem with a Shetland crofter trying to become a millionaire from letting them use his land. Will I be paid big bucks for this? Sadly no, as the cliffs are public land so I cannot charge for that but if they use the house I will receive something. Since it is only one day I am looking forward to the experience more than anything else.

As I went to sleep last night I wondered what else was going to happen this year. It has been full of major media events – two BBC features, a big spread in a leading magazine, and now a movie. Everyone was worried about me being bored. *No chance.*

November 3rd

We are having a terrible storm with high winds. I have been out most of the morning taking pictures over the cliffs. It is dangerous but I took Tom with me to jump in after me up if I got blown over. That's funny because he cannot swim. My lips taste salty, as the sea spray is everywhere. The surf during storms like this is magnificent and one of the most beautiful, exciting sights I have even seen. The pictures do not do the experience justice since so much a part of it is the smell, sound and dampness but they give you some idea.

It took me about an hour to photograph the blowhole on the sea side of the lighthouse. The pictures are not too good but they sort of give you an idea of what it's like. It is very difficult to take a picture of a blowhole spouting spray when you cannot stand still.

November 4th

Yesterday I put some of my pictures on the Internet and was thrilled with the praise I got from my e-mail friends so I have been out seascape chasing again. The wind is strong but it is a sunny day with a few showers. Tom took me down to Hamnavoe and I got some pictures from there along with some more around the lighthouse. I have been taking a lot of pictures of the Eshaness cliffs for my brother, Ray, who is a superb artist and wants to paint the giant surf on the cliffs. The last bunch of photos should have some good ones for him. I tried again to get a rainbow but it probably will fade out in the photograph, as did all of the other rainbows.

A rolled lamb roast is baking in the oven, tatties are cooking on the top and broccoli and cauliflower will round out Sunday dinner. I also have a raspberry sponge cake made with Margaret Macdonald's wonderful raspberry jam.

November 5th

Today brought beautiful sunshine and not too much wind. It is a good fishing day and I hope Tom drops by to take me to the pier. I wish it were closer so I could walk.

We have snow on the top of Ronas Hill. When I put out the trash I looked up and saw Ronas with a nice white hat. Ronas Hill gets more snow than anywhere in Shetland because it is so high. It is fantastic that I can see the mountain from one of the lighthouse windows.

It hardly seems possible that six months have gone by since I was in the USA. Two weeks from tomorrow I will be back in Michigan and I am ready. It is difficult because I miss my family and my dog. It would help if my dog could talk to me over the telephone. She is a nice dog and talented but not enough to talk! Tomorrow I am taking the bus into Lerwick to finish my Christmas shopping since they are having sales. I figure I can get things on sale now that might not be on sale closer to Christmas.

Today I am finishing restructuring *Scottish Radiance* so the search engine can get deeper penetration and working on another story. I am complaining because the writing never seems to end with requests coming from all directions.

November 6th

I just got back from Lerwick where I did most of my Christmas shopping. I was able to get everything on my list except one item so I am in pretty good shape to begin packing for going home.

A calm morning at Eshaness.

Eshaness Lighthouse viewed from a helicopter.

The island of Foula seen from the Lighthouse.

The view from the trout fishing loch.

A red throated diver.

A baby common seal.

More snow coming.

Wave at Bruddans.

Sharma in the lantern room.

Winter storm approaches Eshaness Lighthouse.

Eshaness cliffs in winter dress.

Tom Williamson, Eshaness caretaker, and the 'wee red boat.'

Storm at Stenness.

Eshaness tower and full moon.

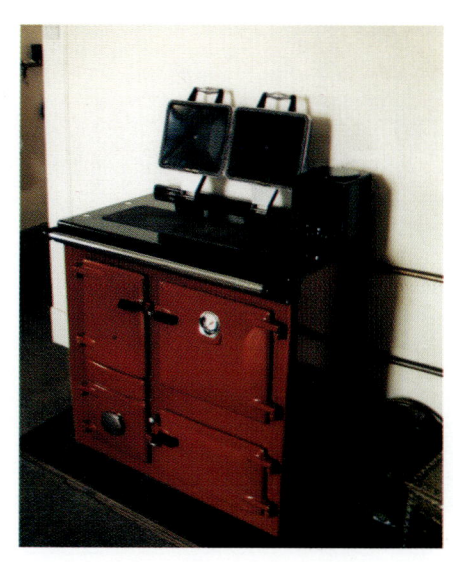

The Rayburn.

Sunsets at Eshaness. Some played their colours upon banks of cloud (above), while others filled the clear sky with their intense hues (below).

The charity shops came in handy as I got a winter coat for £3 that is warm enough to wear to go fishing and a pair of fuzzy Garfield slippers for £1.50. My feet get cold in the house when the wind is blowing hard so the Garfield slippers will feel good.

A second BBC producer who wants to interview me as I leave Eshaness is coming on the 17th and staying with me until I leave on the 20th. I had planned on going to the Sumburgh Hotel so he will have to follow me there, I guess.

Tom and I got stopped everywhere because so many people have seen the article about the lighthouse in *Scottish Field*. I picked up copies for all the people who asked for them and the local frame place is matting and framing a copy of the article for me to put in my office. It should be beautiful.

November 7th

A cold and sunny day with a slight wind has convinced me to hang clothes outside. I want to make use of all the outside drying days I can.

The broody chicken has been released from confinement and I am anxious to see if her broodiness is over. She should no longer want to sit on the nest but sometimes it takes a long time to stop being broody. The chickens peeked out this morning but went back in quickly as it must have been too cold. They are still laying but I soon will have to turn their heater on or they will probably quit.

Last night I went to Tom's to watch *Who Wants To Be a Millionaire?*, visit the caddies and dig up some of my parsnips. The parsnips are really a pretty good size and will add a lot to Sunday dinner. My caddies are fine and are growing but the two smallest ones will probably always be the smallest in Tom's flock. Kara, the middle one who is all black, has a long piece of fleece growing right out of the middle of her forehead which is really cute. Alyssa is a white sheep with black spotted face while Austin is chocolate brown with shades of white and a black face. They loved parsnip leaves.

Miracle of miracles! Tom's dog, Jill, has decided I am acceptable and will now let me pet her and rub her tummy. This was a major breakthrough and I have no idea why she decided to give in after two years.

The BBC producer has decided to leave on Monday morning so that gives me a little more time to close up. I definitely will stay at the Sumburgh Hotel for the night before I leave since the weather is starting to get more and more wintry. I hate to do that but with the potential for icy roads early in the morning it is probably a good idea.

November 8th

What a morning it is. I have three sweaters and two pairs of socks on with a small radiant heater at my feet because there are gale force winds from the northwest so this office is really cold. The forecast was so bad I closed the outside wooden shutters last night, as the high winds are to go westerly. It is pretty dark in the office with the shutters closed. As soon as I have finished my journal I am moving the spinning wheel by the Rayburn and spending the day spinning and listening to BBC radio.

I was woken at 4:00 am by sleet crashing against the wooden shutters on the outside of the bedroom windows. Not able to go back to sleep, I decided to get up have a cup of coffee and read. I read for a few chapters but fell asleep again and did not wake until after 8:00. I always feel a little sluggish after going back to sleep like that in the morning.

After cleaning the Rayburn I braved the elements to dump the ashes and feed the chickens. It was a real battle to get the ashes dumped, as I had to go away from the protection of the lighthouse. It is difficult to walk in this kind of wind, and sleet in your face makes it even worse. The ground was slick in spots so I had to watch where I stepped.

The chickens were fine and the caddy shack quite warm since it is protected by the main house when the winds are in the north. When the winds shift west it will be colder and I might have to turn on the garage heater as it is only going to get up to 42°F today. The chickens were happy and chirping as they ate their food. The one that was broody was on the nest but she got up when I put food in the box. Yesterday before the weather got bad she was outside walking around with the other chickens so I think she is over her problem. Today the chickens are shut up as the wind would blow them away in a minute.

The synopsis of my novel is off to Macmillan today and I am nervous about it. All of the revisions to the novel have made it a first-class story so maybe they will like it. Being the first book I ever wrote, it is too bad it has been neglected with the demand for all of the other books. Well, back to work on cleaning up the synopsis and then to spinning in front of the warm Rayburn.

November 9th

I am again seeing daylight, as the wind has died enough so I can open the outside shutters. Mainland Scotland got lots of snow but we got little in comparison. It is cold outside and feels like winter but the only snow is on Ronas Hill, which is completely white.

When I stuck my head out the door last night to check the weather I was greeted by a huge display of green, rapidly changing Northern Lights. The wind was too severe to go out and enjoy them but they were beautiful.

Sky Digital TV now has ITV on their channels. I have not been able to watch *Who Wants To a Millionaire?* or *A Touch of Frost* for two weeks as something happened to my aerial and all I got was snow on the channels coming through the antenna.

Poor Tom is going to the dentist this afternoon as he has a bad tooth. He does not know if it will be pulled or not. He made the appointment and then it stopped hurting – doesn't it always work that way? Tuesday he has tests at the hospital as part of the physical I persuaded him to get. I hope that doesn't hurt too much or he will blame me.

I have been busy spinning and sitting by the Rayburn listening to music when I am not on the computer. It is a tranquil activity.

November 10th

Another storm has moved in straight out of the west so the sea spray is flying everywhere. The forecast was for sunshine that just might be out there somewhere but right now all you can see is salt spray. I tended the chickens and got some coal but that may be the last time spent outside for the rest of the day.

I want to take a lot of yarn to Michigan with me so I can make some things while I am there. Since the weather is bad I will just spend the day spinning and listening to music.

Tom is at a ram sale so I will not see him today. He is selling a ram that only fathered small weak lambs last year and buying two more rams. He has three crofts with sheep so he needs three males since he does not have a trailer to carry them around.

He had the tooth pulled yesterday but when I called him last night to see how he was he said that it did not hurt at all. I imagine it is sore this morning.

Every day I am getting more and more excited about going back to the USA and seeing everyone. I do not get homesick because I will not let myself think about Michigan but when the time to go gets close then I do start thinking about it.

November 11th

The wind is still gale force and the surf is bigger than last weekend. This morning getting to the chickens was a real chore as the sea spray came over the building. During my Sunday ride I will take surf pictures again, however, the air is so full of salt spray the light has a dull yellow cast. I read in a book once that it is called salt light. It is really strange. Maybe I can get a picture of it but it probably will turn out looking grey instead of the actual yellow.

Cleaning out the refrigerator since I am leaving for a month made Sunday dinner a little strange. We are having cheesy turnips (one of my favourites), a rolled roast of duck stuffed with sage and onion dressing, mashed potatoes for Tom, and another Dundee cake for desert. I have become addicted to duck breasts that I can buy at the butcher here and am hoping I can get them when I go back to the States. I might have duck breasts for Christmas dinner as I leave the day after Christmas and a turkey would leave too many leftovers for Dean.

Sunday is one of my favourite TV nights with *Antiques Roadshow* and *Monarch of the Glen*. Tuesday is another favourite with *A Touch of Frost* and *Who Wants To Be a Millionaire?* I think I have crush on Chris Tarrant, the *Millionaire* host. He is so much more dynamic than the US host. I love all of the BBC mystery series, hopefully no really special ones will be on while I am gone. The non-BBC channels have started Christmas advertising, which is early, but not as early as they do it in the States.

I am reading a great book called *Goats Song* that takes place in Western Ireland on the Atlantic coast. It is so much like here and I really am enjoying it.

November 12th

I put up a web page with pictures taken during yesterday's storm and was so proud because I caught the strange yellow light in some of them. It is a murky kind of yellow when there is so much salt in the air.

It is cold today with sleet covering the ground and now some snow flurries. I am going to take a walk later this afternoon but will need many layers of clothes to keep warm. The sun is bright right now but showers come quite fast these days. It is supposed to be cold tomorrow also.

Yesterday's dinner turned out fantastic with the best dish being the cheesy turnips, which are really easy. Peel and dice the turnips before you cook them. After they are done make a simple cheese sauce (cheese, milk, flour) and put over the turnips. They are out of this world.

November 13th

The wind is still blowing and it is cold outside. The wind chill is 20°F and that is cold for here. The actual temperature is 32° and that too is cold for here. Freezing is unusual for this time of year, or so I am told. Last night as I lay in bed listening to the wind I was not sure I could go to sleep without the wind blowing. It is such a common sound now that no wind noise would seem totally abnormal.

The worst problem I have here is getting something delivered. I finally got my new storage heater for the hall but not without calling the store a couple of times. They sent a truck specifically to deliver the heater since it was so late. The electrician came last night to install it and got almost done before discovering they had not sent enough bricks for inside the heater. Today I have to bug the store again to get the bricks. I had to get my own electrician to install the heater. The seller was supposed to install it but couldn't because of the late delivery. I will ask for a refund on the money I paid for installation. What a nightmare! The best way to get something delivered here is to order off the net or by catalogue and then it comes by regular mail.

Off to Lerwick, so I can finish the Christmas shopping and return my books to the library before I leave. Tom has a test at the hospital so I will spend that time at the library, which I am looking forward to.

November 14th

I'm about to leave to put some new software on Tom's computer and set it up so he can use it in the evening when he is on call. His telephone line needs to be open after five so emergency calls from the fish factory can get through. This has been an ongoing problem since he got the computer. Working on computers is a good inside thing to do on a cold day.

Yesterday's trip to Lerwick had a pleasant surprise. The museum has a huge collection of original negatives by J D Rattar, a famous Shetland photographer who was taking pictures in the early 20th century. I have wanted to buy one of his pictures but they sell for hundreds of pounds so when I heard about the museum collection I went and looked in their archive. They had ten pictures of Eshaness lighthouse and the surrounding area by Rattar. They are going to make enlargements from two of the original negatives of pictures I particularly liked. The enlargements will cost me £10 each. I will have to get them framed but if I can get them framed in the manner Rattar did his, I will have two precious possessions. I am so excited as I love black and white photos and it has been a dream ever since I got here to have a Rattar, but never did I believe I would have one of our lighthouse.

November 15th

What a bloody mess I had last night! For the first time this trip the Rayburn went out without any warning. Its bricks were fully heated so I carefully tried to clear the riddler. The riddler is a gadget that moves the coal around so air can constantly get to it. It took me two and half hours to clear it plus I got burned twice. The electrician came to finish installing the new storage heater in the hall and found me on the floor covered with soot. We laughed about how glamorous *Scottish Field* made living here look. If they could have seen the living room and me last night it would have been a different image. After some assistance from the electrician I was able to get the bloody thing going again and once again it is working fine.

The new storage heater in the hall is a positive addition. It seems so strange to go into a warm hall. During the day I keep the bedroom doors open so they get warm also. When the house is empty it will keep the dampness down in the bedrooms and the Rayburn room. Storage heaters are wonderful as they have constant heat. Our heaters on the wall do well when they are on, but as soon as they are turned off, all the heat disappears which does not work when the house is shut up.

I have begun to pack in earnest and going back to the States is becoming a reality. I have my hotel reservation for Monday night and have confirmed my tickets so all is go.

It is raining today so I will continue to clean and do a little on the computer, as I cannot get outside without getting soaked. It is warm though and the chickens are having a ball running in and out of the caddy shack.

November 16th

I was going to try and make this a positive entry but I do not know how. Yesterday morning our dog, Kiri, was out for her morning romp and somehow she got on the road in the front of our house. Dean tried to call her back but she ran right in front of a truck. She was still alive after she was struck so Dean ran to help her. She was in so much pain she attacked him. At that point she probably would have attacked anything that came close to her. She sank her teeth into both his hands and he may lose the tip of one finger on the left hand. They took him to the hospital by ambulance. Robin and Keith, our neighbours, stayed with Kiri who died quite soon after Dean left.

Dean sees a hand specialist this morning. He stayed with our friends Jim and Val Krone last night. I do not know if he will go back to the farm today or stay with Jim and Val again tonight. I hope with Jim and Val.

I got Kiri as a birthday present the year we moved to the farm. I adored her. She was a big but gentle dog. She had some wonderful and unusual traits. Ever since she was a puppy she howled when the trains passed our house, it was like she was singing to the trains. I will miss hearing that. She also fought a battle with her food dish every day that she usually won. The battle began by her barking at the dish and batting at it with her paw until it fell off of the porch step onto the ground.

I had just started to let myself start thinking about Kiri and going home to be with her and now that has all changed. The thing that bothers me the most is she was in terrible pain for a short time.

I have weathered two other tragedies here by myself – the death of Dean's mom, who was my role model, and September 11th. Both were difficult but they did not hit me as hard as Kiri's death and Dean's injury. We expected his mother, who was 93, to leave us and the WTC was not in our own front yard.

I am not coping well at all. Sleep evades me and I cry all the time. I was up cleaning the house at 4:00 am and I went for a walk in the mist at dawn to let the sea soothe me but it did not work. Most of the time it does not bother me that I am so alone but I would do anything for company right now. Tom has called a couple of times and I am sure he will be up today. To be honest I am not sure how I will get through the day but I will. Tuesday I fly home and it will be good to be back but there will be no big black dog to meet me and my husband is hurt.

Maybe I have been here too long. Maybe I can only take so much isolation and then I crack. I just don't know what is wrong but I am totally forlorn.

I will continue to clean the house and get ready for my BBC producer's arrival tomorrow. If I could reach him I would cancel but he is in London and unavailable. Maybe his arrival will fill the void and help me feel better.

Yesterday afternoon the director, art director and a producer of *Devil's Gate* visited here. I will try to write all about that tomorrow when I am more back to normal.

November 17th

It is a warm, sunny day. It is supposed to cloud over but so far the sun is shining brightly.

Dean's hands are not as bad as we thought. The right one (he is right handed) has superficial puncture wounds with a little deeper one on his thumb. He had to have the tip of his ring finger on his left hand sewn back on. There is good news as he has blood flow and feeling in that finger but it will be a while until we know if the bone will heal. He has a little bit of damage to his middle finger on the left hand but not as bad as the other.

No one will ever know how much I appreciated all of the e-mails and the support that came via this computer yesterday. It helped make a hellish day better.

I am a little recovered today but still depressed. The BBC producer is due any minute so I have been busy cleaning and cooking. He is staying until Monday, just before I leave for the Sumburgh Hotel.

Tom has applied lots of fishing to my depression. We caught 50 fish at Eshaness Pier a few minutes ago, 13 of which were mine. Yesterday I caught 15 and I am not sure how many Tom caught.

Last night I watched *Children In Need* on the BBC and found that very therapeutic. It was fun to watch all the people trying to raise money to help special kids. It made me feel alive again.

The meeting with the film people was really fun. I really liked the director, Stuart St Paul. He is an actor and has been a stunt man and has done a lot of directing, mostly second unit, which as I understand is just as important as the main director for that part of the movie. He is a genuinely nice person and is sending me the screenplay. The art director was busy most of the time measuring things. They have a website which tells a little about the movie which I found fascinating reading. I am a movie buff so I will be interested in watching how the movie is done. They have raised a million pounds to make the movie but still have not signed their stars.

Dean's hand is healing but has been giving him a lot of pain so he is going to ask the surgeon for more pain pills. He did drive himself to Detroit to broadcast yesterday but is now staying with Beth, our oldest daughter.

November 18th

It is a beautiful day in Shetland. It seems that every time we have visitors lately the weather turns good. Maybe I should turn this place into an inn and then we would have good weather the entire time.

Adam Fowler, a freelance producer for BBC, is staying here while working on his feature about the place. Right now he is interviewing someone by phone about fishing in Shetland. Today we are going up into the tower as he wants to record the sounds from there and last night he recorded me taking him through the house and describing the rooms.

I am roasting a chicken in the Rayburn for Sunday dinner along with Shetland cabbage, mashed potatoes, tossed salad, and rhubarb crisp left from last night. Tom will share dinner with us and then we will probably go for a run to show Adam Sullom Voe and the pilot boats.

My emotional stability is getting better every day. I think it is because I am getting ready to go home, along with being busy with Adam. Adam is fun and interesting to talk to because he has produced so many different types of programmes. The most interesting to me was one about Scottish mystery writers. I did not hear it but would love to.

I am counting the hours now until I can go home and see my family and celebrate the holidays. I am fine being away from my family most of the time as they are so busy with their own lives, but holidays are different and I want them near.

November 19th

The Rayburn is out and Adam is gone so I am beginning to pack. Tom is picking me up about noon. Since it is such a beautiful day we are going to poke around the southern end of the island before I check in at the hotel. He is eating dinner with me at the hotel and then will return to finish closing up the lighthouse.

For the first time I had my camera with me when we went up into the tower yesterday. Adam took some pictures of me in the tower. I really like one with the cliffs in the background and hope to use it for the back of books. Yesterday Tom and I took Adam to Sullom Voe where he was able to make arrangements to ride with the tugboats that bring in the huge oil tankers. We came back and had a wonderful roast chicken dinner which Adam and Tom devoured so there are no leftovers to get rid of today. This morning Adam is meeting a *Devil's Gate* staff member to look at a post office for use in the movie. He was really looking forward to that.

My state of mind is confused. I really am anxious to go home but leaving here is always hard, especially when it is a gorgeous Shetland day instead of a storm or the wind blowing like mad. I think there is a certain reluctance to face the farm without Kiri since when I think about that it makes me cry, but it will be wonderful to see Dean, my children, grandchildren and all of my friends.

November 20th through December 29th

This is a summary of my month away from the lighthouse at Christmas. Leaving the lighthouse on the 20th of November I went to the Sumburgh Hotel to stay overnight because the plane left at 7:50 am. It is easier for Tom to take me the day before than to get up early in the morning, especially in winter weather. Tom and I had a nice dinner at the hotel before he left to go back to Eshaness. I actually think staying at the hotel helps make the change from the lighthouse to farm in Michigan easier.

The flight to Detroit was uneventful. In some ways I dreaded the thought of seeing Dean at the airport as I did not want to look at his hand or see his pain, but when I came out of customs it surprised me how happy I was to see him. I tried not to look at his hand and it seemed to work.

Arriving at the farm without a big black dog coming out to meet me was terrible. I completely fell apart and cried hysterically for over an hour. Then knowing I must pull myself together I got busy going through six months of mail. That was enough to bring on more tears but instead it kept my mind occupied. I am not sure how well I did it with bad jet lag but it did calm me down.

The next day I removed all evidence of Kiri from the house including washing the dirt off the wall in the back yard where she lay against the house. This seemed to help my disposition and got me through the first day.

Thanksgiving was the next day and I really enjoyed seeing my family. We went to my oldest daughter's for the day so I did not even have to cook. It was a joy to see how much the grandchildren had grown in both size and ability.

The next few weeks were full of seeing old friends, going to Christmas parties and doing some chores that Dean had not had time to complete. It was a tranquil time and I found myself getting over my grief. Dean's hand was a constant reminder but since it was healing well it did not bother me too much.

Everyone was trying to help us get over the horrid events of Kiri's death. Dot, the Parma librarian, told us about a full-grown golden retriever that had to be kept in a basement because there was a new baby in the house. Dean and I discussed getting the dog and to my surprise he liked the idea of adopting him so McDuff came to our house to live. We worried that he would have adjustment problems but before a day had passed he had stolen our hearts. He was gentle, fun to be around and extremely well behaved. It was a joy to share Christmas with McDuff.

The whole family came to the house the Saturday before Christmas. It was great fun and I enjoyed cooking dinner. Our oldest daughter brought her dog Maxx, who is 13 and frail, as we were going to keep him while they went to Wisconsin for Christmas day. McDuff wanted to play but Maxx just was not up to it so we had quite a dilemma until our youngest daughter's family volunteered to keep McDuff until Maxx went home. McDuff soon captivated Sandy's family's hearts. They had planned on getting a puppy for Christmas but they changed their mind and instead asked us if they could have McDuff. We had come to love that dog in the short time he had lived with us but trying to do what was best for him, we decided to let him stay with our daughter's family. He would have kids to play with and people around most of the time which wouldn't be the case when I went back to the lighthouse and Dean is at work all day. I cried because once again I had lost a dog I loved but the good part was I would see him and get to baby sit him at times.

They aired my audio diary on Christmas Day on BBC Scotland. We were at our youngest daughter's during the first airing so we all listened together. Mark Rickards did a good job of editing and I particularly liked the music. But I was disappointed that they did not use any of the material I recorded. Some of it was lost, but I had sent almost a full tape back with the Australian producer and I expected them to use some of that along with some of the material she had recorded. Instead, they used only the material recorded by Adam Fowler when he was here which mainly focused on the tragedies of September 11th and Kiri's death. Everyone I talked to who had heard it thought it was okay. Maybe my expectations were what was wrong.

The time in Michigan flew by and the day after Christmas I got on the plane to return to the lighthouse.

January

December 30th

After a disastrous trip I finally arrived back at Eshaness Lighthouse. The trip started out with a bang when British Airways upgraded me to first class for the transatlantic part of the trip. They almost never upgrade a coach ticket to first class but because I had so many frequent flyer miles I lucked out. First class is elegant and the seat converts into a bed so you can get a reasonable amount of sleep. To my great delight across the aisle from me was Anthony Hopkins. When I realized who the passenger was I did not know whether to talk to him but he solved my dilemma by asking me, 'Do you know how to get this damn bed opened?' I didn't but we called the steward who did. From then on we chatted some. He looks older in person but he still has those special eyes.

Arriving in London early, I had to say goodbye to Anthony. My plane to Aberdeen was on time so the trip continued to be a good one. Aberdeen had snow on the ground so it looked like a Christmas card as we landed. After many years of flying I always say it is not an exact science. I kept waiting for something to go wrong. My plane to Shetland soon changed to being delayed. When I asked the desk people they said it was snowing in Shetland. One of the other passengers had a mobile phone and called a friend at the airport in Shetland who said it was not snowing but a beautiful day. So back to the desk the two of us went. They repeated their story that snow was delaying us. Another passenger called the national reservations number and was told there was mechanical trouble on the inbound plane to Aberdeen that was still in Glasgow. We kept getting all kinds of nonsense answers from the check-in people until we were finally paged and offered a ride on the P&O ferry to Lerwick. Some crazy people took the offer, since they were told they would be sure to get to Shetland the next morning. Eleven of us knew the weather forecasters were predicting force ten winds by early morning so we opted to wait for the plane, which should get us into Shetland before the winds increased. The ferry people did not get to Lerwick, as the ship had to turn back.

The plane from Glasgow finally arrived and we got on it. We pulled out and went just a few feet before the pilot pulled back in again. It seems we had a generator problem. They asked us to get off and wait in the lounge. I called Tom at the airport in Shetland who said the flight had been cancelled. It was another 30 minutes until the people in Aberdeen told us that piece of news. The next hurdle was finding a place to put 26 people overnight. It took a couple of hours but they finally found a hotel way on the other side of town, which was fine except they could not find anyone to take us there. We had to wait another hour and a half for the bus. Before we left the airport they told us we had to be up the next morning and ready to go by 6:45. It did not come as any surprise that by the time we got to the hotel the morning departure had changed to earlier. It was a classy hotel but all I did was take a shower and go to bed after over 24 hours without much sleep.

When we got to the airport the next morning our plane was supposed to be on its way from Glasgow. Now where had I heard that before? We all went to get breakfast and one of the passengers happened to run into a reservation person who told us our plane was in final boarding. Final boarding! It had not been announced nor was on the reader board. We ran to the plane, boarded and flew to Shetland without a problem.

That should have been the end of it but during all the delay a blizzard had moved into Shetland. I was able to get to Lerwick by bus, but no vehicles could get further north because of drifts on the roads. The tourist board helped me find a B&B and contacted the bus company to get special permission for me to ride on the bus to Hillswick in the morning if the roads got ploughed. (The bus going out usually does not take passengers.) I then checked into a B&B frustrated but safe for the night. The snow stopped around midnight so the bus was able to go the next morning. As I rode the bus I stared out at a magnificent Shetland; sparkling white with snow under bright blue skies surrounded by steel grey water. I do love this place because of all of its natural beauty. Tom met me at Brae with his four wheel drive truck.

I really enjoyed the ride from Brae until we got to the lighthouse road where the truck got stuck in a deep drift. I talked Tom into walking the mile through deep snow because I was desperate to get to the lighthouse.

It was quite a trip from Michigan to Eshaness. Usually it takes a little over 18 hours to get from Detroit to the lighthouse but this time it took three days. It really emphasizes the remoteness of my lighthouse home. But – and this is a big but – once on Shetland you could not have had a more gorgeous setting for the journey.

Tom did not open a faucet inside the lighthouse when it got below freezing so the pipes at the lighthouse froze. I am glad to be at the lighthouse, even with no water and a bronchial cold caught somewhere between here and the USA, as I sit looking out at my white yard bordered by the blue sea.

Physically I feel pretty rotten. I will have to watch myself closely as I have had pneumonia twice.

December 31st

The snowploughs have still not arrived so Tom got stuck down at the bottom of the hill again. He checked on me quickly before he left, not to return until the roads are clear. He is afraid he will get stuck and will not be able to get to his job.

I talked to the Shetland Council road people and they will probably not do anything to our roads until after New Year. For four days I will just have to cope. This is not exactly how I had hoped to spend New Year. Right now I could throw in the towel and call it quits on this remote lighthouse living. That is exhaustion talking caused by the long trip back, tramping around in snow drifts, no water and now a bad cold.

I am still hoping they can plough me out so I can visit some neighbours for New Year's Eve.

January 1st

A huge storm with gale force nine winds is raging outside, but it has warmed up and the snow is almost all gone. The blowhole behind the lighthouse is throwing sea spray high into the air and surf is crashing over the islands – a natural New Year spectacular. I am not up to getting out and taking pictures but the views from the windows are magnificent. Maybe I can take some photographs tomorrow when I feel better.

I am still ailing but I am not any worse so that is good news. Tom is in bad shape since he hurt his knee just before Christmas and can barely walk. He promised he would see the doctor when the health centre opens again. If the knee does not heal he might be looking at surgery.

They did get the road ploughed out so New Year's Eve was spent at Tom's house watching the Hogmanay festival from Edinburgh featuring Scottish music with two of my favourites; Aly Bain and Capercallie. For me it was a festive New Year's Eve.

New Year dinner is a little sparse as I have not been to the store. I cooked roast pork, mashed potatoes, broccoli and cauliflower, and made a bread pudding with lots of currants and fruit. I have lost my Christmas cake. I put it somewhere to keep before I left for Michigan but cannot remember where I put it.

I am excited as I discovered one of the stars of *Devil's Gate*, the movie that is being filmed here, would be Laura Fraser. She has been in *A Knights Tale*, *Titus*, and *Kevin and Perry*, which makes her a seasoned movie actress at the age of 26. In *Devil's Gate* she will play Rachael who is 22. She first worked with the film's director Stuart St Paul on *Small Faces*.

I have seen *Titus* starring my 'friend' Anthony Hopkins but I have not seen *A Knight's Tale*. I found a web site for it and read some of the reviews, which were not good. Laura Fraser was not even mentioned.

I wish I knew who was going to be the male lead. I'm really looking forward to the movie coming to Eshaness because I am so proud of our beautiful cliffs, seascapes, magnificent sky and animal life. The last few days have been difficult but when I look out the window or walk to the cliffs it is all worthwhile. The movie will show the world why.

January 2nd

I started the day off by waking up at 10:00, which is the latest I have slept in 20 years. Dean says my body is telling me it needs rest. I think my cold is a little better but I still don't feel right so another day of babying myself and drinking lots of herb tea is called for.

The Rayburn went out which is not surprising since it went so long without being fed. It is now blazing brightly and warming up the room. Good old Rayburn!

After restarting the fire I went outside to feed the chickens and they were very glad to see me. The wind is in the south and the lighthouse is sheltering the front of the caddy shack so I opened the door to dry it out. I do not think the chickens have ventured outside; it is pretty windy for them. With the bright sunshine and blue sky it does not seem cold until you get into the wind.

Tom is being unreasonable. He can barely get around his knee hurts so much. He called the doctor this morning. She was sympathetic until she told him to get an appointment with the surgery tomorrow. When Tom told her he could not come in tomorrow because he was going to Lerwick she told him not to call her unless it was an emergency. Today is a bank holiday so only emergencies are supposed to go to the surgery number. The doctor was rude but Tom should go to the surgery tomorrow and not go to Lerwick. After he told me this he said he was going out to herd sheep. I have been the knee route and I kept on mine until the damage was so bad I had to have surgery. Tom is probably already there as he will not stay down and give the knee a chance to heal.

The missing Christmas cake has been found. Tom went searching and found it in the clothes closet in the master bedroom. Do not ask me why I put the Christmas cake in my clothes closet. At least it is found.

January 3rd

Tom went to the doctor this morning and had his knee examined and then decided we would go to Lerwick. A free trip to Lerwick is welcome as I need groceries and can always use a day in town.

When we got there nothing was open except the grocery, which had rows and rows of empty shelves (no ferries over New Year). I was able to get all the groceries I needed though. The rest of the stores do not open until tomorrow since they are getting ready for big sales. I might take the bus to Lerwick on Saturday to check out the sales. Before I left for the States I dropped off some pictures for framing and I would like to get those back too.

My cold is not much better and I still have little 'get up and go'. I will take it easy tonight and hopefully by tomorrow things will improve.

It seems strange to be coming home from Lerwick with the sun setting at 2:30 pm. It is 3:30 now and completely dark outside.

I got an e-mail today from a lady who stayed at Eshaness in 1948. She is sending me an article that she wrote which was broadcast on a BBC radio programme. The article tells about her staying at Eshaness on holiday as a child.

January 4th

I have a doctor's appointment this morning so this will be short. My cold has made it to my bronchial tubes causing me to cough most of the night. I am also running a fever so I decided to give up and get professional help. I have had pneumonia twice and I do NOT want it over here.

Tom has lost his voice with his cold and since he is taking me to the doctor it will be a quiet trip except for my coughing. The doctor gave him some new medicine for his knee and hopefully that will help, as he will not stay off of it.

Today I must write my story for *Lighthouse Digest*, which will be a struggle, but deadlines do not go away just because you caught cold.

January 5th

I have a slight pneumonia infection in one lung but I am not too worried as it is only one lung. The doctor started me on a whole lot of medication that seems to be doing some good already but I still have a fever, ache a lot and have almost completely lost my voice. Dean calls me squeaky when I talk to him on the telephone. My energy level is low so I spend a lot of time lying on the couch reading.

I have been back at Eshaness a week and it has been a real struggle with the snow, water and now being sick.

It's a mild sunny day so Tom took me for a ride to get some cough medicine. It was more psychological therapy than anything else. We stopped at a couple of places where I could watch the beautiful surf and even saw a couple of seals. I needed to get out and enjoy what makes this place so special or I might become blue about all the problems. It worked.

Leslie, the attendant keeper, came by for a cup of tea and that was nice. He was topping off the lighthouse batteries so they would be were fully charged in case something happened and he could not get up here with all the bad weather.

Since it was warm and there was not too much wind the chickens came out of their house. All four were outside. I spent a long time watching as they were taking such delight in being free. Tom did not let them out when I was gone since he only made one trip to the lighthouse a day and the weather has prevented them being out since I have been back.

I made pancakes on the Rayburn this morning using a new griddle pan I got for Christmas. It will take a while to learn how to use this pan on the Rayburn. The griddle is cast iron so it takes quite a while to heat up and my first pancakes were not brown but once it finally got hot it did fine. The other side is a broiler and I am going to do chicken breasts on in tonight.

January 6th

I'm late writing today because the Rayburn's riddler was stuck when I got up this morning. Because the ashes couldn't drop through, the fire was slowly smothering. It eventually went out and I had to clean the stove and start another fire. The worst possible calamity is for the Rayburn to go out with the bricks fully heated and that is exactly what happened this time so it took me two hours to do everything. I burned my thumb and a small hole in the rug before I got the riddler free. My health problems slowed me up a lot and my hands were shaking (a side effect from the medication). Once the fire was burning again I called Tom and put off dinner for two hours.

For the first time, and hopefully the only time, I was ready to get on a plane and never come back here, probably because being sick is so difficult here.

Tom came and took to see my doctor, Susan Bowie's, new home. Once the Hillswick Church of Scotland manse, it was built in 1863 and is gigantic. It has seven bedrooms, two bathrooms, three sitting rooms and various other rooms including a maid's quarters. It is in bad condition so they have their hands full. They are putting in central heating as well as putting on a new roof. They were stripping wallpaper so we helped for a few minutes. There are some really interesting designs on those walls and Susan is putting them all in a scrapbook as kind of a history of the house. I told her about my disaster with the Rayburn and she thought with her support and because I am a pensioner we might get a variance (the necesary permission) to convert the Rayburn to oil. The problem is we would need an oil tank and that would require permission from the Shetland Islands Council since the tank would change the outside appearance of a listed building. I am beginning to think a better option would be to put another storage heater in the Rayburn room so we are not so dependent on the Rayburn for heat.

We had baked ham, mixed vegetables, a tossed salad with oranges, mashed potatoes and Christmas cake for dinner today. Tom did not eat too well as he is really feeling poorly so I had lots left over.

January 7th

Tom wants to buy a used tractor so he decided to go to Lerwick to place an ad in the *Shetland Times*. I placed an ad seeking one black and white spotted year-old ewe. Last spring I fell in love with this breed of sheep, with big random black and white spots and long wool. I have not been able to buy one. They look a little like panda bears. If I can find one I will put it in Tom's flock with my three caddies. I found out on the Internet that these sheep are available in the US so maybe I will get one to go along with our black and white cow. (I can hear Dean screaming from here!)

The weather is warm but really windy so I am staying inside. I still tire easily and my cough has not loosened yet.

January 8th

It's a sunny day with a little surf but fairly calm as the wind is down to force five, low for winter. My health must be improving because I woke up at my usual time of about 7:00 this morning. It was toasty warm in bed so I made a cup of coffee and went back to bed to drink it. I could hear the wind but it was just a mild hum so I knew we might have a nice day. Having opened the inside shutters, I was lying in bed drinking my coffee and I noticed that as the beacon swept by the window, its reflection rotated around the bedroom wall. In all the time I have been here I have never before seen this. It was actually beautiful. First, the beacon would sweep by outside and then beginning in the corner by the door a dimmer light would sweep around the wall almost to the window on the other side. If I had seen this before I would have included it in *The Lighthouse Ghost*, my new children's book that is being published. The light was not scary but beautiful.

I am thrilled they are filming part of the movie, *Devil's Gate*, here on Thursday. The Shetland co-ordinator will call me again today to discuss it some more and tomorrow he is coming out to go over the final details. The weather forecast is not too good; rain and strong winds. The winds will produce the surf the director wants but if it rains it could be a miserable day for the production people. I will have my camera out to get pictures of all the action, which will be fun. Tom asked if he could come up to watch and I said yes.

Today is a momentous day as I started the final draft of my next book. My plan is to turn it in before I leave for the States at the end of April. I have developed a writing schedule and should be able to keep to it without too many interruptions like movies.

January 9th

I hung my sheets outside which lasted exactly one hour until it started to mist so they are now hanging on the line inside. I cannot remember any sheets getting completely dry outside since we have lived here. They smell good from the fresh sea air even if they finish in the house.

I spent the morning cleaning the room in the generator house that will be used tomorrow for the film crew's breaks. It had not been cleaned since the lighthouse radio weekend so I dusted and vacuumed. Since I have been sick I have been cleaning the house a little at a time and it looks pretty good so no major problems there.

A blessed event occurred at Tom's house yesterday. One of the ewes had a very small black lamb totally off schedule. Since it is still winter he has moved it inside the steading with plenty of warm straw for bedding. There seems to be divided opinions among our friends about my getting a black and white spotted ewe. There are more positive than negative reactions so Dean, who does not like sheep, is out-voted. He is still screaming 'no sheep'.

On my way back from seeing the lamb there was a beautiful sunset right over Foula. Foula is the most remote island in Shetland and can be easily seen from the lighthouse. I keep trying to get to Foula for a visit but it does not look like I will make it this year. I am curious about Foula because I see it every day and have watched the movie, *The Edge of the World*, that was filmed there.

The Shetland co-ordinator for *Devil's Gate* is due any time so I think I will not start writing on the book until after he leaves.

January 10th

The art crew from *Devil's Gate* arrives at 8:00 am to turn my little home from a lighthouse to an inn and I am so excited. They will be putting a neon sign on the tower and in the three front windows saying Hotel. I wonder what else they will think up? Putting a sign on the tower led to an emergency call to the Northern Lighthouse Board who own the tower. I do not think it will be a problem but you never know with the NLB as they are bound by so many rules. The rest of the crew (25 people including the stars, their make-up artists and costume people) will arrive at 10:30 am give or take a few minutes. They are going to shoot at the 'blink', which is just before sunset. That should be around 2:30 pm depending on cloud cover.

January 11th

I am trying to recover from yesterday. Filming a movie is a kind of organized chaos. There were around 35 people here and they all were either running around like mad or sitting. It is the actors that do most of the sitting, as they have to wait for everything to be ready.

In the early morning I spent most of my time with the art/set people until the main crew arrived then it was the costume, make-up and actors who were in the house. Laura Fraser, the female lead, seemed to be a dedicated actress and was a warm, fun person to be around. Callum Blue, the male lead, was a young, good-looking guy but sort of an introvert who liked to keep to himself. For some reason Callum and I got along well. The costume and makeup people said he talked more to me than to them. It was a strange coincidence that Anthony Hopkins financially supported Callum through his acting education and yet Callum had never met his benefactor. So, I got to tell him about sleeping by Anthony, dear.

The more I hear about the script and the plot the more I think this movie is not going to be a big winner, but, until it is all put together we won't know.

I put up a web page with a sort of pictorial history of the day but I was not able to get outside to take pictures when they filmed at the front door of the lighthouse before Laura runs to the cliffs where Callum's character tries to rescue her. The inside of the hotel will be shot in another location on the island.

Everything went well except for one big mess up. They used the generator house for a tearoom and to store some lighting equipment that shattered Styrofoam all over the floor. They also left the doors open and the lights on. When I discovered this I was really upset because having doors open here is very dangerous as the wind can come along and rip them off. It also took me a long time to clean up the mess. I e-mailed Stuart and Leslie, the Shetland contact, to bring the situation to their attention but I will not hear anything until later tonight.

I am off to see my caddies as I have been at the computer the entire day and am really tired of being in the house.

January 12th

Tom wanted to go look at a used tractor near Sandwick but we drove to Lerwick first so I could get some new library books. He bought the tractor for £1800. It looked okay, ran well, and has been kept indoors so maybe he got a good deal. He is not sure and of course I am no help. We stopped in Brae to get a lorry to pick up the tractor and deliver it to Bordigarth.

Tom's little black lamb got its head caught in the gate in the steading and died. Being weak I guess getting stuck was just too much for it.

I got an apologetic e-mail from the *Devil's Gate* people saying they were sending me something to make up for making such a mess.

I put *Sharma's Lighthouse*, the BBC programme, on the www so my family could hear it. Most everyone in the US missed the original broadcast since during the second airing the BBC server went down completely. The program is copyrighted so I will only leave it on until my family has heard it.

January 13th

Bright sun is shining in the windows and it looks from the inside like it will be a warm day. If you go outside it is windy and feels cold. I may go for a walk to the Bruddans, as I have not been down there since I got back, but the wind will have to ease some first.

Tom is due for dinner since it is Sunday. We are having a stuffed roast chicken, lettuce salad, mashed potatoes, mixed vegetables and a lemon meringue pie that I bought on sale at the store.

I would like to drive to Aith and see the house the movie people are using for their main set but it will depend on how Tom's leg feels.

I am disappointed no one has answered my advertisement for the spotted lamb; usually you get responses right after the *Shetland Times* comes out on Friday. Tom had lots of calls about wanting to buy a tractor. Perhaps everyone wants to keep these unusual sheep. I am finishing an article for the *Shetland Visitor*, which is read by all the tourists who come here. The article is entitled *The Road to My House* and describes the trip from the beginning of Eshaness Road to the lighthouse. It is an unusual and beautiful journey; in many people's opinion the prettiest drive in Shetland with so many unusual sea stacks dotting the shoreline.

January 14th

This week's goal is to get another chapter in the new book rewritten. The day started with a cup of coffee in my warm, cosy bed watching the light sweep across the bedroom. I do miss Dean bringing me my coffee in bed like he does in Michigan. Here I have to wander down the hall to the kitchen to get my own. At least the water is hot on the Rayburn so it does not take took long to make. I think I have figured out what makes the light sweep around the bedroom. It is a reflection from the tower beam on the shiny inside surface of the wooden shutters. The master bedroom is right under the tower so it catches pretty good light.

Yesterday was the first day I felt physically normal since I arrived. It took longer than I would have liked to get over the virus but thank goodness I am finally well. There is good care available but for some reason it is scares me to be here when I am sick.

Tom's leg is not any better and yesterday he could hardly walk. We did not take a ride in the car because it hurts him so much to get in and out. He ate dinner and left. For the first time since I have known him he was really bad-tempered. He will not let anyone help him so he has to continue to chase sheep, etc, and that just puts him in more pain. I am glad he gets X-rays tomorrow to find out what really is wrong. I talked to Leslie and we think we could take care of the sheep with help from his neighbours if Tom has to stay off of his leg for any length of time. The most difficult problem will be dealing with Tom himself as he is really stubborn and thinks *only* he can take care of the sheep. I've got my fingers crossed that he does not have to stay off of his leg for too long.

The sun was out for a few minutes but now it is grey and extremely windy so I will be content working on my new book.

January 15th

I have only a few minutes to write before Tom gets here for our trip to Lerwick and the hospital for X-rays. Tom is convinced they will take the fluid off his knee today.

I went to the door yesterday during a terrible storm and there stood a man with a huge bouquet of flowers from the crew of *Devil's Gate*. Getting flowers delivered this far from Lerwick is unusual. The only other time it has happened was when the bank, who helped us obtain Eshaness Lighthouse, sent me a basket of flowers when I took possession.

January 16th

Sunshine, no wind and warm in Shetland today. I took the opportunity to clean out the caddy shack, now known as the chicken house. I put all the old, wet, used bedding on the garden. Now I have the doors open to dry out the inside before I put in new bedding. The residents were distressed as I kept moving them around but a little while ago they were outside enjoying the day so I guess it was not too much of a trauma.

The medical report on Tom is disappointing. He got his X-rays taken yesterday but it will be ten days until he will know anything because they have to go to Aberdeen to be read. I convinced him to go see our local GP today and hopefully she can do something to make him more comfortable until they can read the blasted X-rays.

January 17th

Another grey, warm day but the weather forecasters are promising sunshine before the day is over. It is calm and so it feels a lot warmer today than it does on a normal, windy day.

Tom went to the clinic yesterday and the substitute doctor was on duty. He examined Tom's knee and said it was probably just old age. The knee was worn out and the only answer would be to replace the knee joint. How does he know that if he has not even seen the X-rays? Tom was upset and I do not blame him. The doctor did give Tom some new pills, which from the description sounded like just another painkiller. From what Tom told me on the telephone last night they do not seem to be working. Tom is really getting depressed so I am taking some time off from writing the book this afternoon to go down to visit him, see my caddies and dig the last of the parsnips.

The new book is coming along and it feels like it will be okay. Somehow when you write something you know if it is going to be a winner or not and I feel this one is definitely a winner. It is like a breath of fresh air for me to be writing something besides a heavily researched non-fiction book. I love writing and I cannot think of anything I would rather be than a writer. The pay may not be consistent but if you have enough books published you have a royalty check coming in quite often which begins to add up. I would like to get enough royalties so I could take time to write another novel. I should check with Macmillan today and see what is going on with my other novel but in this business no news is good news. It definitely has not been turned down or I would have heard by now.

The chickens are over the trauma of having their house cleaned and were singing and strutting around in the new sawdust. It smells a lot better in the chicken house now then it did before it was cleaned.

I have been a little concerned as a car has come up the road the last two nights rather late (after ten) and parked in the car park. I keep the house locked after eight so no one can get in but I keep wondering what is going on out there. Maybe kids making out, but since we usually have no night traffic at all, it is a mystery. It brought back memories of the problems we had a year ago when people tried to break in. That stopped after I put up the new security light.

January 18th

What a gorgeous day. I have sheets hanging on the line and they are just faintly swaying. The sun is bright and the ocean is an indigo blue. I hope to have this week's chapter completed for the new book so I can go fishing with Tom around lunchtime. We are supposed to get terrible storms tomorrow so I will go fishing today and write tomorrow. Writing on Saturday breaks my taking the weekend off rule but things here are pretty much ruled by the weather.

I went to Tom's house for a little while yesterday to see my caddies. They are growing but Alyssa and Kara will never be large sheep. Kara had a sore foot and Tom said he would clean and put medicine on it. Alyssa comes running as soon as she sees me so I believe she will always be a pet but Kara comes more slowly. She is just not sure whether she should or not. Austin just ignores me.

I dug some of my parsnips. I tasted one and it was so sweet. Parsnips are always sweeter after they have been frozen. I probably have a couple more batches still in the ground. Dean loves them and we have had no luck with growing them in Michigan so I guess I will have to dig some when Dean is here in February. Before I leave this spring I will plant more parsnips. They take very little care and I will be back in the fall before they are ready to harvest.

January 19th

It's a beautiful Saturday so I imagine there will be tourists out and about. I plan to work on the book this morning and then off to the Bruddans to visit the seals. Tom went to Lerwick to a ram sale but I decided not to go with him because my top activity is working on my book and if I take any time off it will be to go outside and enjoy the scenery today.

Something nice happened yesterday but it makes life a little more difficult. The Shetland Arts Trust has a new grant in Shetland to increase literary activities. Someone called to see if I would be interested in a part-time position as writer in residence for the Shetland Islands. It was an honour being asked but I am not sure I have time for it. The position is flexible enough that I could spend time in the USA with my family. One thing that is appealing is I would be working with people from all over Shetland. Probably nothing will come of it but I would like to be involved somehow.

I have found an illustrator for my children's book, *Dore Holm*, about how the local sea stack was a living creature long ago. He did a draft for the publisher and it was wonderful to see Dore alive at last. I asked him to make some changes like taking out trees since Shetland has none and making the whale in the picture an Orca since we have so many. I love the expression he put on Dore's face. We are discussing whether Dore's head or nose needs to be a little larger. It is definitely a good beginning.

January 20th

It is raining whales and seals here, an ocean equivalent of cats and dogs. The wind is quite strong too so it is not a nice day for anything but reading.

Tom and I are to leave at noon to go to Aith to see the main set for *Devil's Gate* and then on to Walls to look at some Flecket sheep. Flecket is the breed name for the black and white spotted Shetland sheep I have been looking for. They come in two colour schemes – black and white and grey and white. I finally got a call from a man in Walls who has 20 ewes. He has a type of Shetland chicken that lays blue eggs so I might look at them also. I've never been in Aith (where the lifeboat for the north of Shetland is stationed) or in Walls so it is a journey into brand new territory. I am taking both cameras but if it keeps raining this hard I won't get very good pictures.

Last night green Northern Lights were dancing all over the sky above the cliffs. I know there must be a way to set my 35mm camera so I can get a picture of the Northern Lights but with everything I tried the shutter refused to trip. My inadequacy with my camera distresses me. It was an exceptional occasion but not one I could record but maybe that is what makes it so special.

Dinner is beef pot roast, as Tom and I will be running around most of the afternoon. I put potatoes, carrots, and onions in with a big piece of beef in the Rayburn, which will cook while we are gone. I baked a rhubarb upside down cake yesterday and that along with a tossed salad is dinner.

I've got to go brave the elements to feed the chickens their Sunday treat of potato peelings and carrot scrapings. They seem to know when it is Sunday as they are always waiting right by the door.

January 21st

It's Monday and I am about to hang some clothes outside, as it is warm and not terribly windy. Hopefully they will dry, but as it is not sunny rain could be close.

Yesterday turned out to be a great fun. We found the house in Aith where most of *Devil's Gate* is being filmed and lucked out as they were filming when we arrived. We got to see them rehearse a scene and then shoot it. Stuart St Paul, the director, invited us to have dinner with them so we did. He showed me the rushes of the footage shot at Eshaness and they are great! I talked with Stuart while Tom found a movie star he had always wanted to meet who is playing a minor role. So everyone had fun.

Devil's Gate has been getting some mean press from the *Shetland Times* so I wrote a letter to the editor pointing out how much money the movie is bringing to Shetland and the jobs they are providing. Everyone in the cast came up and thanked me for the letter. They just could not understand why the *Shetland Times* would be so much against them when they were doing so many good things for the islands. I don't understand it myself.

After *Devil's Gate* we went on to look at the Flecket sheep. They were just what I am looking and I found two really cute ones that I am going to try to buy. I talked to the owner last night and hopefully we can pick them up next Saturday.

The illustrator came in with the second draft of the Dore picture and it is just what I wanted. The picture has been sent to the publisher so I am keeping my fingers crossed as they like the story.

January 22nd

Tom has always said I have not experienced a real storm but now I have. The winds went up to 65 miles an hour last night, gale force ten – or storm. It was so noisy I wanted to scream. The plastic protectors on the windows vibrated with a booming sound and the noise from the chimney was not a howl but an explosion. I wanted to see *Taggart*, one of my favourite mysteries, so I turned the volume on the TV up full and tried to watch it but my nerves were jangled from both the noise of the storm and the TV. When I went to bed it took me quite a long time to go to sleep as the noise in the bedroom was so bad. I could actually hear the sea spray pounding on the windows. I do not believe any big rocks were thrown up on top of the cliff but I have not taken time to look this morning.

This morning when I woke up it was dead still. Now there is hazy sunshine and all four chickens are outside running around. It is unbelievable that the weather could have been so terrible last night and so nice today. Either because we are surrounded by ocean or just so far north we get violent storms that never last too long.

I felt safe and secure in this little house. The noise bothered me but the building did not shake or make me feel afraid. If I had to go outside in that fury I would have been scared to death. One thing about Stevenson lighthouses is they are sturdy with three foot thick walls and concrete roofs.

I'm still working on the new book and will be for the next couple of months but today there will be a little fun with the arrival of the library van and the fish van.

January 23rd

We just got back from Lerwick as Tom had to sign some papers related to the croft he is applying to farm. Actually he already farms the Stow croft but it was never made official so he is taking care of the paper work.

Lerwick is looking all 'Up Helly Aa' like. The big event is next Tuesday and I have decided to go. Tom is probably taking me only because we were invited to hang out with some of the movie people who he really likes. Up Helly Aa is such a unique festival it should be in the next book so to be authentic I will go this year. I could paste in the story from last year if the weather gets bad and we cannot get there.

The world-wide launch of new book is going to be at the *Shetland Times* bookstore in late August. I was in talking to Edna Burke, the manager of the bookstore, and found out that the janitor for the bookstore is the Jarl (head man) for this year's Up Helly Aa. Her excitement reminded me to make sure it was mentioned in the next book.

We had lunch at the fish and chip shop where Tom had the biggest piece of haddock I have ever seen. It must have been 14 inches long. If you go inside at the fish and chip shop the food is absolutely wonderful. Carry out is good but it is not as fresh as what you get when you sit at the tables. The carry out has been sitting around for a while. You can have mashed potatoes instead of chips if you go inside and I love mashed potatoes.

Snow is due tomorrow so I should be able to get a lot of work done.

January 24th

We are having a blizzard. A gale force eight wind from the northeast is driving sleety/snow particles. I took the ashes out and fed the chickens but had to be careful, as the parking area was icy. The chickens did not even go near the door. This is supposed to be a quick storm and by Saturday it should warm up again. I have the water dripping slightly so I will not have frozen pipes again. I made a big pot of porridge for breakfast, which warmed me up after I came back from braving the perils of the snowy outdoors. I keep the left-over oatmeal in the refrigerator and reheat it in the microwave so it tastes better than instant oatmeal and is just as quick.

Dean and I have been married 33 years today. He is in trouble as I did not get an e-mail or an e-mail card from him but it is not unusual for him to forget. I sent him an e-mail card and a box of his favourite candy. It disturbs me that for many years we have spent our anniversary in Scotland but for the last few years he has had something related to work that keeps him from being here.

All in all I am not in a great mood as I am fighting with the publisher of one of my books over royalties. They were a month late in reporting my royalties for last year and then the numbers weren't correct. I have waited a month for a correction, which he is now refusing to do. Another problem has been after all my urging (I am not sure how many phone calls and e-mails) to them to have the Internet bookstores well stocked for the airing of the BBC feature – they were not. I contacted amazon.co.uk last week and it took me only three days to get the stock replenished. I hope we can resolve the problems as the book still sells well and I cannot change publishers because I have a contract.

I am not having a good day and it is only early morning. I will begin working on the new book again because that needs to be done and a blizzard is a good reason to sit at the computer.

January 25th

It is really cold, below freezing. Thank goodness the wind has dropped. When I went out to do my early morning chores the most beautiful sunrise was happening.

I ran and got the digital camera, put on every coat I had, and went for a walk to take pictures. One of the scenes showed the lighthouse surrounded by purple with sparkling ice crystals. The lighthouse beacon was reflected in the ice of a tiny lochan. The picture loses some of the impact, as you do not have the sparkle that was part of the moment. I love the picture though.

Dean did not forget our anniversary. We were married at 7:00 pm on January 24th and he called to wish me happy anniversary late in the afternoon US time. He also sent me an email card before the actual US time of the wedding. It seems to me he is stretching the point a little but I suppose he is technically correct.

Macmillan turned down my book, *Northern Lights*, because they think it is too regional for their catalogue. The novel is still being seriously considered, which is more important to me. I talked to Shetland Times Publishing and they want to print *Northern Lights* in the fall, which is probably the best place for the book. I had been hoping to consolidate all of my publishing efforts into one big publisher but Dean does not agree with me. He thinks I get better service from the small publishers and he might be right.

I have to get my company taxes ready to fax to the US. Doing my US taxes is a little more difficult this year being across the Atlantic but thanks to the computer they will get done on time.

January 26th

The weather is about as awful as it could be. The snow and ice started to melt last night but the wind came up and it felt really cold. We have force seven winds (38 miles an hour) and the rain is pouring down. The wind chill is 24°F, which is utterly cold. I did not wear gloves to empty the ashes and feed the chickens because it looked warmer so I almost got my hands frostbitten. They are still sore as I type. From now on I will turn on the computer and see what the temperature and wind chill is before I go outside.

I got my companies taxes done and will fax the forms to my CPA today so hopefully Dean can bring the completed return over here for my signature. It was a good year for the company because of the *Scottish Lighthouses* book. Everything else was down. This is not surprising since September 11th has hurt the economy everywhere.

The morning I am on Warren Pierce WJR radio program in Detroit at 5:30 am US time. It is aired there again on Sunday at 3:00 pm. I have no idea what we will talk about which makes it doubly hard.

After the interview I want to go pick up my spotted lambs and maybe a Shetland chicken that lays blue eggs so I hope the weather improves. We are also planning to stop at a restored Shetland mill, which has Shetland crafts and really good Shetland food. It will be our Sunday outing a day early.

January 27th

It is a bright gentle Sunday with the sun out full and just a breath of wind. It still amazes me how fast the weather changes. I have clothes hanging on the line and they are only blowing slightly. It is cold. The temperature is around 40°. We are supposed to get quite a storm tonight and tomorrow so I am going out to enjoy the nice day before Tom comes for dinner.

The trip to get the spotted lamb was cancelled because of icy, snowy, windy weather. I was disappointed but used the day to work on *Scottish Radiance*. Tomorrow I go back to working on the book so I needed the time for *Radiance*.

The menu today is roast chicken and homemade noodles, mashed potatoes, mixed vegetables, salad, and a Dundee cake. The main thanks for this meal goes to the lighthouse chickens as they furnished the eggs for the noodles and the cake. I still have all four chickens as the chicken being eaten came from the butcher.

Last night I went outside just before bed and it had cleared with a full moon making shadows everywhere. The sky was full of stars and shadowy light grey clouds against a background of charcoal sky. I could hear the waves crashing over at the cliffs but absolutely nothing else. It was one of those special moments that reminded me why I am here. I stood at the door with the beacon going round and round in the beautiful night.

Signed copies of my books are now selling for $65 – $80. Anyone who has a signed copy will be glad they are increasing in value every day. It is amazing to me how signed copies in good repair become so valuable. I would like to someday to collect signed first editions by some of my favourite authors.

Both Misty, our belted Galloway cow, and myself signed some of the *Moonbeam Cow* books. (Misty's signature is a rubber stamp of a cow's hoof). Does that make them even more valuable with two signatures?

January 28th

Another good day to work on the book and *Scottish Radiance* as it is pouring down rain. I was lucky I got the chickens fed, the garbage out and the ashes emptied before it let loose. There is a big debate whether we will be hit by the damaging winds that are causing so much trouble in the middle of Scotland. Some gusts down there are between 70 and 90 miles an hour. I just checked the shipping forecast and it said:

Southerly becoming cyclonic then north westerly seven to severe gale nine, occasionally storm ten, decreasing five or six later. Rain then wintry showers. Moderate

I think I will go out to get coal and shut up the chickens so all is settled in for the big storm if it comes. The lighthouse is so exposed when storms hit we get it the worst.

I hope the storm does miss, as tomorrow is Up Helly Aa. There are more people in Shetland for this event than at any other time of year. The only event which ever rivalled Up Helly Aa was The Cutty Sark Tall Ships Race. Yesterday I could not understand why the car park was so full of cars and people were walking all over the place then it dawned on me Up Helly Aa is this week.

Tom and I went fishing and I caught one pretty good-sized one and a tiny, tiny one that resembled a minnow. We would have stayed longer but the wind was biting cold and my hands began to hurt. I need to start wearing layered gloves just like all the layered clothes I wear. My everyday outfit is sweat pants, a wool turtleneck, a heavy sweatshirt, and two pairs of socks. If it really cold I wear long underwear under the sweat pants and insulated socks. I know it is not actually as cold here as in Michigan but the wind makes it feel colder. The lighthouse is sturdy but when the wind gets really high the house has lots of draughts but most of the time I stay warm. In the evening I cover up with a duvet while reading or watching TV. When I go outside I may have three or four layers under my outside coat depending on the weather. The only problem is it takes me a long time to get dressed.

We are in the final countdown for Dean's visit as he will be here a week from today with luck. After my last trip I am not too sure.

January 29th

It is Up Helly Aa. The worst of the storm missed us but it was really wild here from the middle of the afternoon until early this morning. The waves were breaking over the cliffs in front of the lighthouse for the first time since I have lived here. The spray was being driven 200 feet straight up and the blowhole was like a geyser. A small problem last night scared me big time. I had put the usual amount of coal in the Rayburn before the wind came up. The force of the wind stoked the fire until the Rayburn was showing it was too hot. I was afraid it would explode or something. Dean happened to call while all of this was going on. I had already decided not to put any more coal in it and let it die down. Dean and

I decided it might cool down faster by opening the oven door. It worked, but I had to keep the door open all evening. I did not put any more coal in it until about 2:30 am when I got up to go to the bathroom and then I put in just a little. When I got up this morning I still had a few coals so I was able to get it started using peat. Another lesson learned is to be careful how much coal I put in during severe storms.

An even bigger problem was the noise, which was horrific. I went into the bedroom to read to get away from the rattle of the Rayburn's damper and the howling of the chimney. It was noisy in the bedroom but a more consistent and mellow roar.

There are moments when I wonder why I am here but today it is so beautiful it drives those doubts away. We have a slight breeze of 11 mph out of the north so it is a bit cold. The skies cleared in the early evening and we had a magnificent full moon. I took some pictures this morning when I was out feeding the chickens. This sight once again helped remind me what is so special about this place even if we do have horrible storms. The one with the moon and the beacon may become my all time favourite picture.

January 30th

Up Helly Aa didn't turn out as I had expected. We got into town just before dark so I was able to get some pictures of Vest Maenir, this year's galley. As always it was well done and like last year I felt bad that it would be destroyed but burning the longboat is part of the festival, which has been going on for 150 years. If I had my way they would not burn the beautiful galley but an old wreck. What difference would it make? I think one of the hardest Up Helly Aa jobs must be ship builder, as all of their efforts are burned up in a few minutes.

We ran into some of the *Devil's Gate* crowd on the main street so we ate supper with them. It was enjoyable for a while but then some guy who we did not know joined our table and for him nothing about Shetland was good enough. He treated Tom badly. This is the first time anyone around me had treated Tom in that manner. When you first meet Tom you might think he is just a simple crofter but he is an extremely intelligent, warm and caring person. I was livid and Tom was confused. Later I told Tom not to let the jerk bother him as most of the *Devil's Gate* people have been really friendly but I could see Tom was hurt. Actually I have been surprised we have not seen more of this kind of arrogance from the film crowd but I suppose Stuart, the director, sets the tone and he is friendly and down to earth.

As we were waiting for the procession to start, BBC Shetland news announced a big change in the weather forecast and we were to get snow. After much discussion I decided we would forego the burning and go home, as it is a long way to drive on snowy roads. Tom was afraid I would be disappointed but I wasn't really since I had seen the event last year. It is always exactly the same with a few costumes changes and a new galley. Besides I really do not like to see the galley get torched.

We drove back to Eshaness in the snow, which was not too heavy, and the roads were okay most of the way.

When we arrived at the lighthouse the beacon welcomed us with its rays full of sparkling snowflakes. It was heart-stoppingly beautiful. I probably enjoyed the lighthouse in the snow more than I would the burning of the beautiful ship.

I also realized that the arrogant *Devil's Gate* person didn't bother me any more. I love Shetland and the lighthouse. I am happy here and no idiot who can't appreciate it, or my friends, is not worth a second thought.

January 31st

I have my sheets hanging on the clothes line and at this point they have been rained on four times while I uploaded *Radiance*. The sun comes out after every shower so right now it is really sunny with a bright blue sky. We have a stiff wind so they might be getting dry but who knows. If I go and take them down it will probably not rain again so I think I will gamble and leave them out a little longer. This is a constant problem. I never or hardly ever get my clothes dry on the clothes line. I like the smell of the clothes dried outside and it is nicer inside without wet clothes hanging all over.

Tom's X-ray showed the problem was arthritis in his knee. The doctor said there was nothing she could do about it. She gave him a cream to rub on it and last night he felt that was doing some good. He did not seem too upset as the used tractor he bought arrived and he was having great fun with his new toy. I probably will not see anything of him today, as he will be out playing with his tractor.

Scottish Radiance's new issue is online. After I finish I always wonder how much longer I can continue to invest so much time in the Internet magazine. The site is still extremely popular and serves a good purpose but it takes me an average of four days of constant work at the computer to do each issue. Oh, well it is done for another month.

It was so nice yesterday I went for a walk right after I fed the chickens and got some gorgeous pictures, mostly of the moon. I may be overdoing the moon a little bit but you have to take the opportunity when you get it.

February

February 1st

Tom forgot he had to have his car MOTed (inspected) and he has a colon test this afternoon in Lerwick. I was not going to go with him but he really wanted company so I finally agreed. With Dean arriving on Monday I definitely need to go to the grocery store so he can have all the things he MUST have when he is here, Shetland beer, ginger shortbread and crisps.

A storm is expected this afternoon with BIG winds. The shipping forecast reads:

South west, backing south east for a time, six to gale eight, increasing severe gale nine, perhaps storm ten later, rain or showers.

This sounds like it will be more severe than the storm earlier in the week.

I am buying a pair of headphones so I can at least watch TV while the wind howls. It really bothers me to have the sound on the TV turned up full blast so I can hear it over the damper rattling. It sounds like a battle between different noises is going on in my living room.

The wrap party for the movie is Sunday night and the director, Shetland liaison and the programme co-ordinator have invited us. Each one gave a different time so I am not sure what time we should show up. They are running ahead of schedule and should finish about noon on Sunday. They seem pleased with how it has all gone. I hope I get to see some more rushes on Sunday night, as it will be a long time until the movie is out.

Speaking of movies, *Lord of the Rings* is coming to Shetland. Dean, Tom and I are going to go. We do not have a dedicated movie theatre here but it will be at the Garrison Theatre where they usually present plays.

February 2nd

Sunshine made me think I could hang clothes outside but once out there I realized my clothes would end up in the Arctic Circle as force eight winds are coming out of the south. Not even my storm pegs would have held the clothes on the line. There was spectacular surf and so I got the camera. I am still trying to get the most dramatic picture of the cliff's surf and a picture of the blowhole doing its thing but the wind was so strong I could not hold the camera still. The tripod won't work as it got blown over this morning. There are a couple of sheltered places where I was able to get a few pictures.

The trip to Lerwick was difficult as the weather was horrendous with gales and heavy, heavy rain. I got all of my groceries. Dean will be able to have his favourite Shetland things. On the trip home the sun broke through and the sky was full of rainbows, some of the brightest I have ever seen with many of them being double and triple. It started to rain again just after we got all of the groceries unloaded.

The earphones for the TV work great. I can hear the TV no matter how noisy the wind. I can still hear the howl and the rattle of the Rayburn's damper but it is not overwhelming. I am getting better at judging how much coal to feed the Rayburn in storm conditions and had no problem this time with it getting too hot from a wind driven-fire.

I am working on my book today and if the sun stays out hopefully Tom will take me to get some more storm pictures. As I get nearer to finishing the book I have a better idea of what pictures would best illustrate the book based on the text.

February 3rd

It was extremely quiet when I got up this morning because the storms have finally moved through and there is just a small breeze. You probably get tired of hearing about the wind all the time but that is the one thing I have to pay attention to from minute to minute. When we first started living on Shetland I wondered why everyone always talked about the weather, especially the wind, but the reason is clear; your life could depend on it.

Yesterday afternoon I talked Tom into taking me for a short ride around the area to get storm pictures. His new Ford Mondeo is quite heavy but it was literally rocking in the wind. Jill, Tom's nervous dog, was so upset by the noise she tore all of the plants out of the window and moved some heavy furniture. When Tom called last night he said she had settled down now that he was in the house. She must have been truly scared without him there.

When we were at Stenness waiting for a heavy shower to pass we saw an otter running in front of the wind trying to get shelter. It headed for Tom's lobster creels where we felt it could get out of the wind. Tom has seen an otter once before near there and Dean saw one at the Bruddans which is not too far away so it could have been the same one. I quickly tried to take a picture but all I got was a brown blur. They move fast and he was probably being helped by the wind.

Today is the wrap party for the film. It would be great fun for me but I am afraid someone might act conceited like they did in town on Up Helly Aa night. Tom does not like social events and keeps changing his mind whether he wants to go. When he called last night he wanted to go again but who knows where he will be today. With the improved weather maybe he will still be positive. They are holding it in Aith, which is hard to reach from here so we would be driving a very bad road late at night. Right now I am leaning toward not going but I will wait and see what Tom says.

Sunday dinner is pork roast and gravy with clapshot, pea salad and orange pudding cake.

February 4th

The Laird is in London. He said he got bored so he called me. I can tell nothing has changed. I will be glad to see him. Our weather is supposed to get bad later but I think he will be in before it hits. I hope so.

Tom and I did not go the wrap party. The more we talked about it the more I felt he really did not want to go. He kept trying to tell me he would go if I wanted to but I was just not into it that much. I e-mailed my regrets and got some great e-mails back.

I just baked a rhubarb upside down cake as a welcome present for Dean. We're picking him up at Sumburgh and then Tom is taking us into town for fish and chips before we drive home.

I am really becoming a sky watcher as explained by this excerpt from my next *Lighthouse Digest* column.

> Living at a lighthouse has transformed me into a sky watcher; my eyes constantly turn toward the heavens here. Since trees block the view of the sky on our farm in Michigan I seldom look up.
>
> My understanding of how much I have changed has been pointed out in the last few weeks. While editing my next book, *A Year at the Lighthouse*, (to be published in September 2002), I was astonished how many pages related to sky happenings. It seems the most spectacular events at Eshaness involve sunsets, rainbows, clouds, the Northern Lights, the moon, and of course the lighthouse beacon.

The best way to share these is with photographs so this column contains more pictures than usual.

Eshaness is located on the west coast of Shetland so every night the sun sets over the North Atlantic. Now, I have to admit many times we do not see anything because of clouds or fog but when it is clear at the end of the day, beauty takes your breath away. Sunsets come in all colours including pink, purple and orange.

Shetland has hundreds of rainbows. The frequent rain showers that zip through the island probably generate the large number of these exquisite arches. Yesterday on a trip back from Lerwick I saw lots of rainbows including double and triple ones. They are hard to photograph, as the colours seem to fade in pictures, but my camera and I keep chasing them.

We have the most interesting clouds. Clouds around the ocean seem always to be changing not only in shape but in colour. Probably my favourites are the ones back lighted by the sun.

When the Aurora Borealis, the Northern Lights, takes over the night sky I always dash outside. Standing below the rotating lighthouse beacon I am overwhelmed watching it play in a dancing sky. I knew the farther north the better the Northern Lights are and our lighthouse is as far north as Anchorage, Alaska so we get tremendous displays that take over the entire sky. I have seen red and green Northern Lights but they also come in shades of yellow, pink, and light purple. Northern Lights are one of my favourite sky things but as of yet I have not been able to take a picture of them.

A full moon over the ocean is an incredible sight. Many nights when the full moon casts shadows on the landscape I walk along the road just to be part of the magic. A full moon beside a lighthouse beacon is extra special and the picture of the Eshaness beacon with the moon is one of my all time favourites.

A huge storm has held us in its grip for the last few days but the sun is breaking through the clouds in golden streaks toward the sea so it time to abandon the computer and do some sky watching.

February 5th

Well this is my second try at this entry as Dean deleted it trying to look at some of his e-mail.

I just got him out of bed (maybe I should have left him there until I finished my writing) so he could get his body onto UK time. If you do not adjust to the different time right away you find yourself mixed up the entire trip.

His trip went very smoothly and he even arrived in Shetland early. Tom and I had taken a new road to the airport and arrived just a couple of minutes after his plane so it was perfect. We next went to Lerwick for a fish supper where Tom and

Dean had fresh haddock, chips and peas. I love their mashed potatoes so I had fresh haddock and mash. Dean said it was unpatriotic to eat mash at a fish and chip shop. When we got home we had the rhubarb and ginger upside down cake with a cup of tea. Tom then had to go as he was on duty last night.

Our plan for today is to take a short walk after Dean takes a bath, but since it is pouring down rain I think we may have to revise the plans. It is warm and we have only a little wind so it would be a great day to be outside if it would stop raining.

I cooked a big pot of porridge on the Rayburn so Dean has hot cereal for breakfast. Right now the Rayburn is boiling eggs as the chickens are blessing us with three hen fruit a day. That is a lot of eggs so I will be feeding Dean eggs the entire time he is here. We eat two egg whites and only one yolk to keep our cholesterol down.

The fish van is due today and I am sending Dean out to buy whatever he wants. It will be interesting to see what he comes back with; we may eat fish all week.

February 6th

I'm having trouble getting the Laird out of bed but now he is talking to me so that is progress. It is a beautiful morning with no wind, and warm. This is not supposed to last through the day so Dean should get up and take advantage of it.

We walked to the Bruddans yesterday and saw one lonely seal taking a 'cloud bath'. There was no sun but he or she was out on the rocks soaking up the rays of the clouds. Dumb seal. The surf was pretty spectacular and I took a neat picture of Dean standing on the edge of a cliff with many layers of clothing on just to prove he was here.

Dean bought out the fish van yesterday by getting four monk tails, four fresh halibut fillets and four kippers. Tom is coming for lunch today and I will fix kippers and eggs for them since I am not real fond of kippers. They are too salty. For dinner last night I baked the monk tails in fresh lime juice with freshly grated lime zest on top. I also made twice-baked potatoes with yoghurt and chives and we had a tossed salad to finish off the meal. Desert was coffee later followed by stem ginger shortbread so I am feeding the Laird well.

We went down to the pier to fish but only stayed five minutes as Dean lost his lures and broke the line on my rod. He caught a big buoy that helps anchor our neighbour Ronnie's boat so, as Dean put it, we only caught a buoy so far on this trip.

I had a telephone call from a German television producer who had read my books. They have a producer in Shetland and want to feature the lighthouse. They are coming on Friday to recce. It is neat that Dean will be here to meet the producer since he is the one with German ancestors.

I am off to hang clothes outside to take advantage of such a nice day.

February 7th

Dean is about to see a storm. The wind has been rising all morning and is supposed to swing west and rise to force nine, which is a strong gale. He and Tom are out cleaning the chickens' house and nests before it gets worse. I told Dean I would pay him if he could get a picture of the blowhole. When the wind is in the west the blowhole really does its thing.

Yesterday since it was still and warm Dean got up on the roof and filled cracks, which he thought might be causing some damp in the house. Dean always ends up on the roof when he is here since the views are so great. Tom fixed some broken wires in the fence and I dried clothes outside so we all made use of the fine day.

It looks like the German TV spot might mean some book sales, so two of my publishers who have distributors in Germany want to have further contact with the German television people.

It does not seem possible but the publisher wants a summary of the next book for the London Book Fair where he is going to try to sell foreign rights. As I come closer and closer to finishing the book I realize this year's stay will be over in a couple of months. Most of it I have enjoyed but there have been some bad moments like September 11th, the death of my dog and Dean's injury, my horrible trip back from the USA after Christmas and being sick.

February 8th

I have the house to myself as Dean has gone off with Tom to Hillswick. Tom has an appointment with the physiotherapist and then was going to the shop to get the *Shetland Times* so Dean decided to go with him. Writing the summary of the next book for the London Book Fair is taking most of my time. I just finished a draft, which Dean will look over for me. Hopefully I can send it in today.

Yesterday was a nasty day. Dean got to experience his first big wind storm last night as the winds shifted to the west and really went to it.

Yesterday Dean cleaned the vacuum cleaners. He made a mess but got the task accomplished. In a few minutes I will use them to tidy up a little before the Germans arrive. We are only meeting today so I do not want to spend too much time cleaning but when they come to film I will make a big effort to make this place look spick and span.

We had salt herring and tatties for dinner last night. This is an old Shetland dish and Tom provided the salt herring. I soaked the herring twice before I cooked it with the tatties so it was not as salty as some I have had. I have had enough fish so I am making a meat loaf for dinner.

The two shoppers are back so I guess I will see what they got to go with a cup of coffee.

February 9th

Dean and Tom are about to take off to get my Flecket (black and white spotted) sheep. It is warm and not too windy so it should be a great day for being outside. I cannot go as they are taking the pickup and it is too cold to ride in the back the way I did when Connie was here.

The producer and her assistant from German National Public Television turned up two hours early yesterday and I was still vacuuming the floor. They are doing a series on the Stevensons' lighthouses. Eshaness is the last manned lighthouse built by a Stevenson (David A), so we are probably going to be the last one filmed. The film crew will arrive in April and the program will be aired in September. We certainly have had a lot of film activity for being winter.

My problems with one of my publishers are continuing and now I know what a nightmare it can be to choose the wrong publisher. I have promised myself I will check references carefully on any new publishers I allow to have my work.

Tonight I am making Lobster Newburgh. Tom gave me two small lobsters for Dean to have when he was here. There is not enough meat to serve us each a whole one but between the two I could make a good dish with cream sauce.

While the guys are gone getting the lambs I will finish my summary of the new book and work a little on the main text. I am a little behind so it is a good time to catch up.

There is going to be a Harry Hay auction next week and Dean will get to go. They are advertising tools so this may cost us.

February 10th

(An entry from my husband, Dean.) Sharma says I've been relaxing too much and should get off my … and do some work so I'm writing for her this morning.

I will take this opportunity to correct the record in many areas and provide the truth to counteract some of the scurrilous things that have been said about me in previous sections.

First of all since I am 'The Laird' it is proper and appropriate that I get 'waited on hand and foot' and there should be faster service and less complaining. The situation deteriorated so much last night that I had to pop my own popcorn in the microwave. Actually the food has been great even if the service was a bit surly. When Tom and I got back from picking up Sharma's sheep yesterday she had made lobster salad sandwiches, which is something that I could get used to very quickly. This wasn't done for my pleasure however – the big freezer's compressor locked up and the lobsters had started to thaw. Sharma caught it in time so we didn't lose any food, just will be eating ground beef for a while. The small freezer was about empty so everything from the big one could be moved. Don't know what to do about the big freezer; I'll plug it back in today and see if it might work.

Let me set you straight on 'Sharma's' sheep. I paid for them. Tom and I went to pick them up, wrestled them into the truck, put tags in their ears and then had to chase them when they went into the wrong field when we got them back. Sharma assisted by staying in the car. Tom will have the privilege of taking care of them too. They are pretty and I think it's important to maintain the old breeding lines, too often the old breeds die out and all the genetic advantages that have built up over many years are lost. The older I get the more I'm in favour of maintaining 'old' genetics.

I haven't been fishing since I caught the buoy. Once you've caught something as exotic as a buoy it's hard to get excited about catching common things such as fish. I have a great talent for hooking large, mostly immovable objects such as buoys and rocks so I'm a driving economic force in the fishing tackle industry. If the weather improves I hope I'll get another chance to lose tackle.

The wind picked up yesterday afternoon to about 25–38 miles per hour according to the weather forecast (strong breeze to near gale on the Beaufort Scale). The waves looked about 3 to 4 metres tall (10 to 13 feet) when I walked down to the Bruddans. Sharma doesn't go down there when the wind picks up and she is probably right. I didn't get knocked down but certainly had to walk angled into the wind. It was hard to get used to how fast the wind speed could change. I'd be leaning to counteract a gust and then the wind would almost die and I'd stagger a few feet before I could regain my balance. If you happened to walk behind an outcrop (which could be 50 to 100 feet away) the wind would instantly quit – then as soon as you walked out of the wind shadow you'd get hit again – sometimes in the space of a couple of feet. I really had to watch where I was walking and a couple of times a gust caught me as I was making a step with one foot in the air, which sent me off in a pirouette. It would have been laughable to watch me – probably looked like I had been in a bar all afternoon.

I took some pictures of the spray plumes (they call them 'smoke' here), the clouds and the waves. I could have gotten more spectacular ones but I have to admit I was scared to get too close to the edge of the cliffs. However wild I thought it was the local citizens were taking it in their stride since I saw a seal calmly swimming in the channel between the inner and outer groups of rocks at the Bruddans. It didn't seem to be the least excited about the situation.

I tried to call our friend Robert Macdonald last night but he was at a meeting about the local fair that is held on his farm every year. This fair is one of the largest and most prestigious animal shows in the Highlands but with the rules about foot and mouth in place, if they bring the animals onto the farm he cannot move any of his animals off for 21 days. It would be impossible to not be able to sell any animals during that time so the fair may have to be moved to another site.

I'll sign off now since the weekly farm show is starting on the BBC and Sharma is hovering over this in order to write her rebuttal.

February 11th

It is snowing, it is snowing, the old man is snoring. Actually the old man (Dean) is out wandering around in the snow while I write on the book. We only have a little bit of snow and it will be turning to rain quite soon.

Today I am baking a lemon meringue pie for Dean for his birthday, which is in March. It is a family tradition and since I will not be with him for his birthday he is getting it early. Tomorrow or Wednesday morning I will bake a trifle for Tom and Dean for Valentine's Day. I have not been to town to buy presents so food will have to do.

Yesterday's dinner turned out well. We had roast chicken, clapshot, parsnips and a chocolate whipped cream pudding that we had to eat because my freezer stopped working. Everything was eaten so I guess it was a success.

After dinner we went fishing at Eshaness Pier and Dean caught three very small fish. From Dean's perspective this trip has been a success because he has caught some fish no matter how big.

I took some pictures of my Fleckets who are named Sarah and Jenny after the Macdonald girls. Sarah has four small dots on her nose forming a square while Jenny's nose spots are bigger and more random. Both have beautiful fleece with random spots like Holstein cows. Both should be with lamb as they ran with a Flecket ram for a while. I cannot wait until my herd grows by two.

The caddies were only on loan so these are my first sheep. They seem to be settling in well at Tom's house.

My friend, Judith Friend, gave me two beautiful carved hedgehogs, one of which I brought to the lighthouse. It is on the mantle over the fireplace in the office with a small plaque about living near the sea she gave me a long time before we got the lighthouse. They are sitting beside the picture of my beloved dog Kiri, which I cannot bear to put away. Above the mantle is my brother's painting of Yosemite Falls, which he painted from one of my photographs.

This is a special day for me as it is my dad's birthday. Even though he died two years ago I always think about him on February 11th. For many years I spent this day in Florida with him. There is a big difference between Florida and Shetland in February.

February 12th

I must wake up the Laird as it is after nine. He has been staying up after I go to bed and flicking around the digital television channels. Since we do not have cable TV on the farm in Michigan it is a real treat for him. He wants to clean the chicken house and today would be a good day to do it, as it is clear with little wind. It is cold but shovelling will keep him warm.

We are hoping for a clear night so maybe we will see the Northern Lights. They saw them in Orkney just a few days ago but skies here must have been cloudy and we did not see anything.

Only three more days then Dean will be gone. It has really been fun. Since we did not rent a car we have stayed here most of the time and I imagine when Dean retires this is what it will be like. GREAT! We will need a car then though as I am not sure Dean could go more than a couple of weeks without a newspaper.

Tomorrow we are off to Lerwick for the auction and Dean is developing a list of things he wants to buy. I am going to need groceries as we are out of crisps, cookies, and munchies. The poor Laird has been going through withdrawal. I think he might even be out of beer. On Thursday Dean wants to go to Lerwick to shop for presents for people back in the US and then he will go on to the Sumburgh Hotel to stay the night. Staying in the hotel makes it easier to get the 7:50 flight, especially in winter when the weather is so unpredictable. If we take the bus in we could go see *Lord of the Rings*. Then I would take the bus back to Eshaness and Dean would go to the hotel. It might be a nice way to end his visit.

Off to wake up the Laird and then work a little on the book. I am getting near the end of the draft and have over half of it edited. It is a good feeling when a book starts to take shape.

February 13th

Snow came down in large icy flakes last night so we were treated to a beautiful display of crystals in the beacon streaking across the sky. When I got up this morning I expected to see snow on the ground but there was not one patch of white. It is cold with a north wind but the sun is shining and it looks beautiful.

Dean cleaned the chicken house and put new bedding down for the chickens yesterday. They are a little confused by nice clean bedding as I found them sleeping on the cold concrete when I opened their door this morning. They also did not lay any hen fruit this morning. I guess Dean spending so much time with them was too much of a trauma.

We are getting ready for an afternoon in Lerwick. Dean will do some shopping and I will stock up on groceries. The main reason for the trip is to go to the Harry Hay sale tonight. Dean's list of things to look for has grown quite long. He says if we do not make a list we will forget something. I always just go and when I see something I want I try to get it. The sales are a Shetland history lesson and everyone I have taken to one has loved it. Dean, I am sure, will be no exception.

Yesterday I baked a toffee custard cake for the guys for Valentine's Day. It was to be a trifle but I did not have some of the ingredients. The cake has a rich layer of custard in the middle and then has a toffee glaze on the outside. I have no idea how it tastes but we are supposed to have some when Tom comes to pick us up for the sale.

I need to get back to my book since Dean has finally gotten some of it edited. Dean is standing over my shoulder editing as I write and that is enough to drive anyone crazy. He is off for a walk with my camera so maybe I will be able to write without supervision!

February 14th

I got a bag of conversation hearts, small heart shaped candies with sayings on them, from Dean for Valentine's Day. Dean and Tom got my toffee cake, which turned out to be really first-rate.

Yesterday we went to Lerwick and replenished my depleted food supply along with Dean buying things to take home. It is amazing that now we take home foods we cannot get in the States like brown sauce for our grandson, Branston pickle (made out of beets) and particular kinds of candy.

Dean, Tom and I went to the Harry Hay sale last night after having fish and chips at Tom's favourite take away. I bought some cake pans including a spring form pan, a beautiful glass salad bowl, a nice casserole dish and two handy soup bowls with bread and butter plates. Dean got a set of drill bits, some screwdrivers, a knife sharpening stone, and a fishing tackle box full of gear. The tackle box was most needed as we did not have one and we keep losing tackle when we fish. Tom got a rug for in front of his Rayburn, a set of fishing poles and a collection of oils, greases, and fibreglass (car stuff).

My final purchase was a mistake but turned out better than I thought. I bought seven book compilations of cartoons (*The Broons* and *Oor Wullie*) for our grandson, Austin. Right after I bought them I found out they are collector's items. This morning I checked used bookstores on the Internet and they have doubled in value since being printed, around £5 each when bought new and now more than £10 each. I paid £1 for my seven books. Dean had already decided Austin would not like them as they have lots of Scots language that he would not understand, so I am going to try and sell them through *Scottish Radiance*. With all the Scottish humour they should be popular with ex-patriots. If that does not work then I will sell them to a used bookstore. I often sell my Scottish books to a used bookstore in Nova Scotia.

Today, we are going to see *Lord of the Rings*, which will be my first big screen movie in over a year. They only bring extremely popular movies to Shetland since we do not have a cinema. The films are shown at the regular theatre. I tried to get bus connections so I could spend the night with Dean at the hotel but it is just not possible without having to spend all day in Lerwick and there is no place to go as the library is moving into new quarters. That was a disappointment.

February 15th

Dean just called and told me 'they broke the rubber band on the airplane bringing it in last night' so there is no early morning plane. He is renting a car and is on his way back here. I am glad. It will be fun to have him for another weekend. He is supposed to leave Monday now. A nice surprise, except I just finished washing up his boiler suits and towels.

Speaking of clothes, I had a major fright this morning. I hung Dean's boiler suits (blue coveralls for those in the US) on the line in a gale force seven wind (quite brisk). I came back in, sat down at the computer and looked out the window to see no boiler suits were on the line. I did not see them on the ground and I had a vision of blue boiler suits on their way to Ronas Hill. The wind is in the southwest so they at least would not go to the US or Iceland. When I got outside I found that the lighthouse had stopped their journey and they were wedged into the corner by the tower. When will I ever learn how to get clothes dried here without a major crisis? They are now hanging safely inside and there they will stay until dry. They are heavy and dry slowly so Dean may not be able to wear them this weekend.

Going to see *Lord of the Rings* was a special and wonderful experience. Films are shown at the Garrison Theatre, which is mostly used for live performances. It has recently been renovated and the seats are brand new and quite comfortable. We had wonderful seats right in the middle half way up and Dean remarked it was the first time we ever have had reserved seating for a movie. The sound system was state of the art and we were totally surrounded by the sound. They have a large screen (bigger than most theatres we have been in the US) so it could not have been better. *Lord of the Rings* is a cinematic masterpiece – the visual effects are out of this world, literally. I was impressed with the pure beauty of some of the scenes. We watched the credits and were not surprised to see it was filmed in New Zealand, Australia, the UK, and the US. The actor's performances were top notch. It got something like 13 Academy Award nominations and deserved every one.

It really put me in the mood to get writing on my book, which is destined for a movie. *Lord of the Rings* started out as a book and look what happened to it. I am often frustrated that I spend my time writing guide books about lighthouses when I want to write a novel, but it is my own fault as I choose the more secure money of the lighthouse books. The novel is a bigger gamble. I have no doubt I can write a good one but whether it is made into a movie has yet to be seen. This weekend Dean and I will talk more about my next book being the novel instead of another lighthouse book. It will make a difference in our income in the short term but might make a positive difference in the long run.

February 16th

Dean and I are about to leave to see my Fleckets and caddies. I do like my sheep. The weather is quite windy but not cold.

The Northmavine Up Helly Aa was last night. We thought we might go but I came down with a cold and the weather was really bad. Dean decided we would stay home and watch TV. Since I felt worse as the evening progressed I was glad we stayed home.

Hopefully the wind will die so Dean can get out of here on Monday. Right now I doubt a plane would be able to take off. But it is nice to have him here, especially since I have caught cold. Dean said that it must be tough to be here when you are sick and it really is, as you have to tend the Rayburn, take out the ashes and feed the chickens in the wind and rain. I do not know where I got this cold but I wish it would go back where it came from. Dean does not want it.

Dean is standing by all of the heat sources so he must be cold. He has been proof reading my book at the corner desk by the window where it is draughty.

Little things mean a lot here such as a night on TV with all the programs I like. This is one of those nights so it will be great to just curl up under a comforter and watch some of my favourites; *Stars in Their Eyes, Blind Date,* and *Who Wants to be a Millionaire?* They may not be the greatest quality TV in the world but they are fun. I watch no TV in the States but here I really enjoy it. I call it my culture lesson, as television is very different in the UK.

This afternoon Dean gets the TV to watch Six Nations Rugby. Ugh! I will work on my book or maybe just take a nap.

February 17th

Dean is waiting for me to finish this so we can go for a walk. It is a beautiful sunny, warm and calm day here. I had a virus scare on my computer this morning and it took me a while to deal with that but I just got a clean Norton scan so all is well.

Yesterday was raw and extremely windy. We drove down to Tom's to see my caddies and the Fleckets. The Fleckets were bad. They had gotten through a neighbour's gate and were in his field. Tom is annoyed at the neighbour because he keeps leaving the gate open so Tom's sheep go through.

Dean made a huge pot of Shetland cabbage soup yesterday afternoon. It has swedes, Shetland cabbage, potatoes, onions, tomatoes, garlic, Worcester sauce and malt vinegar in it. I am giving a big pan to Tom and we will have the rest for supper.

We are going to the Weisdale Mill for lunch. It is a converted mill, which has two museums and sells Shetland crafts. It is a great day for a ride and this will allow the guys to get the Sunday newspapers in Brae. We were supposed to go so I would not have to cook since I have been sick but I think the real reason is to get the papers.

February 18th

Dean left about a quarter to six this morning so I have been up a long time. It takes a little over an hour to drive to the airport and he needed to be there by 7:00 am. I am a little worried that his flight did not go with our strong westerly winds. The computer said the plane was on time so maybe it was okay. I should hear from him in Aberdeen if he makes it.

It was really nice to have Dean longer and I almost wish the plane would not go today but he needs to get back.

I did try to go back to sleep; it was so cosy and warm in bed with the wind howling outside. But once awake I am out of bed for the day so I did this month's financial accounts. I just finished and it is a little before 9:00. The rest of the day will be spent writing.

Yesterday it was a beautiful day until late afternoon when the rain and wind started. We went to Weisdale Mill for dinner. Tom and I had chicken roasted in wine and mustard, red potatoes in a yoghurt dill sauce, a wonderful salad of mixed greens with cherry tomatoes and English toffee crème coffee. Dean had a starter of peanut and sweetcorn soup. His main course was roasted pepper and cashew paté on wholegrain bread. He is not a vegetarian but he ate like one yesterday. I was the only one who had dessert; a bilberry tart served warm with cream. Bilberries taste a lot like blueberries but are a lot smaller. Everything was excellent.

I was disappointed the textile museum was not open. It is supposed to have exhibits of weaving, spinning and wool. I will have to go back again to see the museum and of course eat.

The area around the mill is so different from here. It is in a valley surrounded by rolling high hills. A burn (stream) runs down the centre of the valley to the mill and you can see the ocean in the distance. There are a lot of trees including some monkey-puzzle trees. Dean was amazed the monkey-puzzle tree could grow here.

I think I will need to live on coffee to get through the day so I guess I will have a cup before I begin editing.

February 19th

It is the middle of the afternoon and I had to stop working on the book to describe the weather. The sun is out right now but there is a cold north west wind. The sea outside the office window is the most beautiful grey blue colour. There are huge swells with gleaming white tops. If you watch it too long you almost get seasick.

I do not have to worry about watching too long as the sea spray blows up over the top of the lighthouse at times and blocks the view. I was having a cup of coffee with Tom in the Rayburn room and happened to look out the window and saw sea spray coming over the roof. Now that is a storm. I decided the next lull in the storm I would run out and get my coal for the night. I miss Dean already for many reasons; one of which is he would go out and get coal for me before dark. Now I am back to doing it myself.

When I return to the USA I will not miss taking care of the Rayburn. First thing every day when I get up I have to clean out the ashes. It is a messy, dirty and sometimes dangerous job as I have burned myself a couple of times. Then all during the day you have to remember to put coal in it. If it is cold, you might have to feed it every hour or hour and a half, which I see as constant attention. Then no matter what the weather, you have to go out and get coal to replenish what has burned. We have talked and talked about converting it to oil but that is out because of the listed building regulations. Having said that I must admit it provides good heat, lots of hot water, and cooks most meals. It was just while Dean was here to help that I realized how nice it was not to have to do it all by myself.

I decided to brave the storm and get some sunset pictures. It was awfully hard to hold the camera still but the sky was so beautiful I really wanted to try and capture it. I am not sure the pictures do the moment justice but they do show the pale sky.

February 20th

Snow, snow everywhere! We probably got three to four inches of snow last night along with winds straight out of the east at gale force eight (42 miles an hour). The temperature is just freezing but the wind chill is 14°F, unbelievably cold for Shetland.

I think the winds are dying down. When the winds are in the east the quietest and warmest place in the house is the office. With the wind, the snow has drifted fairly high in spots. There is a big drift in front of the gate to the parking area but I just left it as no cars are going or coming today. There was a small drift in front of the chicken house, which I dug out so the chickens could be fed and watered. They did not seemed bothered at all by the wind and snow, as it was warm in their house.

I am a little worried about the weather in the next few days. The direction of the wind is supposed to change but the speed is to increase and we just might be up to violent storm by Saturday, one step below hurricane.

For the first time I was awakened by the sound of the wind. Thank goodness it was 5:45 as I could not go back to sleep. We seldom get winds out of the east so I guess the sound was not only loud but also unusual. Getting up I tended the Rayburn right away as the electricity went off for a while during the night and I wanted to be sure I had heat not dependent on electricity. I also made a casserole of scalloped potatoes and ham that I could put in the oven in the Rayburn if the electricity fails.

Tuesday is always a busy day with the arrival of the fish van in the early afternoon and yesterday was also the day for the library van. It was after two o'clock and neither had come. The roads had been icy early in the morning so I thought they just weren't coming. Then the library van came and just as I started looking for books the fish van came. I did not have any money with me so I had to run back into the house to get money to pay for my monk tails and as I came back out a *Devil's Gate's* costume designer caught me. I really wanted to talk to her but both vans were waiting. So I excused myself, got my fish and got my books. By the time I finished with the books the *Devil's Gate* person had taken off. It makes me chuckle when I think of a person with a piece of fish wrapped in paper in her hand looking at library books; only in Shetland. Most of the time no one but Tom comes here but yesterday everyone came at once. Such is life.

February 21st

Well the winds are still doing their thing. We are at force eight, which is gale force. This should continue for another couple of days then will drop to a slight breeze over the weekend. I had real trouble walking when I fed the chickens and emptied the ashes. I am glad I have the book to work on, as being outside is not an option.

Winter is a great time to be here to write but not so good to enjoy the scenery. One thing I hoped would come out of this year long stay was what times of year I liked best at Eshaness. I still have March and early April to go but the winners hands down so far are spring and fall. Summer is nice but there are too many tourists. It will be difficult to leave here at the end of April with spring beginning, but I need to get home to my family. Hopefully next year I can schedule a spring and fall visit.

Yesterday was spent working on the book until the afternoon when I was going to watch a movie on TV. I thought it would be a nice reward to myself for spending hours and hours at the computer rewriting. Well, when I turned on the TV the digital service was out. I called the service number and they helped me reset the digital receiver. The power dips the night before had turned it off. The thought of not having TV was a little unsettling but not a disaster, as I read as much or more than I watch TV. Tom thought it was a major catastrophe as he watches TV all the time.

After the TV was fixed and I had settled down to watch the movie, the phone rang and it was one of my publishers. We talked about many issues and he seems willing to correct many of the problems so it was a productive conversation. But when we got done my movie was over. So much for rewarding myself for a day working hard on the book.

Maybe I will try again today, as there is a pretty good movie on at 3:30 and no *Ready Steady Cook* later. I realized when I got up this morning the way you enjoy being in an isolated place is to deliberately plan your day. More and more I get up each morning and plan my day so that being alone is not an issue. When I am at the farm I pretty much do the same thing. Dean works a lot of nights so many days are just like here except that I have more telephone contact with friends and family.

This morning before I started on the computer I baked banana bread and muffins, as the fruit was very ripe. Today's schedule is work on the book, take a break for lunch, talk to Tom if he drops by, watch movie and news on TV and then finish the current book I am reading.

February 22nd

It is Friday and the gales and rain are still here. I had hoped I could get outside today, as I am feeling a little claustrophobic. Not that I don't have plenty to do. I have clothes in the washer which I will put on the inside line to dry since outside they would end up in Lerwick as the wind is in the west. Actually when I think about it they would really end up plastered against the lighthouse building.

I have not finished a few changes from Dean's editing on the new book and it is time for *Scottish Radiance* again so I could start on that. I might just clean the house too if I have time after the computer stuff.

It is a good thing the weekend is here as all the work on the computer is bothering my eyes. Last night when I tried to read or watch TV they kept watering. They seemed fine when I looked at them in the mirror but they still fill with tears and I am not crying. Maybe being out in the severe winds causes it but I was only out twice for short times. Hopefully today my eyes will not give me so much trouble. When I get back in the States I will have them examined.

Tom came up yesterday afternoon and we played Mastermind and checkers. He was upset as I beat him every game in Mastermind so I decided to play checkers to make him feel better. It was amazing but I did really well in checkers. He won but not by much, which is a total change as he usually has me on the way to defeat early in the game. I do not think he liked me doing so well. In fact I would bet he went home and practised on the computer. Tom and I have been playing these two games on bad days ever since Dean and I bought the lighthouse.

I would go to Lerwick today by bus if the library was open but they are moving into the beautiful restored church and will not reopen until the first of March. Without the library there is no place to spend a long period of time if I run out of shopping. We are scheduled to go to Lerwick on Tuesday, as the hospital wants to see Tom. He is worried since all he was told is he is to see a surgeon. He is convinced there is something seriously wrong with him. I keep urging him to call our GP and ask but he won't do it.

I am considering writing an Eshaness Lighthouse cookbook. If I have time after I finish the current book I might play around with it in the short time before I go home. Everyone seems to rave about the wonderful meals made out of the things I can get way out here.

February 23rd

I have been out taking pictures, mostly with the digital but some with the 35mm as I think they might reproduce better. I keep taking the cliffs looking for the very best picture ever but the cliffs always make good photos. Maybe if I knew exactly what I wanted it would be easier.

Many of my friends thought the cookbook was a good idea and I even had offers of recipes. I will credit whoever with the recipe used, such as Margaret Macdonald's wonderful Christmas cake. The title for the book could be *Cooking at Eshaness Lighthouse* – original huh? It would be recipes for things cooked at the lighthouse, basically Scotland/Shetland food, ocean based dishes combined with dishes from Michigan and other places that have been served here. An example is porridge with Michigan dried cherries in it. I want to query some of my publishers to see if they would publish it. The most logical place is *Shetland Times* Publishing but maybe another publisher would be interested.

February 24th

Another Sunday has arrived. How do I know? I water plants and cook dinner for Tom. Dinner today is going to be different as I am roasting chicken thighs in a creamy honey and mustard sauce in the Rayburn. I warned Tom that we would not have a roast today. I am making stovies and frozen mixed vegetables will accompany the chicken dish. Pudding is an old-fashioned custard pie. I am making a big pot of chicken broth on top of the Rayburn from the bones of the chicken since last week when Dean was here we had soup on Sunday night and it was great so I am doing it again. It will be some kind of chicken, rice and vegetable soup, since that is all I have in the house.

The gales and frequent sleet showers are continuing so I doubt Tom will take me for a ride. We will probably play Mastermind and checkers. Yesterday I did not do so well at checkers but I seem to always beat Tom at Mastermind now. I saw our checkerboard has backgammon on the back so maybe I will read the instructions and try that. If this bad weather continues we are going to look for a new game at the charity shops in Lerwick.

Last night I had to use the head phones to listen to TV as the wind was rattling the damper on the Rayburn. I watched a couple of network shows but mainly I watched a movie called *Little Big Man* with Dustin Hoffman. I had never seen it before and it was excellent. Even as a young kid Dustin could really act. I taped *Rob Roy* last night so I will watch it when TV is slow this week.

Speaking of films, tonight is the British Academy awards so I am going to be glued to my TV set for a couple of hours while they are on. Maybe my friend Anthony Hopkins will be on, or someone from *Devil's Gate*. It seems more personal to watch the awards after meeting some of the people.

I'm getting a little antsy since I can't get outside very much and have not done anything special. Sometimes I make my own fun by choosing special movies to tape, playing games, or planning an evening around a special event on TV. Books are always not far away but with the main library closed my selection of books not read is decreasing. I am finishing a Colin Dexter Inspector Morse novel and I have a shelf full of Booker prize winners that have not been opened so I might launch into one of those.

February 25th

I have been outside hiking around. The ground is frozen with patches of ice on it but we have no wind. None! I took both cameras but there was hardly any surf and not enough snow for snow photographs. I got one picture of Foula covered by snow that I am going to put in *Scottish Radiance*.

I opened the chickens' door and they immediately ran out. I guess we all felt like caged animals set free. Before I knew it they were on the sea side digging at the grass that was peeking through the snow and they are still outside destroying the grass.

The Rayburn is barely burning, as there is not enough wind to cause a draught. It is cold in the house with the temperature below freezing outside and not much heat from the Rayburn. I have my little portable heaters on but I am still cold. I may have to give in and run the wall heaters. They are extremely expensive to run but today that might be the only answer for any comfort.

I watched the British Academy Awards last night and *Lord of the Rings* was the big winner. It deserves any awards it gets. The programme was such a delight in comparison to the US Academy Awards, with no commercials and over in exactly two hours. The US version is probably more important and you see more stars but I hate how it goes on and on and is always breaking for commercials.

I have been corresponding with Stuart St Paul, director of *Devil's Gate*. They will be making the final cut of the film negative this week and then the music and extra sounds will be added. He is off to Cannes to premier it. Lucky guy! I hope it is really good and the audiences love it since they worked so hard. He was not involved in the awards last night but hopes to be within the next few years.

There is bad news from home as Dean's aunt Mary died. This will be the third sister to die in 13 months with Dean's mom being the first a year ago January. This leaves only one brother. It is difficult when you get to our age and watch the members of the family you've loved and have always been a part of your life leave. Aunt Mary and another of Dean's aunts gave us a loan to buy our first house. A wonderful gesture and one I will never forget.

Got to get to work on *Scottish Radiance* as February is a short month, so I have to do things earlier.

February 26th

I will have to make this short as I am going with Tom to the hospital to see the surgeon. He has no idea what the conference is about but I would bet his knee. He is really worried. It is the unknown that scares us the most. He keeps saying they are going to tell him he is dying. I kid him about it a lot but am also a little worried. He is such a great guy and if he gets sick he is alone.

The weather is really bad with force eight winds and rain. Not a nice day to go to Lerwick but I really need food. I have not been in town for almost two weeks and the cupboards are bare.

I have been discussing the cookbook idea with some of my publishers and they like the idea. We will be doing layouts after I finish the current book.

I have become involved with helping save lighthouses in Nova Scotia. They wanted to follow the Scottish model but have a different design where all lighthouses would belong to one group. This may or may not work. Nova Scotia is such a beautiful place and the lighthouses are magnificent. I have visited many of them and want to help in any way I can.

February 27th

Good news, Tom has a slightly enlarged prostate and gallstones. Since neither is giving him too much trouble the doctor was not too concerned. I am printing a document with descriptions of gallstones, symptoms and preventive measures so Tom can learn more about what is wrong. Tom will have trouble with preventive measures since he eats lots of fatty foods. Needless to say he was quite relieved and we celebrated by having a fried fish supper, which he probably shouldn't eat. Such is life.

I got the cupboards all restocked so eating is a little better around here. Tom tried to get kippers downtown and they did not have any so we stopped at McNabs, who are supposed to have the best kippers in Shetland. They did indeed have kippers and they were cheaper than any place else that we had seen them. I have not talked to Tom to see how they taste but the big find was smoked mackerel in different flavours. They marinate the mackerel in different spices before they are smoked. They had many kinds but I got three fillets, one called Florida that had been marinated in citrus zests, one with rosemary garlic, and the final one with lime and sweet pepper. Tonight I will try one of the fillets. I think I will start with the Florida one which the lady at the fishmonger said was the most popular.

Last night I treated myself to a rib eye steak that I had purchased for a little over a pound. Its sell by date was the day I bought it so they had marked it down. I served it with a baked potato and a tarragon and mustard sauce.

This is a 'would you believe it' story. Tom works for Shetland Island Smolts who raise salmon from eggs to sell to the fish farms. They have millions of fish in their tanks and right now each fish is getting inoculated or as they say here getting a jab. They hire lots of extra people to do the inoculation but it will take a long time. I cannot imagine giving a fish a shot but it's even harder to comprehend giving shots to a million fish. I have seen the tanks and jabbing the contents of one would take months. Tom was not sure what the fish were being inoculated for.

February 28th

A grey gloomy day with off and on snow so I am still working on *Scottish Radiance* and will not be out hiking around so it does not matter. The wind has gone down again but for how long, who knows.

There is a big flap in Eshaness. English fishing boats putting out crab and lobster creels have been spotted off Stenness and the lighthouse. Ronnie, our local fisherman, is irate. Yesterday he was in the car park taking pictures of one of the ships and is going to turn them in. The big uproar is because it is thought the English boats do not have licences to fish here while the local boats have to pay thousands of pounds to put their creels out. If you have a small number of creels like Tom and use the catch for your own consumption you do not need a licence but the full-time fishermen like Ronnie spend a lot of money on the licences. What I do not understand is how they know the English boats do not have licences. I have to give the English ship credit as a rough sea really was tossing it around. It will be interesting to follow what happens next.

The Florida smoked mackerel I had for dinner last night was so good just thinking about it makes my mouth water. I think I cooked it too long as it was a bit dry but the flavour was delightful and not salty. I will try the other two later this week and I have not had my weekly monkfish from the fish van. I am going to stir-fry it and then add a sauce of orange juice and zest. Served over brown rice it ought to be pretty good. The idea of writing a cookbook has made me more adventurous with what I cook.

Some big positive publicity must have happened yesterday for *Scottish Lighthouses* since the sales of the book were really high and also sales of *The Last Lighthouse* went up. It is frustrating that I cannot find what was said or where.

I've got to write the reader's letter for *Scottish Radiance* and then it is done for another month except for spending the four hours it takes to check links and do the search engine registration. What a pain!

March

March 1st

I am taking a day off from writing to do something that I have wanted to do for a long time; putting all of the Eshaness pictures on one website so my publisher and I can access them from anywhere. I have room on one of my servers so it is worth the trouble. I might eventually open the site up to the public so they can flip through them. Before I go back to the USA I will be selecting eight of the best for the new book. As I move the pictures around I guess I am working on the new book because I have to look at the pictures, sort and name them.

The weather is windy and cold again. Many of the neighbours, including Tom, are getting depressed because of what they call 'awful weather'. I am not down in the dumps as I have so much to do that I am constantly busy but if I stopped working it might bother me.

The fight over fishing rights is continuing. Yesterday while I was uploading *Scottish Radiance* I heard a helicopter outside. It is not unusual for the coastguard helicopter to be in the area but this time it stayed a long time. It was just hovering off the end of our point with its door open. Ronnie was in the car park and there were two other cars parked just down the road. The helicopter stayed quite a while with the door open and then took off. Tom thinks the boat or boats that were causing the problem were being photographed but I could not see them. They could have been below the cliff where it would have been impossible to see from the house. What they will do with these photographs is yet to be known. Ronnie is determined they are going to stop unlicensed boats. Everyone in the neighbourhood seems to be upset about it.

Tom is due soon with the *Shetland Times* and maybe something about the fishing problem will be in there.

March 2nd

It is a cold, bright day with a light dusting of snow on the ground. Tom called and wanted to know if I wanted to go to an estate sale at the south end of the island. He has to go in that direction to look for a hay bale fork for his new tractor. I said yes, since it would get me out of the house and away from the computer.

I am debating whether I will start using an Internet videotape rental program. I can get videotapes of the newest movies, which come by mail and cost £3.49. I might try it and see how it works.

Yesterday I worked all day cataloguing and moving my Eshaness pictures to the Internet. I am still at it as they take a long time to upload and I have lots of pictures. Hopefully I can pick out the ones for the book next week. Now that March is here we are counting down to the due date of next book. I will begin final proofing and plan to submit the 95% of the document by mid April. It is hard to believe it is time for me to begin thinking about going back to the States.

This weekend I am writing a story entitled *The Movies Come to Eshaness* for *Lighthouse Digest*. I read the script of *Devil's Gate* yesterday while I was uploading pictures and it is pretty dramatic. If the actors did a good job, combined with Shetland scenery, they should have a first-class film. I have been staying in touch with Stuart St Paul by e-mail so I can keep up to date on the film's progress. They should be done with the final print this week, as they want to take it to Cannes. They keep adding to their website (http://www.devilsgate.shetland.co.uk/laura_large.htm), which has a great picture of our lighthouse. They called Eshaness 'The End of the Earth Inn' in the film.

March 3rd

A bright sunny day but every once in a while it rains so hard you cannot see two feet. It is windy but warm. If you are out in the sunshine protected from the wind you do not even need a coat. Washing clothes would have been nice today but they would have blown to Norway, as that is the direction of the strong wind. I am hoping to go for a walk after dinner.

Yesterday's sale had lots of nice things but way too many people for a small community hall; it was hard to see what was being sold. I bid on a wooden Shetland chair that was not the type I really wanted. The chair I want has wings to keep draughts from your shoulders. The chair for sale was in only fair condition and being not exactly what I wanted I pulled out of the bidding before it finally sold for £110. The second item was an antique teapot shaped like a sheep dog. The head came off to pour the water in and the brewed tea came out of its mouth. Bidding was brisk but I finally got it for £12 then I watched in horror as the auctioneer dropped it. It was not broken but badly chipped on one ear. I asked if I could get it for a reduced price since it was damaged but was told no so I gave it back in frustration. Tom had to run an errand and then go to work so I did not get a chance to bid again and there were still some beautiful dishes to come. The best thing about this little episode is I did not spend any money.

Dinner is not the usual Sunday roast. I boned two large pork chops and pounded them thin. Then I cooked the bones and the trimmings from the chops with onion to make a broth. The broth I added to breadcrumbs sage, egg and grated carrots to make a stuffing. I then rolled the thin chops with the stuffing inside and will roast them in the oven. The rest of the meal will be mashed potatoes, cooked fresh carrots and orange segments with a brown sugar sauce. The pudding is a sponge cake with raspberry jam and whipped cream in the middle. Not a bad effort with what I had around here.

My friend Kay found this review of my Irish Lighthouse guide book yesterday and it made me smile.

> Ireland possesses almost 1980 miles of varied and often dramatic coastline, so lighthouses have long played significant and crucial roles in the island's coastal landscape. From the first lighthouse at Hook Head, County Wexford, established in the fifth century and manned by St Dubhan, to the twentieth-century total automation of all Irish lights, these structures have guided and protected seafarers for centuries. The author takes the reader on a lively and insightful tour of 36 lighthouses, starting at The Baily near Dublin on the East Coast and finishing at the 112-foot Haulbowline tower in Carlingford Lough in the north. The histories of the lighthouses and descriptions of the surrounding localities are combined with illuminating anecdotes and accounts of adventures at sea. With 58 beautiful colour photographs, including stunning aerial shots from renowned lighthouse photographers, this compilation is a visual delight; and with a detailed introduction, list of all Irish lights by date of establishment, glossary, bibliography and map, it forms an indispensable companion for all lighthouse enthusiasts and visitors.

This kind of review helps keep a writer going.

March 4th

The wind is gale force nine and I could barely stand up when I took out the ashes and fed the chickens. I no longer wonder why the ferries to the far islands stop running around the middle of February. The worst of winter seems to be from the middle of February until the end of March. The ferries start running again in April so maybe that means the weather will clear by then.

Sunday dinner was a huge success with the stuffed pork chop being particularly good. Today I made a pot of potato and leek soup for lunches this week. Soup in the refrigerator makes easy lunches when I am so busy at the computer.

I just finished this month's column for *Lighthouse Digest*. My *Lighthouse Digest* stories are another type of journal of my stay this year.

> I would never have thought a big screen production would come to Eshaness and definitely not in the winter, but for one bleak and windy day in January, Eshaness Lighthouse was turned into 'The End Of The World Inn' for the film, *Devil's Gate*.
>
> *Devil's Gate* is the story of a girl named Rachael who returns to her island (not called Shetland) home when Rafe, an old boyfriend, falsely informs her that her father, Jake, is dying. Arriving on the island she meets Matt who lends her a hand. The story is full of mystery, dark secrets, and shady characters. When Rachael needs a place to stay for a night she goes to The End Of The World Inn. The hotel has no room for her. In frustration she rushes to the cliff's edge to be called back from destruction by Rafe.
>
> The role of Eshaness in the film began when its director Stuart St Paul, art director Sarah Beaman, and location manager/unit manager (Shetland) Leslie Lowes checked the area in December. After looking around and watching the Eshaness footage in Scottish Lighthouses they determined Eshaness Lighthouse would do just fine. Sarah measured all the various parts of the building, which would need to be added to or changed to transform the lighthouse into an inn. The director determined he wanted dramatic surf along with a beautiful sunset, which, if the weather was right, we could supply. The scenes at Eshaness were only of the outside of the building with the inside of the Inn being shot in another location.
>
> With the art department crew arriving before eight o'clock, the actual day of shooting started early. The first task was to hang a large sign on the tower saying 'Hotel' along with dressing the windows with neon signs to make it look more like a bar/inn. The hanging of the sign was the most difficult as the wind was blowing hard that morning. The art crew, with the help of the Eshaness caretaker, Tom Williamson, got it done so quickly they had time to come into the house for a cup of tea before the next group arrived.
>
> The next crew to arrive were the stunt, costume, and make-up people. They would be staying in the house with the cast involved in the scene taking place at the lighthouse. The production team try to keep the actors comfortable so they can concentrate on their parts. The costume and make-up personnel were never far from the actors.
>
> Then we had to wait for the main contingent that was coming by convoy, as they were filming as they came to Eshaness. Surprisingly they arrived pretty much on time. It was after the whole crew was here that I became convinced that movie making was organized chaos. From a spectator's point of view it

seemed everyone was running around without any order to his or her madness but it soon became evident there was a definite system in place.

The two stars involved in the Eshaness scenes, Laura Fraser and Callum Blue, soon appeared in the house for a hot drink as it was getting colder and nastier outside as the day progressed. I found them friendly and really enjoyed our conversations as they waited for their scenes to be set up.

The other thing that struck me about the making of a film was the amount of waiting as various departments got everything prepared for the next step in the process. This probably affected the actors more than anyone else, as they did not get involved until everything was ready. It did give me a lot of time to talk to the people in the house. Most of our conversation centred on movies and lighthouses. They educated me about movies and I taught them about lighthouses. Everyone, without exception, was fascinated with being inside a lighthouse and many wanted to go up in the tower but few made it because of the busy schedule. Many of the crew have returned to Eshaness to have another look.

It was a fascinating experience for me as I love big screen films and plan to write a script for one in the near future. Since then I have seen the rushes of the footage shot at Eshaness and it is beautiful even if the lighthouse does look a little strange as an inn. The one thing they captured is the remote grandeur and beauty of a lighthouse sitting on the edge of the sea.

Whether *Devil's Gate* is a success at the box office is yet to be seen. But, if you are a lighthouse lover, you should see the film since it dramatically portrays what is so beautiful about these magnificent buildings we all like so much.

March 5th

For a few minutes this morning I thought that I would get out for a walk but just as I was getting ready to leave a storm roared in with heavy-duty winds and stinging sleet. It is fairly calm and sometimes sunny but then terrible blasts of wind, rain and sleet come.

I baked fruit scones for Tom since he announced yesterday that I had not baked scones for him since I came. That is not true but he has been sort of neglected because of all the book stuff I have had to do so I decided to make him feel better by making some goodies.

We are finishing the details for *Northern Lights*, the lighthouse book on Shetland and Orkney, to go to the publisher, *Shetland Times*. We hope to have it out by fall. My text is all written and edited so all I really have to do is respond when needed from here on out. There are always a few changes in the text, photograph selection, cover design and back text that I get involved with.

Today in my e-mail I got pictures of the posters for *Devil's Gate*. They said they would give me one for my office wall, which tickled me.

I started Iris Murdoch's Booker prize winning book *The Sea, the Sea*. The author is the subject of the movie, *Iris*. I only got through the introduction before I doubted whether I wanted to read it. Instead of lauding isolation it says isolation can drive you insane and does not bring peace but despair. Being in such an isolated situation I decided I should not be exposed to the premise of this book so I stopped reading it. It will get packed and taken to the States to read when I am not alone.

Last night the wind rattling the plastic protectors on the windows, the sleet clicking as it hit the window and the damper rattling on the Rayburn gave me a strange sort of peace. I felt secure inside this strong building but I suppose I could have just as easily felt trapped and afraid. I have learned that living in isolation is totally an exercise in mind control. You can interpret it as peace and an opportunity to feel close to nature or you can feel trapped and yearn for people around you. Most of the time I feel tranquil but it is harder and harder, especially when I cannot get outside and enjoy the beauty, to not feel a little yearning for more human contact. Tom and I came to the conclusion that February and March are not desirable times to live at the lighthouse. I always wondered why the former owner, Sandra James, said she would not spend a winter here alone but now I know.

I am getting along just fine because I have so much to do on the book but without that stimulation I would have to dig deeper. Along that line I think I will start spinning again as it is a type of exercise and I love to do it.

March 6th

Signs of spring are beginning to appear since two of my favourite birds have returned. For the last week I have seen a few oystercatchers and yesterday Tom took me down to Stenness beach where there were hundreds of oystercatchers.

As we were coming back to the lighthouse we saw a flock of lapwings at the bottom of the hill by the cemetery. I tried to take their picture but they would have no part of it. I got my bird book out and checked to see if we would have any more birds coming in great numbers soon but it looks like most of the sea birds will not start to return until the end of March.

We have had huge flocks of starlings and the European blackbird around for weeks but they are not so much fun to watch. The plovers have been back for a while but not in the large numbers you see later in the spring.

The wind is down to what my chart calls a gentle breeze. I may just put on my waterproofs and go for a walk later. I can dress for the rain but cannot cope with wind like yesterday which was even rocking Tom's car.

The new book is coming along and I have a printed copy of the edited pages. The last edit is done from a printed copy of the entire book to catch duplications and those last few errors. Dean is working on editing the rest of the pages. With luck I am going to be able to hit my target of submission in mid April with the exception of the last chapter and the introduction. I am debating whether to stay here a few days into May to finish editing those. It would get me back in the States a few days later but the book will have been put to bed. I will decide later. The next book is longer than anything I have ever written being about double *The Last Lighthouse*.

March 7th

We are just getting ready to set off for Lerwick. Tom has to get feeder rings in which to put his silage bales for the sheep. They have been unavailable on the island for weeks. It is difficult to live on a remote island where everything has to come in by ferry. As Dean always says we are at the end of the delivery chain.

I am going to the opening of the new Shetland library. They moved from a sort of ugly block building to a historic church, which took years to renovate. They even replaced the stained glass windows. I cannot wait to see it and to get some new books. I have read everything here as they have been shut for two months. I just checked amazon.co.uk to see what best-selling new books were out so I could look for them.

The weather is sunshine and showers but cold. A shower just went through but the sun is back out. I hope we have more sunshine in Lerwick.

Last night I cooked pork side meat until it was really crispy and then removed most of the fat, made a lettuce and orange salad with vinaigrette dressing, and had boiled potatoes. For some reason it was a great combination and tasted so good. No dessert was served as I am trying to maintain my weight while I am getting little exercise. I have been able to do it but it has been a fight. No cookies or crisps have been in the house since Dean left.

March 8th

The wind is gale force eight again but the sun keeps peeping in and out and it is pretty warm with temperatures in the 50s.

I just took two loaves of bread out of the Rayburn. I found a recipe for people who get to the store infrequently. It takes flour, one teaspoon of sugar, dried yeast and water. I just had two hot pieces hot with jam and butter. Not too bad for such a simple recipe. I let the loaves raise too much in the lower oven today so they are not perfect bread shape. Next time they will look better. I am going to keep baking with the recipe until I get it perfected for the Rayburn and include it in the cookbook.

Scottish Field printed the second article based on their trip to the lighthouse – this time about Shetland in general. There is a gorgeous picture of the Eshaness cliffs on the front cover. I knew the cliffs would eventually end up on the cover, as they are one of the most beautiful seascapes in the world. Tom was absolutely thrilled as there is a small picture of his house on the first page of the article. It is not the best view of his house but you can tell it is Bordigarth. Another important picture is the pony with the Tina Turner hairdo. Connie named this pony when she was here. They took so many pictures of the ponies it would have been a huge surprise if there was not a pony picture in the magazine.

The magazine has sold out everywhere in Shetland, which frustrates me as I have people back in the States who want a copy. With the picture of the cliffs on the front it is too easy to spot and they actually sold faster than the first one with the lighthouse in it.

The Shetland Tourist Board should start paying me a salary for promoting this island.

Tom's new fork for his bales broke last night and dropped a bale right in the middle of the road. I hope he can get his money back.

March 9th

I got up at 6:30 am as it was already light. I have watered all of my plants including re-potting two, baked a Dundee cake for tomorrow's dinner, dusted the house, taken out the ashes, fed and watered the chickens and taken a bath including washing my hair. I just finished answering my e-mail and it is only ten o'clock.

I have absolutely no idea what is making me so productive. Maybe it is my desire not to work on the book today and treat myself to a movie marathon this afternoon. BBC is running *Citizen Kane* and another Orson Welles movie. *Citizen Kane* is a great movie and it has been a long time since I have seen it. The sun is shining brightly but the wind is still fierce so no long walks today.

Speaking of wind, the *Shetland Times* came out yesterday with the weather statistics for February. We had 11 days of gales (almost half of the blasted month), which is a record. That, coupled with 76% more rain than usual, does not make a great February. I should not write off Shetland winters completely with this February being such an unusual month.

Brahma is broody again. I kept hoping she would get off the nest and act normal but no luck. So Brahma is now getting the anti-broody treatment, in a cage sitting on the floor for five to six days. I will let her out for a little while in the morning to eat and drink. She is wise to all of this and I had a little trouble catching her this morning.

Guess I will pay my bills and then I can fix some popcorn and settle in for a movie afternoon.

March 10th

It is Mother's Day in the UK. I sent myself some fragrant flowers in a basket, which will bloom in the house before I put them outside. They didn't arrive, so much for my UK Mother's Day. I guess I will have to wait and celebrate back in the US with my kids and grandkids.

Tom is coming early today, as he has to return the silage bale fork to the farmer/blacksmith who made it so he can fix it. This will take us by Brae, where the shop might have some copies of *Scottish Field* for those who asked for them.

Sunday dinner is duck breast with celery, orange, onion and sage stuffing, mashed potatoes, tomato salad and the Dundee cake I baked yesterday. Everything is ready to put in the oven to cook while we run Tom's errand. Oh, by the way, the stuffing is made out of the last of my homemade bread. I have a sourdough starter seasoning and will make sourdough bread next week.

I have a dilemma and cannot figure out what to do. My current book will be finished in April and out in the summer and another already written that will come out sometime in Spring 2003. So that means I will have nine books providing income. I am also going to do the cookbook so there might be ten. Three children's books are accepted for publication but who knows when they will be out.

I want more than anything else to write a novel about the lighthouse keepers who were made redundant. If I do that I will have to not write any lighthouse guide books for at least a year. With nine books selling I should have a good enough income to support Eshaness. Without a new book coming out for a couple of years (could take a year to publish after writing) will my name become forgotten and sales slip? I will still have my monthly columns in *Lighthouse Digest* and *Scottish Radiance* that reach thousands but most of those readers have my current books.

This whole issue really began to bug me more last night. I have always liked John Thaw who recently died and I have been watching TV re-runs of some of his greatest roles. Also one of my favourite big screen actors, Kevin Spacey, was interviewed on television last night. More than anything I would like to see my words put into action by a talented actor.

The basic question is whether I take a year off from writing high demand commercial books and put all my efforts into *Keepers No More* (working title for the book about the two brave redundant lighthouse keepers) for the next year. This book is a big gamble, as I would have to get it published and sold to a studio. Because my success as a writer came rather late in my life I feel like time is ticking away and it might never get written.

March 11*th*

I am about to experience the worst storm since we have owned the lighthouse. When I went out to dump the ashes from the Rayburn I had to hold on to something to stay on my feet. I went from the lighthouse to the water tower to the fence and then I was able to walk a few feet to the rocks where I empty the ashes. The winds were *only* 65 miles an hour from the southwest. I thought getting out was bad but it was nothing compared to getting back against the wind. I put my black bag of trash in the bin so it would not blow away. I was so glad to get back to the solid walls of the lighthouse. Getting out to the chickens was difficult only from the door to the garage. The garage protected me from the wind so I was able to get it open to feed and water the chickens. I had to stay inside the garage for ten minutes to allow the broody hen to eat and drink. The howl of the wind was deafening but the chickens seemed to pay no attention. It was cosy in the garage with the chickens clucking softly. It was like the wind was a big orchestra and the chickens the chorus.

Back in the house I decided this was definitely a soup day so I put a big pot of potato and leek soup on the Rayburn. Just putting the soup on to cook made me feel safe and secure. The clothes washer runs at night so I had to hang the clothes on the inside line which also helped me ignore the roar of the wind.

The weather forecast was:

South westerly storm force ten veering northerly imminent, decreasing severe gale force nine soon.

Great! Severe gale force nine means the winds will go down to 55 miles an hour. The surf around the stacks is so wild you cannot see Moo Stack. Waves are crashing over it and the mist and spray was so heavy the stack was lost to sight. I just went to check on the soup and it is raining so hard against the window in the Rayburn room you cannot see beyond the glass.

I have so many layers of clothing on I sort of waddle. I do hate being cold. All of the heaters are working fine, keeping the house at about 62° and considering the wind speed that isn't too bad. The office is one of the warmest places, as it has no southern exposure but when the wind turns north it will be cold too. Then I will have to put on another layer. What I need for working at the computer are those gloves with the fingertips cut out.

Would I rather be somewhere else? The thought does cross my mind (taking the trash out this morning) but most of the time I can't think of anywhere I would rather be. Usually from the windows you get the most incredible views and outside the office window is a blue grey sea with long white-topped waves. Today the ocean is rocking so much you could get seasick just watching it. I can tell the wind is still in the southwest because of the direction the ocean is plunging.

March 12th

One of my e-mail friends told me that they only wanted to hear good things from the lighthouse and I should quit complaining but my e-mails are the true story of what happens at Eshaness and sometimes that is not good.

For about half an hour last night the wind was still. It was so strange dropping from the tremendous howling to nothing. Then just as quickly it went back to screaming and I had to wear earphones to hear the movie.

I went to bed with the wind squealing in the lighthouse tower as it always does when the winds are in the north but it is something I have become used to.

I fell asleep right away, but about 3:00 am I was awakened by a low thunderous, exploding, crashing sound that ran together so it sounded like a continuous drum roll of dark and horrible thudding. It was terrifying to wake up to such a sound. When I was fully awake I decided it was the Plexiglas protectors on my bedroom windows making the ghastly noise. They were being beaten so hard they never had time to fully recover before they were hit again, which caused the continuous booming noise.

I then heard doors rattling all over the house and sounds like things were being moved around. I was petrified. Was someone in the house? Had something gone wrong with the Rayburn? Was a window damaged? I was scared stiff to leave my warm bed to find the source of all these strange noises but logic told me no one in their right mind would be out in these winds so I got up and begin to walk down the hall. There was a dreadfully cold draught and when I reached the end of the hall and turned I was facing the full force of a very wintry stream of air. One of the doors to the outside was standing wide open. As a result all the doors in the house were being opened and slammed by the force of the wind. I was scared I would not be able to get the outside door shut since I could barely walk against the icy air streaming into the house. It took a while but I finally got the outside door shut and the bar across the doors to lock them. By then I was soaking wet from the rain, sea spray or sweat and shuddering with cold and fright. How did that door get open? That had never happened before. I had not locked it but I know it was tightly shut when Tom left and no one had used it since.

We have had trespassers twice before so it was possible someone had opened that door and come into the house. Since there was so much noise, it was hard to pinpoint any unusual sounds. I peeked into the Rayburn room where there was a nightlight and could see nothing moving so I went in and got a hammer out of the closet. At least if someone was here I would have something to protect myself. I went from room to room, always scared that when I turned on the light I would find someone, but I didn't, thank God.

Freezing cold, I went back to bed. Once snug in my warm bed I was hoping I could go back to sleep but the loud noise at my window continued. Then I heard another sound like someone knocking on the front door. The front door was locked now so I was safe inside but what if someone was outside needing help? Deciding I could look through the peephole I once again went down the hall. When I reached the door there definitely was something knocking but when I looked through the peephole there was nothing. Not willing to open the door again I went into the kitchen and got a big glass of Dean's whisky. I hate whisky but I thought it might knock me out so I could go back to sleep.

Back in the warm bed and with the help of the whisky I fell asleep. I awoke this morning to the same noise from the bedroom window and the knocking at the front door. When I went out to feed the chickens I realized the wind was so strong that unless the door was locked it could blow open. An outside latch that holds the doors open in good weather had been swung around by the wind causing the knocking. It all seemed so simple in the daylight but in the dark of the night it was completely different.

It was the most terrifying night of my life due to a combination of the nervousness caused by the strength of the storm, the noises it created and the door standing wide open in the middle of the night. To give myself a little credit I did not once consider just pulling the covers up over my head and hiding. Neither did I have visions of ghosts running around the house.

Today I am exhausted and wish the winds would ease so the noises would go away. The gales are still with us only they have changed direction.

Currently the winds are above 80 miles an hour so we are at storm force and approaching violent storm. I did not make it out to the dumping ground for the ashes but did make it to the chickens since the generator building stands between the chicken house and the wind.

I am going to spin and write a review of Stuart St John's last movie, *The Scarlet Tunic*, for a website. I watched it last night and felt the scenes were beautiful and the story was not bad but there was some bad acting. I do not know if the bad acting is a sign of bad directing or not. Maybe I will look on the Internet and see if I can find anything about movie directing.

March 13th

What erratic weather. Today could not be a nicer spring day with blue sky and a glassy, light grey blue ocean. Tom came and picked me up for a short trip to Brae. When the weather clears everyone gets outside.

The big topic of conversation in Brae was this week's storm. My episode might have been one of the worst but everyone had problems. Tom's skylight was jumping up and down and he could not find anything in the house to tie it down. He looked outside and saw a small piece of string on the fence so out he went dressed only in his birthday suit to get the string. Some people had shingles blown off and almost everyone I talked to was woken up many times. They all looked at me and said it must have been awful at the lighthouse. So far I have just said 'yes' and not told anyone the story of the door.

Tom tested the door yesterday and found that the latch was worn. It will hold if you shut it hard but if rattled a few times it loosens and comes open. I am searching for a new latch but it will be hard to find, as it is a big, antique solid brass one. Dean suggested I contact the Lighthouse Board, as they may know where I can get one. As long as I remember to bar the door we will not have a reccurrence of the other night.

I am burning peat in the Rayburn now with a little coal because the high winds of the last few weeks burned coal twice as fast as normal and yesterday I discovered I was almost out. The coal people cannot deliver until next Tuesday so I am going to conserve as much as possible until then. I can use peat as long as the wind stays light. Peat produces a lot of heat but does not last very long.

March 14th

I have no water. No, it is not freezing again. The water authority is flushing all of the lines and it is my turn. They will turn it back on by night so it is a short-term thing.

All four chickens have been out running around in the sunshine. It seems my broody treatment has worked as Brahma is acting like a normal chicken again. It was really pleasant to see them pecking in the grass and strolling along.

Speaking of chickens, I experienced close up and personal the laying of an egg yesterday. No, I did not lay it. When I went out to feed the chickens, Sussex was sitting on the nest and kept making all kinds of cooing and soft clucking noises. All of sudden she let out a series of big cackles and jumped off the nest, leaving behind a steaming brown egg. Then she strolled over to get something to eat. I guess laying an egg is all in a day's work for a chicken. I know what you are thinking. I must be really desperate to get big pleasure out of watching a chicken lay an egg but it was a first time experience for me. You get your entertainment where you can at the lighthouse.

I have a loaf of sourdough bread rising in the Rayburn, which is still burning peat while the wind is down, as I really like the smell it leaves in the house. When cold and nastiness arrive again I will go back to coal. In days gone by it must have been common to have the house smell of peat and yeasty aromas.

March 15th

Another loaf of sourdough bread is in the bottom oven of the Rayburn. Tom was here yesterday when I took the first loaf out and he loved it so I am making another one for him this morning. The Rayburn is great for baking bread. The bottom oven is perfect for raising the dough and the top oven bakes it beautifully. The loaf is more moist than when I bake it in the electric oven. The different type of stove does make a difference. I would love to have an Aga at the farm in Michigan since I now know how to use them but they are just too expensive. The Rayburn was over £1000 and it's not the most expensive model.

The sourdough starter that I am using is made out of potatoes and the bread recipe uses only the starter, butter, milk, flour, sugar and water. Living so far from everything without a car I always have butter, dried milk, flour, and sugar on hand. I usually keep a loaf of bread in the freezer but homemade bread is so much better. It makes me feel extraordinary to smell a pot of soup simmering accompanied by the yeasty smell of bread rising.

The sun is shining but I do not have any desire to go outside, as the wind is fresh. That is a term which I did not understand for a long time but it means slightly windy and cold. Today it is cold but I have the door open for the chickens because the wind is in the south so they do not get anything through the door but sunshine.

The technicians were here yesterday because the radio in the lighthouse is not working. One of them was from Sweden and we talked lighthouses for over an hour sitting on a rock out by the cliff. If and when I start the Scandinavian lighthouse book I will have lots of contacts. The lighthouses in Scandinavia are so different in appearance to the ones I have seen in Scotland and Ireland.

The new book is moving along. I was considering staying in Shetland a couple of weeks longer to finish it but I have decided to keep my airline reservation for the last day of April. The final editing will be done in the USA. It really feels good to see a completed manuscript taking form as I add the edited chapters to the final document.

March 16th

Yesterday was a bad day. First they were flushing the water system in this area and so I was without water for most of the day then Dean's schedule is too busy for him to finish editing my book. I tried to hire a couple of my editor friends but they are already busy. My new publisher gave me what I consider a perfect contract and would really hate to miss my deadline on the first book with them. I will have to work night and day for the rest of my stay to do all five rewrites that are a part of my writing process. It doesn't help that this is the longest book I have ever written (around 120,000 words).

I was proof reading last night and the electricity went out. I thought it would just be a power dip but it stayed out for most of the evening. I have kerosene lamps but there was not enough light to read proofs by. The electricity was off so long the lighthouse beacon was barely visible as the batteries ran down.

By then I had the most unbelievable headache. It could be one of two things – anxiety about the book or the peat smoke from the Rayburn. I am going to stop burning peat when I am in the Rayburn room. As to the book I will do the best I can.

When I told Tom last night that my time for doing play-like activities might be over he was upset. I think he was hoping that if I got the book done by the first of April I could really enjoy the last few weeks of my stay. He has been working on getting the wee red boat ready to put in early before I leave, depending on the weather of course.

We had planned to go to an estate sale today for my weekend outing. He said I needed to get out and away from the book for just one day. He is probably right. Maybe if my head doesn't hurt too much I can proof read tonight.

Tomorrow is St Patrick's Day. A tradition in the Krauskopf household is green mashed potatoes so I will have them to celebrate the special day.

March 17th

I wonder if everyone is wearing green today? It is a beautiful blue day in Shetland so that is as close as we are going to get to green. The sun is bright and quite warm but there is a cold wind. I might try hanging clothes outside, which will probably bring more wind but it is worth a try.

St Paddy's menu is green mashed potatoes, smothered chicken, mixed vegetables and a herb salad. Dessert is one of my homemade rhubarb pies. I think it is the last bag of rhubarb in the freezer so it will be next trip before I get any more.

This morning I realized how self-sufficient I am. For breakfast I had toast made out of my sourdough bread with my own rhubarb ginger jam. The pie comes from my rhubarb via the freezer. I grew the herbs on the windowsill. The potatoes I bought from a local crofter. The only thing that is not home grown is the chicken. By the way if you have never had smothered chicken, you roll the chicken, bone and skin removed, in flour seasoned with salt and pepper, brown it in a little oil in a non-stick pan, remove the meat from the pan and make a cream gravy out of the dripping then put the chicken back in and cook it slowly in the Rayburn. I use just a little sunflower oil for browning and dried low fat milk for gravy so it does not contain much fat but tastes like it does. It is one of my mother's recipes and it is super.

We went to the sale yesterday in a drenching, cold rain. It was held in a small double garage so once again it was packed. When we got there Tom immediately recognized the house as the home of Willie Gifford, the last keeper at Eshaness. After finding that it was Willie's sale it became a much more important sale to me because I wanted to get something that had been at the lighthouse. I decided on a couple of birds made out of shells and a wooden box that was very old. The birds are really beautiful and now are on the shelf in the bathroom with all the rest of my shell stuff. I bought a box of dishes so Tom would have some soup bowls and there were some other odds and ends in the box that I could use. Near the end of the sale I saw them move up a big metal box with handles that I immediately recognized. I had seen ones like it at other lighthouses we had visited. Northern Lighthouse Board staff use similar boxes when they are working on rock lighthouses and I think I have seen them being unloaded off the helicopter. I really wanted that box and was hoping that no one else suspected what it was. When bidding started only one antique dealer jumped in and he finally dropped out so I got the box for £14. I talked to Willie's daughter-in-law and she felt I was right about the box. Tom and I searched carefully and could not find any identifying marks. It had been painted many times so any marks would be under layers of paint. My thought was it was such a utilitarian thing the NLB probably just bought them by the hundreds and did not bother to mark them. It was much cared for by Willie, as I have no idea how many times it had been painted.

So yesterday's sale was probably the most important one I have been to in Shetland.

March 18th

Because rain was coming down and the north winds were howling Tom decided to go to Lerwick. He always says bad days are good days to go to Lerwick. I am not sure I agree with him as I trudge around in town in the rain and cold but beggars cannot be choosers so I went to town. I wanted to get lettuce, vegetables and meat but I didn't get much meat as I decided I should eat as much seafood as I can in the next few weeks. The fish van will become my main grocery store until I leave. Last night the BBC finally aired the *Antiques Roadshow* that Tom and I went to last spring in Lerwick. Tom invited me down to watch it on his big TV. We were hoping to see someone we knew or maybe even ourselves in the audience but no such luck. They did show a few nice scenes of Shetland including one of our Da Drongs. I am kind of disillusioned since I talked to some of the people who were filmed during the *Roadshow* at my book signing afterwards and found they were invited to participate. I always thought people brought in things and it was a coincidence if they got filmed. I am sure there is some of that but some is staged.

Yesterday was a beautiful spring like day. Tom went home early after dinner to paint the trim on his house and I did some proof reading from hard copy outside in a sheltered spot where the sun was shining on me. It felt like summer. Shetland has the most changeable weather but that is just part of being here.

Last night I stayed up late and watched a movie that is part of a BBC countdown to the Academy Awards. They are going to carry the Academy Awards live but it will be in the middle of the night so I can either stay up or video tape it to watch the next day. I am going to have to make a decision in the near future about what book (besides the cookbook) I take on next. The London Book Fair was this week and my publishers will be back and ready to move on the list for the next year. I am leaning more and more towards taking a year to write the novel about the lighthouse keepers.

I had some pictures developed in Lerwick, which has made me aware I need to get busy on the final selection of pictures for the next book. Some are easy to choose but deciding which is the best storm picture of the cliffs and Bruddans is really tough. I am still trying to get a good picture of the chickens.

March 19th

Sunshine is sparkling on the blue grey ocean and it looks really warm until you go outside. The wind is out of the north and goes right through your clothes. I think I will not take the long walk I was contemplating when I got up this morning.

Trout season is open and we are beginning to see fishermen in the lochs.

Last night just before I went to bed I peeked out to see what the weather was like and there was a canopy of the brightest stars I have ever seen. The sky was literally covered in gleaming white dots. When I looked to the north there was just a hint of green Northern Lights, like a ghostly shadow dancing across the sky. It was too beautiful a night to go to bed so I put on my robe and went for a short walk around the parking lot. I could hear the surf lapping at the foot of the cliffs but that was the only sound. It even got to the point where I resented the interruption of the beacon as it illuminated the surrounding area and me. It was a special moment but finally I got cold and that drove me inside to go to bed.

The weather situation has been a contest between the wind and my sanity. I think that I am winning as I still think this is one of the most beautiful places in the world.

March 20th

Trout season officially opened on the 15th of this month so I decided to reward myself after I finished rewriting two chapters of the new book and go fishing. But it is Shetland and it is early spring. A few minutes ago it started snowing really hard with gigantic fluffy flakes. It took only about ten minutes for the ground to become white. I will have to think up another reward for getting my two chapters done. Yesterday when the library van came it started to snow while I was in the van and I got absolutely soaked coming back to the house.

What I have not figured out in the eleven months I have been here is how to handle a day with a forecast for sunshine and showers. One thing I have learned is the front gate might be too far to venture with that forecast. I am still hoping the sunshine will reappear so I can go fishing.

Yesterday the fish van had tuna and swordfish steaks. They do not usually have these types of fish, as they are not caught around Shetland. The van has an arrangement with an Aberdeen fishing outfit to trade Shetland catch for tuna and swordfish. I bought a tuna steak and grilled it on top of the Rayburn in my new grill pan. It was wonderful. I added a lettuce salad and a baked sweet potato, quite an elegant meal for just me. Tonight I will have my weekly monk tail.

It is hard to believe there will be only one more visit from the library van before my year will be over. Today she had three cookbooks with old Shetland recipes for me. I am going to try as many dishes as I can before I leave which will give me some interesting things for a lighthouse cookbook. That book should be fun to write, as it demands that I try any new recipes before I put them in the book.

I will start my new novel about redundant lighthouse keepers when I get back in the States. I will not take any lighthouse guide books contracts for a year. If the publisher is willing to wait 18 months for a text I will talk to them about it. Hopefully the other books will keep selling. Dean has gone along with me on this. The one stipulation he made was he was not editing the new book.

Dean edits my books before submission. He spends hours doing it and deserves a lot of credit. Using the review function in Microsoft Word, we can do it via e-mail. I especially appreciate him doing it for the next book, as it is his busiest time for the university.

The most difficult part of writing a book for me is the rewriting. I go through each of my manuscripts five times, making changes each time. It is a tedious and nerve wracking job. You get so tired of it you want to scream. I could drop part of my process but then I think it would weaken the books. All authors I know get a feeling of pride when the final book is done but just before submission absolutely hate the work and doubt everything in it.

Today two chapters will be put in what I call my submission copy and I will not have to look at them again. That is progress and worth a cup of coffee.

March 21st

Yesterday afternoon I got my fishing rod ready for catching trout before anyone else comes out here and catches them. I put on a new fly that was in the fishing tackle box Dean bought at the sale. Tom is supposed to come up this morning and we will give the lochs a try. But when I got up this morning big, lazy, fat snowflakes were coming down and the ground was completely covered with snow. There was not a hint of wind but it definitely was snowing. Today is the first day of spring and we have snow. Oh, well.

When I went out to feed the chickens the sun was out on the front of the lighthouse but it was still snowing on the back side. I took some pictures of this strange, still, snowy Eshaness morning. In one picture, you can see how calm it is by the lighthouse's reflection in the lochan and in the background you can see the sky black with snow. It was unlike any morning I have ever experienced while at the lighthouse. I wonder how many other types of morning there are for me to see.

The big question is will the trout be hungry and biting on a snowy morning? It is unbelievably calm day. That might make it easier for the trout to see the flies.

The Rayburn and I baked sourdough bread again yesterday. The bread is wonderful and makes the best toast in the world. I will just keep baking it so I can have toast everyday.

March 22nd

I have added a new activity to my early morning routine. I empty the Rayburn's ashes, feed the chickens, and then take off for one of the nearby lochs to fish for trout.

It is not only the fun of fishing but I need the exercise so it gets two things done at once. We have bright sunshine but quite a cold north wind. At the split lochs down the hill from the lighthouse there are a couple of sheltered areas to get away from a north wind so I will try there.

Actually there is another reason. Yesterday when Tom came up to check on me we also went down to the split lochs to try a little fishing. We would have tried the lighthouse loch, which was closer but there were already two fisherpersons there. I thought about telling them that we owned the land around the loch and they were trespassing which is technically true, as we do own about a 3-foot square of land where the windmill used to be that supplied the lighthouse water. But since they might have got upset we went down to the split lochs.

Tom tried one loch and I tried the other. I cast my line out about three feet from the edge and since there was little wind the bobber was dancing up and down just a little. Standing in the sunshine my mind was wandering and then I happened to look down at the bobber. It was more than just bobbing but was under water. I immediately jerked the line thinking I had a fish. The line stayed down a couple of seconds and then I could feel it let go. Thinking I had a fish interested I reeled in slowly. As the bobber got closer to shore I could see a trout following my line. I stopped reeling in and hoped he would bite. That fish just swam around my bobber right in front of me and had the audacity to turn so the sunlight was gleaming on his silver tummy. I did not move the line or myself thinking he would bite again. All of sudden he turned his tail and swam away. I almost jumped into the water and swam after that arrogant fish. Oh, by the way, he was a big one to boot.

I was devastated. That was the first trout bite of this year and I lost it. I expected Dean to feel sorry for me but he was just angry that he was not here. To be honest I have so little experience catching trout that I never know what to do. Should I use worms or flies? Where to cast? How fast to bring the line in? How to set the hook? I keep asking all of the trout fisherpersons around here and they say it is just a matter of luck.

I am determined to catch one of those fish before Shetland's annual fishing contests start. They always use a couple of the lochs around the lighthouse, as they are some of the best fishing in Shetland, or so they say.

March 23rd

Saturday has arrived and it my day off from working on the book. So I am working on the April and May issues of *Scottish Radiance*. It is hard to believe but right after the May issue goes online my year here will be over and I will be back in the States. Because I am travelling on the last day of the month I am trying to get a head start on the magazine so the last few weeks will not be so hectic.

I did go fishing for a few minutes this morning but my line tangled so I came back early. It was so calm the lochs were like mirrors. You could see reflections of the clouds and the oystercatchers flying overhead. It is nice to have the oystercatchers back with their weird call.

Last night I stood for a long time at the bedroom window and looked at the silver trail of moonlight on the calm ocean with tears streaming down my face. I do love the ocean and will miss it greatly when I return to the farm. Dean often talks about how hard it is for him to leave here and I believe it will be even harder for me to leave this time after such a long stay. But I miss my family and will be glad to get back to them. I keep remembering what my partner for ten years, Jim Bruce, always said, 'All things must end so new things can start'.

There is always a mixture of joy and sadness when I leave the farm or the lighthouse. The sadness of leaving people and places and the joy of going to another loved place and people. It is just the consequence of buying the lighthouse. When I think about this subject the words of my Luath publisher echo in my mind, 'Welcome home from home'.

But, as Tom is always reminding me, the lighthouse is not going anywhere and will be here when I return. In fact one of the things I have to do today is get my tickets to return in mid-July. I will only be staying until the end of September but it should be great fun with a book launch and the second lighthouse radio weekend. Dean is coming for two weeks, Connie Harper and her husband are talking about coming, and a couple who won a weekend at the lighthouse in a *Scottish Radiance* drawing competition will be here. Summer is nice because there is lots of fishing and many trips in the wee red boat.

I guess doing two *Scottish Radiance* issues is making me think about all of this but I do not want to dwell on it, as it would spoil the last month I am here.

Hopefully, if it does not rain, Tom is taking me to some lochs too far away to walk to and those trout had better watch out.

March 24th

No fishing this morning, as it is a stagger around day with an extremely strong wind out of the south. The chickens stuck their noses out the door and turned around and went back in. They were still happy as on Sundays they get potato and carrot peelings. That is yum-yum food if you are a chicken.

I cannot decide what to do about the Academy Awards tonight. They start at 12:45 am and run until 4:45 am or later. The most logical thing for me to do would be to tape them and watch tomorrow morning but if I do that I cannot turn the computer on before I watch them or it will spoil all of the fun since I have news updates e-mailed to me all the time. This is the first time in a long time I have not seen all the movies nominated for best picture. *Lord of the Rings* is the only one so I am pulling for *Lord of the Rings*. Stuart St Paul and I have been discussing the various nominations via e-mail and that has been fun. His is a much more knowledgeable viewpoint than mine.

The Dutch magazine which was interested in doing a spread on the lighthouse has decided not to do it. It seems we are not the type of property they usually cover, meaning we are not posh enough for them. It made me mad that they should think Eshaness was not good enough for their stupid magazine. I should have sent them a copy of the *Scottish Field* article.

Sunday dinner is roast chicken, mashed potatoes, carrots with dill, sliced tomatoes and a chocolate and Michigan dried cherry cake. Next week being Easter I will have to think of something special. I have some ham (gammon) in the freezer so it might be some kind of ham meal, traditional Easter fare.

March 25th

Tom decided to make another one of his unplanned trips to Lerwick so I just got back. As it was Monday the shelves in the grocery store were pretty empty but I was able to get a nice leg of Scottish lamb for Easter.

I have been fighting a bladder infection for the last two days and I think it is going to win. Today I am really under the weather. I slept in the car all the way to Lerwick and back and after I get this written I am off to bed. If I am not better tomorrow I will go to the doctor. All I really need is a prescription and I will be on my way to recovery. This has happened before when I am pushing myself too hard and don't drink a lot of water and do not stop to go to the bathroom enough.

I taped the academy awards and watched them this morning before I left for Lerwick. I have found that is the very best way to watch them. You can fast forward through long-winded speeches. The BBC did interviews during the commercials and it was great seeing the academy awards without commercials. Since the only movie I had seen was *Lord of the Rings* I have no idea whether the right people won. One small problem was I set the recorder for a half hour longer than the program was supposed to run but I did not get the last of the programme. It must have run a great deal longer than planned. They are running a summary on BBC tonight and I will watch that.

March 26th

I just got back from the doctor. I met Dr Beard, the regular doctor's substitute, for the first time. I liked his laid-back manner and gentle approach. We sent off a urine sample to the lab in Lerwick to make sure the prescription he gave me was correct. I am running a fever, which is responsible for my sleeping all the time. I slept for four hours yesterday afternoon, watched a little TV, went to bed before ten, and fell right to sleep.

An interesting twist was the urine sample kits, which I send to the hospital at Lerwick to check recovery. They are really neat with a preservative to keep the sample from changing during the time they are in the post. They seem to have everything figured out to serve isolated people.

Tom ordered me to stay inside and not go out into the cold wind. He said that the cold wind might blow around the bladder, chill it and make me worse. I laughed and laughed. I do not think that would be a problem but it would make a hilarious cartoon.

It is sunny but not warm. The wind is blowing at force six to gale force eight out of the south west, which is more than fresh or breezy.

I am going to try and work on *Scottish Radiance* a little but would not be surprised if I take another nap this afternoon. I need to get better by tomorrow morning as I am being interviewed and filmed for the trailer of the DVD version of *Devil's Gate*. Right now I look really bad and am not able to think very fast but at least it is on film and not live. The director can cut out anything I mess up.

March 27th

I am waiting for the camera crew, who were supposed to be here at 10:00 am and it is now 11:30 am. It is really a bad day for filming, the winds are at gale force eight and it is raining, but maybe it will improve by the time they finally get here. Right now it looks like the sun might break through so I have my fingers crossed.

I feel a little better today but still need Tylenol to keep going. I do not think the antibiotics have had much effect so far. I was up every two hours going to the bathroom last night so I did not get much sleep. Maybe after the crew leaves I can take a nap.

Yesterday at the doctors I saw the most beautiful poster of The Drongs from Scottish Natural Heritage. I just ordered Shetland posters of The Drongs, Croft Land – Shetland, Wildflowers at Clickimin Broch, Gannet, Razorbills, Otter, Corncrake, Sphagnum Moss, Common Frog and Marine Life from them. Don't ask me what I am going to do with so many posters but I will figure out something.

I also talked to the managing director of the *Shetland Times* regarding publishing *Northern Lights*. I hope to have all the arrangements made before I leave for the USA. The *Shetland Times* is talking about having it out by October, in time for the Great Lakes conference. Two new books for the conference will be exciting and keep Dean busy selling while I speak.

There is the film crew, finally, so I have to go.

March 28th

Fog is letting just a little light through the windows. I was hoping when I got up this morning we would have sunshine but it looks like a drape of light grey silk on everything.

Last night I started to feel about 40% better. This infection has really hung on. I am not sure if the drugs are strong enough or my run down condition is responsible. The new doctor had much to say about how tired and worn out I look. He suggested lots of rest but as I told him you cannot rest when a book submission is just around the corner. I will rest when the book is submitted around the middle of April.

The TV crew announced they wanted to do the interview out by the cliffs. They must have been out of their minds as we still had gale force winds but they really wanted to do it that way, so I put my coat on and out we went. I must have been about two feet from the cliff edge and that would have been scary without the wind. By bracing my feet I could keep my body from swaying. Once I was stable they began asking questions. That part was easy. The interview was for the *Devil's Gate* trailer so the bad weather was appropriate. Since the movie is one of the most interesting things I have done this year it was lots of fun talking about it.

Maybe I should consider a new topic to write about. If I wrote about something besides lighthouses I would be able to do interviews sitting by the fire or with a cup of coffee in my hand. I might even be able to have my hair beautifully done. But for now I have to go out and stand on a cliff in a gale. All people will notice is the surf action so it really does not matter what I look like. This is not the first time I have done this insane thing. I did an interview with the BBC at Noss Head in a gale and pouring rain but at least there was a wall to protect me from the ocean even if I was soaked to the bone.

March 29th

It's Good Friday and it could not be better here. I was out with my fishing pole at the lighthouse loch before 7:00 am. There is no wind. The loch had the reflection of a few puffy clouds floating in it. The only ripple in the water was the trail behind a large red-throated diver. The diver was calling. They have an eerie call like the North American loon. The difference between the two is the diver has the sound of waves playing softly in the background.

I actually have clothes on the line that are not even moving. I was out chasing the chickens trying to get a good photograph for the book and ended up with a once in a lifetime picture of a still clothes line at Eshaness. I still do not have any good outside pictures of those stupid chickens. Getting all four of them with either the ocean, the cliffs or the tower in the background is the goal but so far no luck. They just do not stand still long enough or one has their head down or their tail feathers facing me.

I feel pretty normal (or as normal as I get) this morning. I will work on the book and finish *Scottish Radiance* but it is the beginning of Easter weekend so I am going to goof off after that. While I was fishing I thought how lucky I was. I do not have to get in a car to find beauty, peace and fun; I just go out the front door. Yesterday the big news on BBC was all the car wrecks as people began their migration to a resort for the long weekend. I have the best resort in the world right here. I cannot wait until Dean retires and he can be here with me.

I want to bake Tom some hot cross buns. It will be a real struggle whether I stay inside to bake or take off with the fishing pole again. The problem with fishing is by the time I left the loch at 7:45 there were already two other people fishing there and another had taken off for Houlland. This is the first holiday since the season began so I imagine we will see lots of fisherpersons and probably a mob of tourists so finding a place to hide may be the best plan.

March 30th

Hot cross buns are baking in the Rayburn and the whole house smells yeasty. I used a Scottish recipe out of an old cookbook and hope the rolls will be as good as the ones my mother used to make. They are an Easter surprise for Tom.

The fog is starting to clear and it looks like it will be a sunny, beautiful day. I did not go fishing this morning since it was so misty and the wind was quite strong. *Scottish Radiance* has taken up most of my time since I got done in the kitchen. Easter dinner is going to be lamb with rosemary sauce, clapshot, devilled eggs and gingered carrots plus a trifle I baked.

It is a bummer that *Scottish Radiance* has to be uploaded on Easter Sunday but that is way the dates fell this year. It always goes online on the last day of the month. I have to check all the links and write the reader's letter and then I can relax a little. There are lots of tourists in the car park already so I will try to stay inside.

Yesterday I went over to Tom's to see my caddies and Fleckets, and just enjoy his view without any tourists. The caddies are full-grown sheep but Kara and Alyssa are still small. I hope that they are not too small to have lambs, as then they would be a liability for Tom. There is no problem with Austin since she is the biggest of last year's crop of sheep. My Fleckets are totally spoiled. Tom feeds them sheep nuts so whenever they see any activity near the house they come running. I keep hoping they will have their lambs before I leave but it is not likely as most Shetland lambs are born in May. Tom will just have to send pictures of them.

The hot cross buns just came out of the oven and as soon as they are cool I will put the traditional white icing cross on top. Here they put a cross made of dough on top and bake it with the rolls. I guess my rolls are a Scottish-American cross.

March 31st

My first Easter at Eshaness. It is in the 50s with only a slight breeze. The sun is bright with a little mist still around the cliffs from lots of surf. I took a cup of coffee and a hot cross bun out on the rocks and had a little picnic, which is not a bad way to spend Easter. I was driven back into the house by the arrival of two cars at the car park. A wonderful day and a holiday probably mean we will have lots of visitors today. Yesterday while sitting at the table proof reading the book I was startled when six people went by the sundial. Now the weather is improving there are lots of strangers around. Maybe I will have Tom take me for a ride to somewhere off the beaten track after dinner.

One major change in Easter dinner is I mashed the rutabagas alone and made parsley potatoes in cream sauce with peas. Parsley potatoes just sounded more spring-like to me. One problem was the potato I used falls apart after it is cooked so I have a new dish, which looks like mashed potatoes with peas and parsley. Oh, well, it tastes good.

I discovered a big problem in the chicken house when I went out for my coffee break. Rock was sitting on the nest trying to lay an egg and Brahma was sitting on top of Rock also trying to lay an egg. It was so funny I almost doubled over with laughter. I ran to get the digital camera so I could catch this rather hilarious moment forever but by the time I got back Brahma had jumped down. This is getting to be an old story, chasing those chickens around with the camera. There are four comfortable nests but those chickens only lay in two of the four and mostly just one nest. Only when that nest is occupied do they go to the other nest. But, will they lay in the other two nests? Not the lighthouse chickens. They are very particular.

It is difficult for me to be away from family on holidays so I am trying to keep busy. Tom is bringing some daffodils and worms. The Easter bunny sort of found me as not everyone gets worms for Easter.

It is only a month until I get on the plane to fly back to Michigan and the year is over. It does not seem possible.

April

April 1st

Today is a bank holiday in the UK so I am going to make it half a holiday at Eshaness. I am working at the computer until the sun comes out and then I am off trout fishing taking along a good book to read.

Tom must not have been feeling well yesterday as he only ate dinner and then left so I had Easter Day all to myself. I was sort of depressed and upset at first but after giving myself a good talking to, I decided to do all the things I like to do. I totally self-indulged by first reading a funny book, then watching an old black and white movie on TV and finally going down to the loch and fishing for an hour and a half. It turned out to be a great day.

We had had some rain early afternoon but the evening turned out to be sunny with a fresh wind. I was able to find a sheltered spot and using a worm Tom brought me for Easter I just cast out the line and sat on a rock. Sitting there I realized how lucky I am and that I should not let myself feel bad because I am not doing what everyone else was doing on Easter. I would really like to catch a fish but the best thing about trout fishing is it gives me an excuse to just sit outside and enjoy my environment. I could hear the ocean and a few oystercatchers flew by but otherwise I was alone. The water in the lochs is so clean you can see the bottom so I watched for a trout to come by. I did see one jump as we have midges out already. A trout jumping is a beautiful sight and just added to the magic of the moment.

As I begin my last month in the year stay I have learned that living in isolation is great if you are at peace with yourself and are happy doing your own thing. Where I get in trouble is when I compare what I am doing with what I think others are doing. Like yesterday when my family was eating Easter dinner I was fishing on the loch. If I dwelt on not being with my family I could get depressed but instead I went outside and enjoyed the beauty of Eshaness. One problem is that I work at the computer all the time but I am getting better at not doing that. I will write some this morning but only until it quits raining. If you spend all of your time working I think the quality of what is produced goes down.

The rain is continuing but if it clears I will get to do outside things otherwise it will be books and movies this afternoon. Not a bad way to spend a day.

April 2nd

I have been out for my daily constitutional, better known as trout fishing. Actually I am getting exercise by walking to the loch, even if I never catch a trout. When I arrived at the loch I saw male and female eider ducks swimming in the sunshine. Last night I saw a red-throated diver.

Tom came by yesterday to take me over to see the house he is building for the lighthouse chickens. It is in his fenced back yard. He is even putting in a small swinging door so they can come and go at will. The idea that my chicken house will be empty and become nothing but a garage distresses me. It has been a good home for four chickens and three lambs.

Yesterday the lambs were let out from the small park where they have been confined all winter so when we drove up to Tom's two of my caddies were sitting on the concrete by his house. They still prefer stone or concrete to grass for napping which means they have not forgotten their caddy shack. There were only two caddies because Tom made a mistake and took Kara over to one of the other crofts. He promised he would bring her back so she could be with her family. I worry about her since she is the smallest of the three.

The residents of the caddy shack have been a special part of this year. I loved raising the lambs even though they became a nuisance after a while. Watching the chickens is real entertainment and it is nice to have something to say good morning to each day.

The funniest part of the whole caddy shack scenario is that before it was home to lambs and chickens it was home to a Rolls Royce. Colonel James would probably rise up from his grave in the cemetery down the hill from here and haunt us if he knew we replaced his Rolls with lambs and chickens.

April 3rd

I am a little bleary-eyed and brain-dead as I have been working non-stop on the new book. The last couple of weeks before a book is submitted I get really uptight and jumpy. It is at this point I begin to think the book is no good, having seen it so much, and everything starts to run together.

Tomorrow my monthly column for *Lighthouse Digest* is due so I have been working on an article about the box I bought at Willie Gifford's estate auction. The following is a short excerpt from the article.

> Curious about the box's history I finally called the Scottish Lighthouse Museum and talked to one of their staff. The staff member had been a lighthouse keeper for 32 years and as we talked I found out he had been trained by Willie Gifford, the owner of my box. I started to give him the measurements of the box and he immediately stopped me and described it down to its black matte interior. He explained it was a dry stores box that was used to keep the lighthouse's high value tools and items. The box was kept locked and the key was the principal keeper's responsibility.
>
> One of my assumptions had been that my box had probably moved from lighthouse to lighthouse with Willie because of the handles. But in fact a dry stores box was kept in the generator house of each Scottish lighthouse. Willie must have taken the Eshaness box after the lighthouse was automated, as there would no longer be a need for it. So instead of getting something that belonged to a keeper who happened to be the last one at Eshaness I had in fact gotten Eshaness lighthouse's dry stores box. It could have been at the lighthouse since it was commissioned in 1929.
>
> I am pleased that the box has come back to its home and now proudly sits once again in the generator house. My biggest dilemma is what to do with it in the future. It is a historic item and should be given to the local museum or the Scottish Lighthouse Museum. But for now, I think I will keep it at Eshaness and when we have our open house every year, put it on display. I will put a note in it with a description of what it is and if anything should happen to me it should be give to the local museum.
>
> The best part of this whole story is not knowing what I was doing I brought something that was a part of this lighthouse's history back to where it belonged.

What a joy it was to find out I was right about the box.

April 4th

Tom has decided to go to Lerwick so I am going to bum a ride. A trip to Lerwick with Tom is so predictable. As soon as we get near the harbour and the power plant he goes to the farm store to buy supplies for the sheep. Then we stop at the Co-op to buy groceries. I think it might be safer for the food if we stopped on the way back but he does not like to navigate the roundabout at the Co-op. Next is the vet where we stop to get medicine for the woolly gods. Finally we find a place to park under the fort on Commercial Street. The area around Commercial Street is the old part of Lerwick and my favourite. The beautiful old stone houses go down the hills to the harbour. Walking on Commercial Street is difficult as it is narrow and cars are allowed to use it. They are talking about making it a pedestrian mall but so far have not. I love to go to the *Shetland Times* bookstore and all the charity shops.

The trip usually ends with a fish supper at the chippy. After the food we drive home. The drive is quite pretty so it makes a good outing. I need to be away from the book for a few hours as it is beginning to wear me down.

I have a big bouquet of daffodils on my table. Most are from Tom's garden but some are from the lighthouse. I am making progress on the lighthouse having flowers.

April 5th

I was up and about at 6:00 am. It was light and I had many things I wanted to do before the television coverage of moving the Queen Mother's body to Westminster, which starts at 10:00 am. I want to watch this sad event because it is an important moment in UK history. I am so pleased Princess Anne is breaking the tradition of only male members walking behind the coffin. It is hard to be here and not get caught up in the country's mourning for a great lady.

Before 8:00 am I had clothes on the line, soup cooking on the Rayburn and had answered my e-mail besides working on the book. I will continue to work on the book off and on during the events in London.

I did something wild and wonderful in Lerwick yesterday. Last year I bought a small print of Leslie and Tom's mother's house. The last time I was in Lerwick I saw they had another small one so I went in to get it for Leslie as a thank you for all the help he has given me while I was here. When I went to pay for it I saw a large watercolour of Tom's house behind the cashier. After chasing Tom for 30 minutes I finally found him and took him to the store. He was so thrilled to see a good painting of his house. It was too expensive for him to buy so I bought it for him. It was probably too much money for me to spend but I knew he really wanted it. He has done so much for me during the last year I felt it was justified.

The watercolour is correct down to every detail including the little white truck. The artist is from Canada and was here on holiday and did some Shetland pictures. This is an original not a print. I wish she had done the lighthouse as I think she is pretty good. I kept threatening Tom that I was going to keep the picture. But I scanned the picture and printed an A4, which is really pretty good so I will frame that.

All the way home from Lerwick, I kept saying it is Leslie's fault I bought the picture. If I had not gone to get his print I would have not have gotten the bigger picture. Actually, even though I am little poorer I am glad I bought it.

April 6th

Today the USA and Canada celebrate their Scottish heritage with Tartan Day. I spent some time looking for a Tartan Day card for the readers of *Scottish Radiance*. The selection was not very good so I ended up making my own.

It is warm but foggy today. Being a weekend I am going to try and stay away from working too much on the book but I am only one chapter rewrite away from submission. I cannot explain how excited I am about having it done. A big task is completed and well done if I do say so myself. It also means I can enjoy being at the lighthouse without feeling I should be working on the book.

Somehow I made the BBC Shetland Radio news last night. They announced *A Year at the Lighthouse* was about done and that it would premiere in Shetland in September. I have no idea where they got that information. The only possible source is the *Shetland Times* bookstore but I have not told Edna that the book is about done.

Yesterday I decided against considering the Shetland writer in residence position. I want to get on with my writing and not feel obligated to do other things. It would have been fun but I have other priorities.

April 7th

I am off to Whalsay, so this will be brief. Tom and I have wanted to visit this small island, which has the most successful fishing fleet in Shetland, for ages. Today is the day. We have no wind so the 30-minute ferry ride should be a good one. It is a roll on, roll off ferry better known as a RORO, run by the Shetland Island Council. We can drive the car on and just sit in it while we cross the sea. I am excited to be going to a new area of Shetland. I have all the cameras out so maybe I can put some pictures on the Internet.

Sunday dinner is not the usual. I made a big slow cooker full of scalloped potatoes and ham with a cheese sauce. I have golden buttons, which is sliced carrots and parsnips cooked in butter for the vegetables. For dessert I have a pineapple upside down cake. Even if we are gone we should have a nice meal. I am taking coffee and cookies in the car for the trip.

It is important I get out of here and see some new things. I have been here long enough that when I took the ashes out yesterday I didn't even notice the cliffs. How anyone can get used to such beautiful scenery is beyond me but I seem to be doing it. I always wondered why the people here never really noticed the magnificence but it just sort of fades away after a while. I made a promise to myself that I would not let that continue so I stood and watched the cliffs for a few minutes this morning. Until I leave I am going to start focusing on where I am and how spectacular it is.

April 8th

Rain is coming down softly so I will wait to go fishing as it is supposed to clear and warm up. If I get my writing done early this morning then I can fish or at least be outside the rest of the day. I want to dig up my garden and plant some carrots and parsnips. I am also starting some gazanias from seeds as they did so well last year.

Whalsay is one of the most wonderful places I have been on Shetland. I had hoped to see a whale as they had seen many from the ferry last spring but Tom thought it was too early. Ferry rides are one of my favourite things and it makes you really feel like you live on an island. Since I fly into Shetland all the time I do not get the island feel.

When Whalsay came into view the first thing I noticed was the harbour, which is full of fishing boats of all sizes. Two of the seven giant Whalsay fishing boats were in. The other five will be returning soon as fishing for them does not start again until mackerel season in August. The others might be in Lerwick getting repaired as we saw two on our last trip to the big city.

The harbour town is a mixture of beautiful, large new houses and old croft houses. As we drove away from the town I was struck with the beauty of the well maintained stone dykes. I did not see one that was in bad repair.

We drove to the north end of the island where the Whalsay Golf Club is located. It is a heather golf course out in the middle of nowhere. At the golf club we saw some happy golfers, the Out Skerries ferry on its outbound trip and two beautiful red-throated divers in the loch.

The road ends at the golf club so we slowly drove back looking for some daffodils blooming by one of the stone dykes to photograph. When I finally found what I wanted Tom parked down the hill and I walked up to the dyke. As I was taking the picture a man came out of the house behind the dyke and chatted with me. He invited me inside the dyke to see his garden so I had Tom come up too. As we talked I asked him if he was fisherman on one of the big boats. He was not only a fisherman but the captain of the Zephyr. He was a quiet man and explained he had had four Zephyrs. Each one was bigger than the previous one. The current one cost £10,000,000. He has three partners. He gave Tom and me some beautiful purple primulas from his garden. Tom is going to put them in his garden and when I get back in July I will move some of them to the lighthouse.

Another peculiar thing about Whalsay is you see the strangest collection of cars on the road. There were lots of Mercedes and Audis that you hardly ever see on the Shetland mainland because they cost so much to buy and run. You also see the small cars and pickups that are common to the mainland. I think this exemplifies what Whalsay is all about; an island of fishermen, some involved with the big boats who became rich, and some who are struggling like the rest of the Shetland fishermen. Whalsay is a wonderful place and I want to go back next summer when the entire fishing fleet will be in. I am now bugging Tom to take me to the Out Skerries before I go back to the USA. There is one of the most beautiful Stevenson lighthouses on the Out Skerries and it is another great fishing island but alas has no big boats. The only other big fishing boat is the *Altaire*, which is docked in the north mainland near the lighthouse.

April 9th

It is the most glorious day here. Hardly any wind is blowing and the sun is out bright and warm. The lighthouse chickens are lying on the sidewalk in the sun, which must be a first. I have spring fever so I planted some seeds to start inside. Tom can take care of them and plant them in the garden later, which means I will have some flowers blooming when I get back. Yesterday Tom dug up the garden in preparation for planting carrots and parsnips.

I am about to go outside to hang up clothes and then will work on the last chapter of the book until the Queen Mum's funeral starts. After the funeral I am going to go over the text one more time. Since it is a hard copy edit I might take it down to the loch and read while my worm waits for a trout. Notice I did not say while my worm caught a trout.

Someone asked me when the editing stops. The content rewriting is all done and you just come to a point when you have to stop. The final edit looks for typos and words that the spell check missed. There might be some reworking by the publisher but usually I do not have too much of that as I have edited so hard on this end. Submission is planned for Friday. I am going to have the biggest celebration I can arrange. It might just be a whole day of trout fishing. After the book is in I am going to play and work on the cookbook on the bad days.

April 10th

This bleak, cold and misty day is a blessing as it makes it easier to stay at the computer. Getting up at 7:00 am and beginning work early means the new book minus the last chapter and introduction is finished. Today I finalize the picture selection and go over it one more time on the computer screen. Tomorrow if all goes well today I am sending everything via e-mail. I am always nervous when I submit a book, even books under contract when I know the publisher wants it and is waiting for it. Maybe I should forget the last quick screen edits but I might find some little things. One thing for sure is there are no big issues left. I feel confident of that.

Tom wanted to go to Lerwick tomorrow and I asked him to change the trip to Friday so the book would be in. Now I think we can still go tomorrow, as the book will have gone to the publisher. Maybe that will keep me from trying to change anything more.

Macmillan turning down the novel this week is causing part of my anxiety. The book got to the highest level (no small feat) but the final decision was it did not have the type of story that would sell large numbers of books. They were highly complimentary on my style and how the book was written. It was a disappointment I have experienced before and might again as I keep sending new books to publishers.

By all definitions I am a successful writer in the non-fiction field but I still want to write novels. If I think about it I am not sure why. Maybe it is because I love to read novels.

My first reaction to the novel's rejection was that my decision to write the novel about lighthouse keepers might be a bad one and I should start a new non-fiction book. But I know there is an enormous market for a novel about lighthouse keepers and how their lives were changed by automation because of the huge number of questions about keepers I get by e-mail and at conferences. I will begin the novel after I get back to the USA.

The fish van had scallops yesterday for the first time since I have been buying from it. The scallops here are larger than the ones I get in the USA. Last night I treated myself to fresh scallops cooked in lemon garlic sauce. They were really good.

April 11th

Visibility is improving as I can see the sundial. Yesterday the fog was so heavy I could not see across the driveway. It is raining pretty hard, all in all not a nice day so I am going to Lerwick. Tom always likes to go to Lerwick on bad days so he does not miss any good weather to work on the croft.

My picture selection for the new book is done. What a job that was! I will probably add more before it is sent in. I tried to pick out the best pictures that went well with the narrative. A beautiful picture of Moo Stack is my choice for the front. It might not have enough colours but I really love the dancing light in it.

The book is still sitting on my computer and on many back up disks as I have decided to take one more look at it and submit tomorrow. I found just a few little things yesterday and might find a few more today when I get back from Lerwick.

I have just three weeks left at the lighthouse. Planning what I want to do is next on my agenda. I will not have a book to write so I can do anything I want. While in Lerwick I am picking up some new library books for the rainy bad days. Trout fishing, hiking and gardening head the list of things I want to do outside. Also I want to try some new recipes to put in the cookbook. Sounds like it will be a fun time.

April 12th

I have had lots of positive feedback on the picture selection for the new book from my e-mail buddies. The photos do a pretty good job of showing the most often mentioned things in the book. I have decided to add a picture of the wee red boat and a red-throated diver as they are mentioned a lot.

As we drove to Lerwick yesterday I was amazed how many new salmon farms are being put in the voes. Actually I thought the number would be decreasing because they are constantly having problems with disease and it has been proved that the farms are polluting the seabed. Another big issue was the escape of thousands of salmon in Lewis a couple of weeks ago. The fear is the escapees will breed with the wild salmon and we will have no more pure wild salmon. What bothers me most of all is how they change the look of the voes. The seascapes are what makes Shetland so unique and to have it spoiled with hundreds of cages is discouraging. Along with the salmon there has been a huge increase in mussel farms. They are not as large so they do not do as much damage to the environment. Next they are going to start putting in scallop farms. Two are planned already. What I want to know is will we in a few years know what it is like to taste fish or shellfish that was caught in the ocean instead of raised in a cage?

Speaking of shellfish, the fishmonger is now selling cooked crab claws and guess who is having them for lunch?

April 13th

A Year at the Lighthouse has gone to the publisher. Or as least 95% of it has as I still have to finish April and the introduction. I dedicated the book to each of my immediate family for putting up with my year long absence - Dean, Beth, Norbert, Alyssa, Sandy, Darren, Austin and Kara. I got an e-mail from my husband this morning that I forgot Misty, Steak (Michigan cows), farm chickens, Petey (Dean's new cat) and McDuff, who now lives at Sandy's. I did forget to mention Kiri because she was alone a lot while I was gone. So Dean's note helped me remember to put her in the acknowledgements.

How do I feel about not having to get up and work on the book? Absolutely on top of the world as they say in the UK. Writing a book is a lot of hard work and takes endurance. It sounds glamorous and fun but only the creation fits that description, the rest is long hours at the computer doing tedious work. I must admit the next steps are definitely fun – seeing the published book and doing all the book signings. That will not be until later this summer.

I have started on the cookbook. Last night I made a wonderful crab salad out of the crab claws I bought in town. They are just like the ones Tom catches. I also made a bacon and green pepper pizza from scratch. Today I baked a Michigan dried cherry chocolate cake for Sunday dinner. I will take pictures of that tomorrow with the rest of dinner. I am asking anyone who has recipes to please send them my way. I have limited resources most of the time but I can buy some special ingredients in Lerwick.

Tom is taking me to the island of Burra today to celebrate the book's finish. Actually he says that is the reason but he is also going to check out some used double glazed windows that are advertised for sale in the *Shetland Times*. No matter what the reason it will be fun, taking me to another area in Shetland where I have not been, and getting me away from the computer. It is a beautiful day with bright sunshine, hardly any wind, but a bit cold.

I had better gather up the cameras and actually get away from the computer.

April 14th

It is Sunday and I seem to be a little under the weather. Last night I had a badly upset stomach. Today it is better but I feel tired and achy. Dinner today is turkey fillets in a creamy Dijon mustard sauce baked in the Rayburn, cauliflower and broccoli, mashed potatoes, and Michigan dried cherry chocolate cake.

The trip to Burra was fun. It is a small island off the lower west coast of mainland Shetland near Scalloway with many new houses, which I thought ruined the character of the beautiful little island. Being so close to Lerwick and Scalloway it is understandable why so many people have chosen to build there. Access to the island is by a one-lane bridge so it is really easy. Tom told me it used to be a rich fishing island like Whalsay but we found out only one small boat is still fishing. The minor lighthouse is quite famous because it is so easy to see. It is run by solar panels, as are almost all of the NLB's minor lights. I happened on a black guillemot swimming near the pier. In Shetland they are called tysties. This was the closest I have ever been to one and he had the cutest bright orange feet.

I dropped the long-range lens for my 35mm on the concrete pier. I will have to take it back to the USA and see if I can get it fixed. I cannot get it fixed here as they have to send all camera repairs to mainland Scotland and it takes weeks.

Leslie brought me some photographs taken when Eshaness was built. One with the tower just begun is my favourite. The quality of the photos is not too good as they were taken in the early 1920s and my copies were scanned into my computer from a copy off someone else's computer. Leslie is going to try to get the original photos for me to scan directly. My big question is whether David A Stevenson is one of the people in the pictures since he usually supervised construction in person.

April 15th

I have been out hiking in the hills with fishing pole in hand and my backpack on, containing a book and a can of worms and fishing net hanging on the outside. It is a bright and fairly calm day but cold with the temperature around freezing. I saw ice on some of the smaller bodies of water. I read my book for a while and then picked up and moved to another loch since there were no fish around.

A fence is being put between the lighthouse and the Bruddans. They started it on Saturday and I have been upset every since. The fence will run from the high point over the Cannon (a huge crevice near the Bruddans that makes noise from the waves) straight up the hill to the lighthouse. The government wants to protect the cliffs and the flowers that grow around them. I support those goals but it is depressing me greatly to see what were open hills fenced off. I imagine it is how the cattlemen in Texas felt when they started fencing their range.

The fence was to go all the way to the lighthouse's south fence but they couldn't because that would cut off Hydro Electric's access to the lighthouse's transformer, which is east of the garage. So the fence will be about three feet short of ours leaving room for a truck to get through to the transformer.

They are having a terrible time getting the posts in around the lighthouse, as the rock is so hard. Tonight they are bringing a big rock crusher out to try and break through. It is almost like the land is fighting back. I am sure man and his machines will win. I may ask Tom if I can come visit him and my caddies tonight while they are beating at the hill.

Closing on a more positive note, a farmer told me that he has three belted Galloway cows (or they might be belted crosses). Another farmer on Shetland had a whole herd of belties but he is now raising Shetland ponies instead so Dean might be able to have belties here if we can find a little land.

April 16th

The fence building is continuing. Last night they used a huge caterpillar type tractor that drove a metal rod into the rock. The ground did put up a good fight and they were not able to finish putting the holes all the way to the edge of the cliffs. They will probably return tonight to finish.

Tom came up and talked to the guys doing who didn't seem to be the least bit upset about fencing off the hills. What they are doing is a part of the Ministry of Agriculture, Fisheries and Food subsidy for sustainable farming better known as ESA. Farmers in designated areas of special biological, landscape or historical interest voluntarily agree to farm less intensively or undertake prescribed conservation practices in exchange for a fixed annual payment per hectare. The areas the programme is designed to protect are of national environmental significance whose conservation depends on the adoption, maintenance or extension of a particular form of farming practice. In these areas changes have occurred or there is a likelihood of changes in farming practices that pose a major threat to the environment.

The grants usually cover 60–80% of capital costs if the work is carried out within two years. In most instances the crofter must keep the sheep off the area fenced for a period of time.

Most of the farmers around here are jumping at the opportunity to get the subsidy, so what is going on is all about money. Tom has four plots in the programme, which he has fenced. Not one farmer that I have talked to really cares about the flowers or historic things they are saving, they just want the subsidy.

I still struggle with whether the fence out here was needed. There is some grass but it is mostly rock and no flowers to speak of except sea pinks so there is really nothing to protect from the sheep. However, though it is not a stated part of the programme, it does protect the cliffs from the tourists.

April 17th

My clothes are horizontal on the clothes line but the sun is bright. While I was out hanging up the washing only Ronnie and I were about. With the stiff wind Ronnie's boat was really jumping around.

The saga of the fence continues. Yesterday I was even more upset when the library van lady told me that most Shetlanders did not even notice a new fence when it was put up as the island is literally covered in fences. The fences are becoming a part of island life even if they do not fence in or out anything. They did not work on the fence last night so I had a peaceful evening without the thudding of a machine disfiguring the rocks. I hope they miss their deadline and the fence is not completed until after I leave.

This afternoon I am off to Lerwick with Tom. He has a bowel test at the hospital. I really wanted to stay home but Tom seemed anxious for me to come along. I did not see him yesterday, as he had to stay close to the bathroom as they are cleaning out his system for the test. He has to go a day and a half without food since his test is late this afternoon and he says he is starving.

While he is at the hospital I will go to the library and research recipes. I am having a ball working on the cookbook. This morning I ordered two books, which were recommended by Charlie Simpson who used to write a newspaper column on using Shetland fish and vegetables. The *Shetland Times* published a book of his columns called *In Da Galley*. It is full of great recipes and hints on using Shetland things. One of his recommended books was out of print but I found a slightly damaged one on the Internet and the other one I found new on amazon.co.uk. It is too bad that I didn't start on this project sooner as I would have been able to try more fish recipes but when I get back in July I will be all prepared to go to at it in a big way. Today I am picking up the ingredients for ling curry, which sounded particularly good. Tom catches ling all the time so it is one dish we can have over and over again.

Dean loves to cook so we can continue working on recipes for the cookbook back in Michigan. Maybe we can't do the seafood but we can work on other dishes that will be included. The UK bestseller list has a big percentage of cookbooks.

April 18th

Tom survived his tests. He was uncomfortable for a while afterward but he was able to eat.

I got up all excited about working in the garden today. It was supposed to be a nice day but turned out fairly cold and grey but that did not stop me. I think I will not plant my carrots and parsnips until this weekend. After we move the chickens to Tom's house I will put the manure from the chicken house in between the planted rows and work it in. The daffodils I forced in the house earlier are planted now in some sheltered spots and I still have a basket of daffodils blooming on the table that will need to be transplanted outside.

My parsley, chives, and some perennials are being hardened off with a few hours outside every day. I will place them in a sheltered corner sometime next week. My big debate is whether I should put the geraniums and some plants I started from seed in the lobster creel greenhouses. I suppose it is worth a try as otherwise they will just linger in the house and die. Yesterday was probably my last journey to Lerwick this trip and I bought the usual food to take back to the States. I laugh every time I think that food is the souvenir I take back and forth.

While working in the garden I surveyed the progress on the fence. The posts have now been placed all the way out to the edge of the cliffs and the fence will definitely keep people from accessing the puffins unless they climb over it. That is a big positive as far as I am concerned. They have not put in the posts right in front of my south window. I just hope it does not spoil the view too much.

April 19th

The hot plate part of the Rayburn is full of pots. I have a big pan of fish stew simmering on the hottest area. Next to it is the kettle so I can have a cup of coffee when I finish this and next to the kettle is a pan of parsnip soup I made with the last of the parsnips that will be my lunch. The stew and the soup will get their pictures taken for the cookbook if they turn out okay.

Yesterday I took off for the hills and wandered around for over three hours. Over the last year they have become so familiar. The hills have become a comfortable place for me which is in such a contrast to how nervous I was on my first trip when I turned back trying to get to Houlland Broch because I could no longer see the ocean or the lighthouse. Today there were oystercatchers, fulmars, ringed plovers, and ordinary seagulls around. I saw my first flower in bloom; tiny daisies like flowers no bigger than the end of my little finger with yellow centres. Spring is definitely on the way.

Today I think Tom is going to take me to North Roe, which is too far away for me to walk. The big appeal for Tom is both a good trout loch and an ocean fishing beach close together so we can try for either type of fish. Tom's legs do not allow for him to do much hiking so this sounds like a perfect place for him.

Looking out the window last night just before bed there was a great silver circle on the water in the middle of the horizon. Actually it was nothing more than a break in the clouds that allowed moonlight to peek through and shine on the ocean. Many little things in my ocean world are spectacular.

April 20th

A bleak and cold morning is keeping me at the computer.

I spent yesterday fishing with Tom. It was not a good day so we used his four wheel drive pick-up to get part of the way to Houlland Loch and got rained on before we could get back to the truck. We did not see one fish.

I have finally convinced Tom to get a sheep dog so hopefully by the time I return he will have a working dog.

Today I have baked the cake part of a Boston crème pie and inventoried the freezer. I might have enough food to make my meals varied and interesting for the last week I am here. Tom keeps hoping I will have all kinds of things left because he gets it. There is very little chance of that.

I keep thinking they will work on the fence but so far no one has shown up. That is great, as I hate watching them. Tom and I walked the perimeter of the fenced area and they still have a lot to do before the end of the month. While we were walking the fence we saw what looked like three puffins in winter dress on the ledge where they live in the summer. If they were puffins something is really wrong, as they should not be back for another two or three weeks.

April 21st

This is the next to last Sunday at the lighthouse before I return to the States so I am cooking Tom a fantastic dinner; a big roast chicken with sausage stuffing, mashed potatoes, fresh broccoli, and a Boston crème pie. The chicken is in now, as Tom wants to get me out of here for a while.

Yesterday the farmers took a digger out near the cliff edge and started breaking up the rocks to break pieces to put along the bottom of the fence to keep the sheep from going under. But the fence is being put up so nothing will happen to those rocks since they are rare and designated a site of special scientific interest (SSSI). According to the current law those areas are not be damaged or abused. In a thousand years the sheep would not do as much damage as the digger. I put some pictures on the Internet. They are pounding and scraping around the puffins' main nesting area. The puffins are not back yet but who knows what damage has been done to their burrows and the cracks they live in.

Another issue is the area they are bludgeoning is above some deep-sea caves. The rocks do not look fragile but the whole area is full of deep cracks and it is not unknown around here for a whole bank to fall in or break off. The most recent example is Dore Holm losing a large area from one side.

Tom is anxious to get me away because I am so angry about the fence that he is afraid I am going out to tell the farmers off. He need not worry, as my anger is not directed at the farmers, they are only doing what they were told to do. My big debate is whether I am going to try and do anything about what is happening.

We are incomers and I do not want people to get angry with me for taking a controversial stand on something. We have been so careful not to act like the typical incomer. Also I think it is too late to do anything since most of the damage has already been done. Probably the most important thing is if I start something I will not be here to see it finished as I have only one week left before I leave.

Scottish Natural Heritage (SNH) has jurisdiction in situations like this. The following is from the regulation.

MANAGEMENT AGREEMENTS

Where it can be shown that the special interest of an SSSI may be damaged by an otherwise viable operation, SNH has the power to enter into a management agreement to compensate the owner for not proceeding with the operation. However, it is SNH's long-term goal to move the focus of management agreements from compensatory payments to payments for positive management.

After some more thinking and talking to Dean tomorrow I will telephone Scottish Natural Heritage, the ESA program coordinator, and maybe the RSPB (birds) manager to see what they have to say about all this.

April 22nd

Monday morning and it is raining off and on. I am hoping it will be more off than on so I can work outside.

Well, I talked it over with Dean and Tom and decided that I would find out as much information about the fence as I can and do a story on it. Tom became very supportive of doing something when he found out I was not going to have a confrontation with the farmer.

I thought about what I would do all day yesterday and decided I would start with the ESA programme. That turned out to be the Scottish Executive Department of Rural Affairs. I talked to the man in charge of the programme today and asked for information for my story. The conversation was friendly and helpful. The person I talked to became worried immediately when he heard the digger was out on the rocks because the basalt lava is a protected SSSI area. We agreed that the farmer was only trying to get the job done but the ESA person soon concluded there were other ways to go about the job. He promised the head people would be out this week to inspect what is going on. It helped that the person I talked to hikes around here all the time and loves the area.

Dean wants me to find out who owns the land around us. He would like to buy it to keep this kind of stuff from happening again. Tom should be able to help me find the owner.

Tom made a valid point yesterday. If I wanted to build a new fence around the lighthouse I would be stopped immediately as we are a historic listed building but no one was stopping these people from destroying irreplaceable rocks.

April 23rd

First an update on the fence. The digger has been removed from the cliffs. I do not know exactly what transpired but the farmer came early this afternoon and began working on the part of the fence not touching the cliffs. They left and then came back at dusk and moved the digger, which is now sitting outside my window at the new fence's gate. I imagine the ESA people might be coming today to look at the fence. I doubt there will be any more major developments. I think the fence will be finished without the digger being involved and that will be that. I do want to find out more from Scottish Natural Heritage about SSSIs since we live in the middle of one and do not want to see a repeat of the fence problem.

Tom went to Lerwick without me today. I think he was upset I did not go but there is absolutely nothing I need from Lerwick and would rather spend the day here, especially if the weather clears. Right now it is raining but the wind is only a fresh breeze. I was able to get my lobster greenhouses set up with geraniums and petunias before the rain started and I have hardened off my parsley and chives so I planted them in a sheltered area. The only thing left to do with the garden is plant the carrots and parsnips which I will do when we have a really still day so the seed won't blow all over. One of last year's rugosa rose sprouted and I am keeping my fingers crossed it will survive.

A tragedy struck that may have big repercussions. One million ready to sell fish at Tom's hatchery died. Yesterday Tom had a call telling him he could have the night off as the fish were all dead. He was told the main power lever stuck around 11:00 am and they could not get it loosened and the fish died. Tom cannot understand how that could have happened in the middle of the day with a full crew working. He keeps muttering they could have found a way to get oxygen to the fish with all those people around. Tom spent the last month tending alarm after alarm, as the fish were getting too big for the tanks. Tom is also a shareholder in the company and he is wondering what the financial repercussions will be. He thinks the fish would have been insured as they had a small loss once before and they got insurance money but we are talking between a £500,000 and £1,000,000 loss depending on the current price of the smolts. Tom came up and we talked a long time. If the company fails he would lose his job.

April 24th

Dean and I have another dependent. Late yesterday afternoon Fiona Bruce Flecket was born to my sheep Jenny Flecket. She is the cutest thing I have ever seen with randomly distributed black spots all over her. I tried to page Dean to announce he had just become the proud guardian of Fiona Bruce Flecket but the page did not get answered so he will not find out until this morning.

It is really nice to have some positive news since this week has been sort of a bummer with fence problems and the death of a million fish. Tom wanted to take me to see the dead fish last night but I passed.

It is really a good morning here. The sun is shining brightly and the wind is not blowing me over. It may be too windy to plant the carrots and parsnips but I could certainly go for a walk.

The fence is all done except for the gates. The view from the house has a few fence posts between the window and the islands but it is not too bad and the fence will keep some people away from the puffins since not everyone will try to get around. Hopefully that issue is all over.

I've got to run as I have a big pot of cream of broccoli soup on the Rayburn made out of the broccoli stalks and chicken broth from Sunday. It is great that you can eat soup in Shetland all year round.

April 25th

Sunshine and a rather brisk breeze are drying my clothes. I am washing things like jackets, which will not be used again until the next trip.

Today is a sad day for me as my chickens are moving to their new house at Tom's. We are moving them at noon. I will probably cry because since the caddies left the chickens have been my constant companions. One thing I have learned is I like having animals around.

I had a remarkable time talking to Scottish Natural Heritage personnel and the Scottish Executive's Rural Affairs division that is in charge of the ESA program. I found out that two ESA staff came out and inspected the cliffs before they instructed the farmer to take the digger off and never to use it there again. Everyone I have talked to believes the ocean will destroy the fence within a couple of years and some think the sea will rearrange the rocks that were broken off and moved in the first winter. The personnel of both agencies were helpful and concerned about the environment. I even finally found out where get you soil tests done around here. The Rural Affairs people want to meet with Dean when he is here this summer hoping he might be able to get involved after retirement with some of their efforts.

Shetland Islands Council is working on finding out if we can buy the land around us.

Now all I have to do is write my *Lighthouse Digest* story about the fence. So I shall begin that now before I move the chickens.

April 26th

Well, it is just a few fulmars and myself at the lighthouse. Tom came with the pick-up and we put the chickens in the hedgehog cage and took them to Bordigarth. They sat quietly in their cage during the short ride and loved their new house, which even has a window. It only took them a short time to wander from the house into the yard, which they found delightful because it was full of green grass.

There is one small problem. Tom's goose is sitting on her eggs in the same yard with the chickens and the gander is extremely conscientious about protecting her so he keeps running at the chickens. Tom may have to put up a fence between the chickens and the geese.

I took some pictures of Fiona Flecket who is really growing. She is about the cutest thing going and Jenny is a really good mother.

After the chickens were moved I came back and cleaned out the chicken house, which will have to go back to just being a garage. I got three quarters of it cleaned before I ran into a steel bar and badly bruised and scraped my arm. It is really sore this morning so I will have to wait until tomorrow to finish it.

Leslie was here last night to say goodbye and we had a great chat. I got notification yesterday that the lighthouse board is going to paint and redecorate the tower in June. Finally!

April 27th

Salt spray and small rocks are bombarding the lighthouse. I can't see out the windows as they are covered with salt. I tried to take a picture of the spray coming through the blowhole but no luck. I cannot go outside to try and take a picture as I was turned back by the wind when trying to take the ashes out this morning. The wind is from the north west so the office and the master bedroom are cold but it is not too bad in the Rayburn room.

I have been invited to the opening of a new art gallery near the Eshaness Pier tonight. Tom is going as my guest. The small croft that has been renovated for the gallery faces straight north west and is right near the water so I am not sure we can even reach it.

The man in charge of property for the Council is coming to the house after the gallery opening to talk about land purchase. We lucked out and the land surrounding the lighthouse is not a croft so a purchase is possible. The big question is whether we can afford it. The best option would be to buy the land in front of the lighthouse to the loch toward the east and then south to the split loch and straight west out to the sea and back up to the lighthouse. That would take in the fenced area and I do not think the farmer on the land will agree to sell. We would not buy the rocks on the sea side of the lighthouse because of liability issues.

Sarah Flecket had twins last night just before the storm started. My Fleckets are such smart sheep. Tom was able to move her and the twins into his steading. I have not seen the new Fleckets but Tom thought there were one boy and a girl. The boy would have to be sold but the girl I can keep. Tom was not sure about colour but he thought they had the usual black Flecket face with a white strip between the eyes, all black backs, and their legs and feet white. If the wind settles down I am going to go down and see my sheep's first set of twins.

April 28th

It is a gorgeous day in Shetland. I was up early and planted my carrots and parsnips, as there is absolutely no wind.

I visited Sarah Flecket and her new family. They are really cute. Spot Flecket is the male. He gets his name from the big black spots that circle his eyes. His legs are all white and he has mostly white ears. Jackie Bird Flecket has a black spot around one eye but the other side of her face is all black to under her chin. She has one white circle on a front leg, black spots on her back legs, which are white, and white tips on her ears.

The female baby Fleckets are named after Jackie Bird and Fiona Bruce who are my favourite BBC newsreaders. Tom is considering keeping Spot so maybe he might get a name change to Hugh Edwards.

I bought a small print of Calder's Geo for £15 at the open house as no one was buying anything and I felt sorry for the young couple. The man from Shetland Island Council did not come, probably because of the bad storm but overall they had a pretty good crowd.

Our last Sunday dinner is duck breast rolled with stuffing in the middle, broccoli, tossed salad, mashed potatoes and rhubarb upside down cake.

April 29th

In some ways this is a sad day as it my last full day of the year at the lighthouse. I am here tomorrow morning but only to get up at 5:30 am and drive to the airport. The house is pretty much ready. I have to turn off the refrigerator and finish cleaning it and the fire in the Rayburn is slowly dying. I am letting it burn up its coal so it can be easily cleaned in the early evening. Tom and I were going to go out to eat but I had just the right ingredients to make macaroni, ham and cheese. Along with a shredded lettuce salad and cooked carrots we will have a pretty good meal. No dessert but that is okay.

Staying here makes it easier for Tom to check for lambs. One was born yesterday and I got to take care of it by giving colostrum, warming it by the fire and mixing up milk if needed. The mother eventually accepted it so it did not become a caddy. I would have felt badly if I started taking care of it and then had to abandon it.

A small strange white bird with black trimming is hanging out at Tom's house. I tried to get some pictures, as I have never seen on like it before. Someone told me they thought it was a petrel.

April 30th

I can no longer see the ocean because I am sitting at my computer at Hilltop Farm in Parma, Michigan. Shetland is close as I am listening to last night's news on Radio Shetland.

It was a perfect Shetland day when I got up 5:00 am. There was a magnificent sunrise. Tom drove me to the airport. We saw many lambs and one tiny newborn Shetland pony. All the way to the airport I felt insane to be leaving Shetland when spring was just beginning.

My trip back to the USA was a frantic run from one airplane to another. The Shetland plane left on time. When I arrived in Aberdeen there was a two hour delay because of bad weather in London. That meant I was going to miss my transatlantic flight. The desk people were told the weather was starting to clear so they put a notice on my record regarding my tight connection and hoped it might help. They loaded us on the plane so as soon as we got clearance we could go. The notice on the record did help because when we finally arrived at Heathrow they had a cart waiting to take me to my transatlantic flight, which was still waiting on me. I made it but my luggage did not as it is still in Heathrow.

It seems strange to be back at the farm. I had a great time during my stay at the lighthouse. It certainly does not seem like I was gone for a year. I keep wondering how Tom's lambing is going and how my Fleckets babies are. I bought my ticket to return in July and I cannot wait.